PRAISE FOR AMERICA INVADES

"An intensive compendium of America's interactions, both good and bad, with other countries that rightly leaves out the philosophizing."
Kirkus Reviews

"This informative yet entertaining history text presents a factual account of United States military involvement throughout the world."
Foreword Reviews

"Provides a perspective and approach to American history that should be brought to the attention of every U.S. citizen."
Midwest Book Review

"This is a fresh new approach to military history. I was astonished by many of the things I learned about Americans fighting throughout the world. Don't let the provocative title fool you, every American who cares about the military should read this book."
General Barry McCaffrey, US Army, (Ret.)

"History but entertaining"
Gerard Richardson, MBE
Founder Whitehaven Festival

"With wit, insight, and no small amount of shock and awe, Chris Kelly and Stuart Laycock have come up with a fascinating compendium of American military invasions around the world. The writing is brisk and chatty, the history is fascinating, and the message is arresting no matter where you are on the political spectrum. This should be required reading by American presidents."
William Dietrich
Author of The Three Emperors: An Ethan Gage Adventure

ITALY
INVADES

HOW ITALIANS
CONQUERED THE WORLD

CHRISTOPHER KELLY AND STUART LAYCOCK

BOOK PUBLISHERS NETWORK
Changing the World One Book at a Time

Book Publishers Network
P.O. Box 2256
Bothell • WA • 98041
Ph • 425-483-3040
www.bookpublishersnetwork.com

Five percent of all sales from Italy Invades will be donated to military charities.

10 9 8 7 6 5 4 3 2 1

Printed in the United States of America

LCCN   2015946827
ISBN   978-1-940598-72-7

Kelly, Christopher (Christopher Robert), 1959-

Italy invades : how Italians conquered the world / Christopher Kelly and Stuart Laycock. -- Bothell WA : Book Publishers Network, [2016]

pages ; cm.

ISBN: 978-1-940598-72-7 (hardback) ; 978-1-940598-73-4 (perfectbound)
Includes glossary and index.
Summary: Offers a global tour of Italian military history, arranged by country, from the Roman Legionnaires to George Custer's 7th Cavalry at the Battle of Little Big Horn to modern Italian Eurofighter Typhoons, including Italian Americans fighting in WWII.--Publisher.

1. Italy--History, Military. 2. Italy--History. 3. Italy--Foreign relations--History. 4. Italian Americans--History, Military.
5. Italians--United States--History, Military. I. Laycock, Stuart. II. Title

DG482 .K45 2016   2015946827
355/.00945--dc23   1510

Editor: Elizabeth Barrett
Cover Designer: Blaine Donnelson
Book Designer: Melissa Vail Coffman
Production: Scott Book
Indexer: Carolyn Acheson

Cover art: Front—Roman legionnaires with Roman standard; Emperor Marcus Aurelius (161–180 AD); il condottiere (professional military leader during the Renaissance). Back—The Bersaglieri (Italian elite infantry).

Dedicated to the ladies ... Nina, Maria, Clare, Oona,
Isabella, Lizzie, Katie, Aurora, Maria, Catherine and Suzanne

Che l'antico valore
Nelli italici cor non è ancor morto.
                    —Petrarch
(For ancient valour
Is not dead in Italian hearts)

TABLE OF CONTENTS

FOREWORD

As an Italian American kid growing up on the East Coast, I had plenty of exposure to my grandparents' nation of origin.

My grandfather on Mom's side was outspoken, confident, and humorous. He owned Romano's Bakery in Rutland, Vermont, had ten children including Mom, and a small dog that hung around the kitchen and drank water out of a coffee cup. When the dog begged at the breakfast table, Grandpa would let out a huge laugh and say, "Get your own cup." Nick Romano was a tough businessman but a softy when it came to his grandchildren. One day I asked him for a jelly donut. Instead of giving me one, he taught me how to use the donut filler and set me up with a part-time job. To this day, I can't look at a powered jelly donut without thinking of my grandfather.

My mom's youngest brother, Ralph, was my favorite uncle on that side of the family. He was the first professional radio broadcaster I ever met and, in fact, was my inspiration for going into the media business. After Uncle Ralph retired at age sixty-five, he became a stand-up comic, doing free shows for nonprofit organizations for the rest of his life.

My dad's family lived close to us in Norwalk, Connecticut. Every Sunday, without fail, we visited Grandma and Grandpa Ventrella on Aiken Street. Grandma made homemade pasta under the grape vine just outside her kitchen. Chickens roamed the yard freely, and several cats lived in the barn next to the large garden and the old-fashioned well. There was a party every Sunday at Grandma's.

My uncle Louie, Dad's brother-in-law, was my favorite on Dad's side of the family. He ran a lawnmower repair shop in New Canaan, Connecticut. Uncle Louie was always whistling, always seemed happy, and loved talking about his favorite team, the New York Yankees.

Both sets of grandparents immigrated to the United States in the early 1900s, so both of my parents were born in America but spoke fluent Italian. That made it difficult for us kids to decipher what they were talking about at times.

My dad owned Ventrella's Barber Shop in Norwalk; taught me the trade; and over the years, we worked side by side. He also taught me everything I needed to know about Italian culture.

I learned about the difficulty of growing up Italian in America in the early 1900s. There were less than flattering nicknames tagged on my dad and his siblings when they were growing up. I heard some of it myself in the 1950s, but it was mostly from kids with bad manners, ignorant parents, or both.

We learned to follow Italian heroes of our time, like Joe DiMaggio, Yogi Berra, Phil Rizzuto, and Rocky Marciano. Frank Sinatra, Perry Como, and Mario Lanza were favorites among my older relatives.

My dad told me stories about the war, and how Hitler and Mussolini teamed up for a while before both were crushed by the Allies.

Most of my uncles on both sides of the family served in the US Army or Navy during World War II, but honestly, I never gave much thought to the Italian Army. Oh, I heard all the jokes, but I never considered Italy was much of a factor in military history.

That's why *Italy Invades* is such an exciting and somewhat nostalgic adventure for me. I only wish my dad were still alive to share this wonderful book. I can imagine him and me standing out in front of the barber shop, the red, white, and blue pole spinning away, and Dad telling me how proud he was that Italian Americans made up one-twelfth of US fighting forces, and that Italy's own military had seen action in fifty different countries.

In fact, I can see him telling his next customer the same thing.

—*Tony Ventrella*

ACKNOWLEDGMENTS

We would like to thank our friends and family whose assistance made this book possible. I (Chris Kelly) would particularly like to thank my aunt Catherine Townsend for her generous gift of *An Adventure in 1914*. Vincent Driano, my brother-in-law, has been hugely helpful in organizing our various Invasion projects. Major Jack Coughlin, USAF, (Ret.) has been a fantastic support on many book tours. Thanks to Blaine Donnelson for design assistance and building our first-rate websites: www.americainvades.com; and now: www.italyinvades.com. A big #12 thank you to Tony Ventrella and his wife Mika. Thanks to Elizabeth Barrett for her meticulous editing of our efforts. Thanks for advice along the way from Matteo Pierattini, my Bersagliere friend. Thanks to Matt Cail for assistance with social media. Thanks to Erin MacDonald-Birnbaum for PR support. Thanks to Melissa Coffman for her professional layout design of our work. Thanks to Anna Whitehouse for her assistance with our *Italy Invades* tour.

Special thanks also go to many institutions that have aided us along the way, particularly the RAF Museum Hendon, the West Point Museum, the Museum of Flight (Seattle), the National Museum of the US Air Force (Dayton), the National Naval Aviation Museum (Pensacola), Arles Archaeological Museum (Arles, France), the French Foreign Legion Museum (Aubagne, France), the Grand Curtius (Liège, Belgium), and the Ufizzi (Florence, Italy).

Any flaws you find herein are entirely our own.

INTRODUCTION BY CHRISTOPHER KELLY

A FEW YEARS AGO, A SON ASKED HIS FATHER, "Dad, how many countries have we invaded?" Stuart Laycock, the father, having studied classics at Cambridge, wrote a book to answer the question properly: *All the Countries We've Ever Invaded: And the Few We Never Got Round To*. Laycock's book documented how Britain managed to invade or fight conflicts in nearly 90 percent of the world's countries over the course of its history. It offered a chapter on every country in the world and a short summary of Britain's military involvement with that country.

I read Stu's book, reviewed it, and forwarded him the review. We met for a pint in London where we both live and became friends. As an American, I was curious about how America would compare to Britain when considering the topic of invasions. We coauthored *America Invades: How We've Invaded or Been Militarily Involved with Almost Every Country on Earth*, in which we demonstrated that Americans have invaded about 45 percent of the world's countries and have been militarily involved with nearly all the rest. America is a military superpower that spans the globe with alliances and complex relationships.

Stu and I each have strong connections to and affection for Italy. Stu learned Latin, studied classics at Cambridge, has visited Italy many times, and has authored or coauthored several books about Roman and post-Roman Britain. My wife is an Italian American with roots in Calabria. We have a holiday apartment in Florence and are frequent visitors to Italy. My great-grandfather, Thomas Tileston Wells, visited the Italian Dolomites in the summer of 1914 just as World War I was breaking out (see an Appendix which contains an extract from his never before published *An Adventure in 1914*). He believed that Riva on Lake Garda in the Dolomites "is one of the most beautiful places in the world." So it was natural that our thoughts turned toward Italy.

Italy has been the eternal birthplace of empires intent on conquest. Ancient Rome was a great world empire and had a profound influence on all those that followed in her wake; just think in terms of architecture, government, and language. How many countries did the Romans invade?

Niccolò Machiavelli was the philosopher of invasions. He offered this advice to future princes: "A ruler, then, must have no other aim or consideration, nor seek to develop any other vocation outside war, the organization of the army and military discipline. This is the only proper vocation of the man in command."

Just how many countries has Italy invaded? Start asking this question and you will likely raise many an eyebrow. Perhaps a snicker too. "You're writing a book about Italian military history? That'll be the world's shortest book!" The Italian fighting spirit has been much maligned over the years. Stuart and I believe it's time for a reevaluation.

This negative view of Italians' military prowess is largely derived from their disastrous experience in World War II, when Mussolini thrust them into a war for which they were ill-prepared. When Mussolini declared war on the Allies in June of 1940, he thought he had placed a wager on the favorite to show, and that Italy would augment her empire by collecting easy territorial gains. Instead, he had bought Italy a long-shot ticket that would place her in a desperate battle against three great industrial powers—the British Empire, the Soviet Union, and the United States. Moreover, the Allied propaganda machine perpetuated a narrative of Italian military incompetence despite the bravery of the Italian soldier and a surprising number of Italian victories.

The years after 1945 served to cement the idea of unmilitary Italians, rather than to shake it. Despite the armistice of 1943 and the successes of Italians fighting in the Co-Belligerent forces on the side of the Allies, Italy emerged from the war bitterly divided politically. The nation had suffered massive loss of life and destruction of infrastructure, which yielded an entirely understandable cynicism about Mussolini's militarism, his dreams of empire, and the devastation the war had brought to Italy. Unlike in 1918, Italy emerged in 1945 as one of the war's great losers.

Italians themselves have been their own sharpest critics. When his son modified the uniforms of their Neapolitan troops, King Ferdinand of the Two Sicilies said, "My dear child, dress them in white or dress them in red, they will run just the same." The great Italian patriot Garibaldi, in a moment of doubt, wrote that his countrymen were a "generation of hermaphrodites." Mussolini declared that Italians were "a mediocre race of good-for-nothings only capable of singing and eating gelato."

Italy has had a troubled, sometimes tragic, history. Rome lived by the sword and died by the sword. From the fall of Rome in the fifth century AD until the nineteenth century, Italy was, as Metternich put it, "a geographic expression." Politically, it was divided into many different principalities and smaller states. To tourists, Italy is a land of unmistakably ancient history and tradition, but in terms of modern statehood, Italy, united in 1861, is younger than the United States.

In Alexandre Dumas's classic novel *The Count of Monte Cristo* (published in 1844–45), the Abbé Faria is asked by Edmond Dantès why he is imprisoned. The Italian cleric answers, "Because in 1807 I meditated the scheme Napoleon wished to realize in 1811; because, like Machiavelli, I desired to alter the political face of Italy, and instead of allowing it to be split up into a quantity of petty principalities, each held by some weak or tyrannical ruler, I sought to form one large, compact, and powerful empire. ... Italy seems fated to be unlucky."

Why was Italy unlucky? Why did she struggle for so many years to become a nation?

Machiavelli, who wrote *The Prince* in hopes of obtaining a job from Lorenzo de Medici, insisted that Italy lacked proper leadership. He wrote, "Italy is hardly lacking in raw material for the man who wants to give form to it. The limbs are healthy and strong; all they need is a head to guide them. Look at how much stronger, defter and more skillful Italians are than foreigners in duels or small skirmishes. But when it comes to armies they can't compete. Because they are badly led."

Some would say Italians have always been their own worst enemies. In ancient Rome, Republicans fought against the followers of Julius Caesar after Caesar's assassination in the senate in 44 BC. Rome suffered through numerous civil wars, coups, and power struggles. According to legend, Romulus slew Remus. The Guelphs fought the Ghibellines. The Florentines battled the Sienese. The Venetians duelled with the Genoese for mastery of the Mediterranean. Garibaldi's Redshirts needed to invade the Kingdom of the Two Sicilies to finally unite Italy into a modern state. After Mussolini's arrest in 1943 and the Italian defection to the Allied side, World War II itself became a civil war for Italians that has left lasting scars on the face of Italy.

Mussolini claimed to use *The Prince* as his guidebook, but he crucially forgot Machiavelli's injunction that, "Wars begin where you will, but they do not end when you please." In April 1945, after enduring over four years of a ruinous war, Italians assassinated Mussolini and his mistress and resumed singing and eating the world's finest gelato. One of Mussolini's sons, Romano Mussolini, even became an accomplished jazz pianist in postwar Italy.

Has Italy been a victim of history?

Giuseppe Mazzini, the patriot of Italian unification, rejected the notion of Italian victimhood, proclaiming that Italy was a fortunate land with a special destiny. He asserted the greatness of Italy, saying,

> *There are not five Italies, or four Italies, or three Italies. There is only one Italy. God, who, in creating her, smiled upon her land, has awarded her the two most sublime frontiers in Europe, symbols of eternal strength and eternal motion - the Alps and the sea.... Rome shall be the holy Ark of your redemption, the temple of your nation.*
>
> *... Rome, by the design of Providence, and as the People have divined, is the Eternal City, to which is entrusted the mission of disseminating the word that will unite the world.... Just as, to the Rome of the Caesars, which through action united a great part of Europe, there succeeded the Rome of the Popes, which united Europe and America in the realm of the spirit, so the Rome of the People will succeed them both, to unite Europe, America and every part of the terrestrial globe, in a faith that will make thought and action one... The destiny of Rome and Italy is that of the world.*

Italy was no mere "geographic expression" to Mazzini.

In spite of its disastrous fate in World War II, Italy has had an amazing record of military success, achievement, courage, and extraordinary leadership. We cannot ignore thousands of years of military prowess. Italians have, sometimes peacefully, sometimes militarily, transformed the world.

Consider, for example, a sample of points about Italian military and political prowess:

- The Roman army was, by far, the most powerful and successful fighting force in the ancient world. Roman armies, in fact, invaded or fought in at least fifty-one different countries, or 26 percent of all the world's countries, by modern geographic reckoning. This is an astonishing tally considering that this happened before aviation and that the Romans were only aware of three of the world's continents.
- The map of Roman military conquests influenced the development of languages around much of the world. This is why French, Italian, Portuguese, and Spanish are romance languages. The word *pistol*, for example, is derived from the Italian town of Pistoia. The popular type of pasta, fusilli, is closely connected to *fucile*, which means rifle, and the English word *fusilier*.

- The Italians have often been at the forefront of military science and engineering. The Romans reduced the fortifications of their enemies with ballistae, onagers (wild ass), scorpios (crossbows), battering rams, and elaborate siege towers. In his notebooks, Leonardo da Vinci, despite his revulsion at "the cruelty of men," sketched designs for the helicopter, the parachute, the armored car or tank, and the submarine. The first aerial bombing raid was made by the Regia Aeronautica (Italian Royal Air Force) in Libya in 1911. Giulio Douhet (1869–1930), author of *The Command of the Air*, was a visionary proponent of air power in warfare. In 1943, Admiral Minisini and twelve engineers and technicians were pinched by the OSS and brought to the United States to develop the modern submarine.
- Italian generals have been among the greatest military leaders in the world. To this day, Caesar's *Commentaries* is used as a teaching text at military academies such as West Point. The great conqueror Napoleon once said, "Io sono Italiano o Toscano, piutosto che Corso" ("I am more Italian or Tuscan than Corsican"). The ancestral home of the Bonaparte family is in San Miniato in Tuscany. Garibaldi's Thousand Redshirts managed to conquer Sicily, defeating an army that initially outnumbered them by forty-two to one. President Lincoln was so impressed with Garibaldi's Italian generalship, he offered him a command in the Union Army during the US Civil War.
- The design for the American Pentagon is based on Italian star fortification plans used during the Renaissance.
- Many popes based in Rome directed Christians to embark on crusades to the Holy Lands. Alexander VI, a Borgia pope, imposed the Treaty of Tordesillas, which split South America into Spanish and Portuguese bits in the fifteenth century. The Papal States had their own armies for many centuries. Pope John Paul II, with his special insight into Eastern Europe, helped to steer the West to victory in the Cold War.
- Italian explorers played a major role in the Middle Ages and the centuries afterwards, opening up the world to contact with Europe.
- In 1915, one hundred years ago, Italy joined the Allied cause in the First World War. By 1918, after bitter and brave fighting and massive losses (over 462,000 combat deaths), Italy had liberated the north of its country from Austro-Hungarian rule. Italy was one of the major victorious Allied powers at the Versailles Peace

Conference, both respected and keen to spread its political and military influence farther across the Mediterranean basin.

- The largest invasion in world history has an Italian name—Operation *Barbarossa* (*Barbarossa* means *redbeard* and was the nickname of a Holy Roman emperor.) To their intense regret, Italians participated in Hitler's disastrous invasion of Russia, and Napoleon's as well.
- Since the Romans, Italy has fought or done peacekeeping duty in at least fifty different countries, or 26 percent of the world. In 2010, they were involved in peacekeeping missions in twenty-two different nations.
- The Italian diaspora (running mainly from 1850 to 1955) had a profound impact on much of the world, including both North and South Americas. As a result, Italian Americans, who made up about one in twelve American servicemen in World War II, have fought in even more countries, including some missed by the Romans and warriors from Italy.

Italians are literally and figuratively an "outgoing" people. They built and trod the Roman roads. Many traveled on the Silk Road to Asia in search of wealth. Others used the sea as their road. From Marco Polo to Christopher Columbus, they have been some of the world's greatest travelers, explorers, and adventurers. Italian pilots took to the air with the dawn of aviation.

Since the end of World War II, Italy has enjoyed relative peace in the world and has rediscovered other aspects of her ancient heritage. She rebuilt herself from the rubble of that war by launching a series of commercial and cultural invasions. In the postwar world, Italy's much reduced armed forces have served honorably as Blue Helmets with UN peacekeeping missions around the world.

Italians have done more than just their military duty—they have kept singing and enjoying life. Italian opera is performed not only at La Scala in Milan, but also at opera houses from Sydney to Shanghai to San Francisco. Pizza is consumed worldwide. Italian wines are quaffed around the globe. Italian fashions cut *una bella figura* internationally. Bright red Ferraris roar though the streets of Beijing.

Modern Italians have largely beaten their swords into plowshares. They have exchanged their uniforms and togas for Armani business suits, their sandals for Tod's shoes. In this way they continue to conquer the world.

These new Italian invaders are the softer side of globalization. But they cannot hide the true history of Italian military activity around the globe, a history that is far more extensive and has far more effect than most people realize.

The modern state of Italy has existed only since 1861. In this book, however, we have concentrated on Italian military activity in a much wider sense, to give a broad picture of the Italian people at war.

The Roman Empire eventually stretched across many peoples and many lands. At that time, most of those fighting in its armies were not ethnically Italian, and even many of its emperors in the later period were ethnically non-Italian. However, Italians remained important in the imperial hierarchy, and Rome remained both a key political, ideological, and spiritual (both pagan and Christian) focus, even with the rise of Constantinople. Therefore, it seems legitimate to include Roman campaigns within this book.

Similarly, we have included the activities of political entities that existed within the boundaries of modern Italy, such as the city-states of Genoa and Venice.

We have also considered the activities of Italians fighting in armies apart from those of Italian entities; and since Italians have immigrated to many lands around the world, we have included some key military actions by those of Italian descent who were citizens of countries outside Italy. We have paid particular attention to Italian Americans; but this is not primarily a history of Italian Americans, and therefore we have not attempted to cover in detail all the large number of military operations carried out by Italian Americans.

We have defined an invasion as conducting armed action in the land, sea, or air of a country beyond the boundaries of Italy. And we have classified the geography of the world in terms of today's nation states since those are the boundaries that are generally of the most significance to today's readers.

In a small book such as this, it is not possible to include *every* invasion and military action by Italians around the world, but we hope the selections we have made will help with the important job of reevaluating Italian military prowess and what it means to be Italian.

Finally, we are aware that some have questioned whether Christopher Columbus really came from Genoa, and have suggested other origins for the man. In this book, we have kept to the traditional narrative of his birth. We are also aware that some have questioned whether the word

America really derives from Amerigo Vespucci. Again, we have kept with the narrative that this is the origin of *America*.

Emperor Marcus Aurelius wrote in his *Meditations* that "life is warfare, and a visit in a strange land." We hope that our readers will enjoy exploring the many lands that Italian warriors have visited over an amazing history.

AFGHANISTAN

Y ES, ITALIANS HAVE FOUGHT IN AFGHANISTAN.
It is conceivable that Italians first reached the territory of what is
now Afghanistan with Alexander the Great (see Iran).

Certainly, Italians were in that area in the Middle Ages. For instance,
Marco Polo himself traveled through Afghanistan.

But it was in the nineteenth century that Italian soldiers first had much
impact in Afghanistan. Italian mercenary officers commanded elements of
the Persian forces besieging Herat in 1837; and Italian officers serving with
Sikh forces were also active in Afghanistan. General Jean-Baptiste Ventura
(Giovanni Battista Ventura), born in Modena in 1794, played a part in
the decisive Sikh victory over Durrani forces at the Battle of Nowshera in
Afghanistan in 1823.

Mussolini had plans for Afghanistan, seeing in it the potential for
spreading Italian influence in Central Asia. During World War II, anti-
British activists from the region broadcast to Afghanistan on Italian
Radio Himalaya.

But, of course, it is since 2001 that Italian soldiers have been most
active in Afghanistan. The 9/11 attacks in America killed ten Italian
nationals and many more Italian Americans. The first Italian troops arrived
in Afghanistan late in that year. Over the years since, thousands of Italians
served in Afghanistan, and at least fifty-three Italian service personnel lost
their lives there. Once again, the western region of Afghanistan saw the
arrival of Italian officers, this time taking command of Regional Command
West and basing their headquarters in Herat, rather than besieging it as they
had in 1837. Italian troops are still at their Herat base. From August 2005
until May 2006, Italian General Mauro del Vecchio was in command of
the International Security Assistance Force (ISAF). Italian aircraft have
also been active in Afghanistan. For instance, by December 2013, Italian
fighter aircraft had flown over three thousand sorties in Afghanistan.

And it wasn't only in the Esercito Italiano (Italian Army) in which
people with Italian heritage served in Afghanistan. Many Italian Americans
served bravely there, including Salvatore Giunta and Jared C. Monti,
both of whom were awarded the Congressional Medal of Honor for their
courageous actions.

ALBANIA

I T IS SITUATED JUST ACROSS THE ADRIATIC SEA FROM ITALY, so not
surprisingly, Italians have invaded Albania, and have invaded it a lot.

When the Romans first encountered what is now Albania, the
southern part of the country was part of the Kingdom of Epirus, while the
north was controlled by the Illyrians.

In the third century BC, as Roman power expanded, the Romans
looked across the Adriatic to the lands on the other side. The Illyrians
irritated them with piracy and the murder of an envoy. In 229 BC, the
Romans invaded Illyria. A short, successful campaign gave them the peace
deal they wanted and left them in control of the port city of Dyrrachium,
now Durres, in Albania.

In 219 BC, after the Illyrians again conducted widespread sea raids,
Rome attacked and again won. Finally, in 168 BC, Rome achieved a
decisive victory over southern Illyrian territory. Then in 167 BC, they
also sacked the Kingdom of Epirus. Further fighting in the area would
follow during Roman civil wars, such as when Pompey tried to defend
Dyrrachium in 48 BC.

Soldiers from Italy invaded Albania on numerous occasions during
the Middle Ages. In the Battle of Dyrrachium in 1081, Robert Guiscard,
Duke of Apulia and Calabria, defeated Byzantine forces and captured the
city before advancing inland. A few years later, Byzantines recaptured the
city, but William II of Sicily captured it in 1185. The Venetians occupied
the region after the capture of Byzantium in 1204 in the Fourth Crusade,
and established the Duchy of Durazzo (the Italian name for Durres) before
losing it again to the Despotate of Epirus. It then passed through the hands
of a number of other parties before ending up as part of Venetian Albania.

However, the Ottoman advance spelled the eventual end of Venetian
power in Albania. In 1466 and 1467, the Venetians campaigned alongside
Albanian leader Skanderbeg against the Ottomans. But Skanderbeg's
death greatly reduced the Venetians' ability to resist the Ottoman advance.
In 1501 the Turks took Durres.

In November 1915, Italian troops returned to Durres, landing there
to assist with the evacuation to Corfu of the retreating Serbian Army. And
in 1916, the Italian Army occupied much of southern Albania. The Italian
Army advanced north into the rest of Albania in October 1918, capturing

Durres again, as well as Tirana. Italian plans for a protectorate over Albania sparked the Vlora War in 1920, which forced the Italians to withdraw.

In 1934, Mussolini tried to intimidate the Albanian government by sending an Italian fleet off its coast. Italian troops invaded again in April 1939; and in a few days occupied the country, uniting it with Italy, and placing Italian King Victor Emmanuel III on the throne instead of King Zog.

From Albania, Italian troops invaded Greece in 1940. A Greek counterattack forced them to retreat, and they found themselves fighting on Albanian soil again. The German invasion of Greece in April 1941 removed any threat from the Greek Army to Italian control of Albania.

Albanian resistance fighters increased in strength during the war and, after the Italian armistice with the Allies in September 1943, some Italian troops then joined the Albanian resistance to fight against the Germans.

In 1993, a few years after the end of Communism in Albania, Italian troops arrived yet again, but this time to help maintain order. More forces arrived in 1997 to help control the flow of illegal immigrants from Albania into Italy.

During the Kosovo crisis in 1999, Italy sent thousands of troops into Albania, both to help deal with the refugees fleeing to Albania from Kosovo, and as preparation for moving land forces into Kosovo.

Albania joined NATO in 2009. Italy has helped provide Air Policing services over Albania.

ALGERIA

THE ROMANS REFERRED TO THE NORTHERN PART of modern Algeria as Numidia.

The area first became a concern for them during the Punic Wars (see Tunisia), when different Numidian factions supported different sides in the war. One king, Masinissa, allied himself with Rome at a crucial point during the Second Punic War, and as a result managed to make himself king of a united Numidia.

However, Masinissa died in 148 BC; and Rome's destruction of Carthage in the Third Punic War in 146 BC left Rome in control of Carthaginian territory—mainly what is now Tunisia—and a neighbor with the Numidians.

In the late second century BC, Jugurtha, a grandson of Masinissa, became the dominant force in Numidia, fighting off competitors to take control. In the process, however, he fell out with Rome. A messy series of conflicts followed, which resulted in the Romans teaming up with Bocchus I of Mauretania, located to the west of Numidia, to defeat Jugurtha. Jugurtha was marched through Rome in chains and then killed. Bocchus I was rewarded with a chunk of western Numidia.

The Numidians got involved in Rome's wars again when Caesar clashed with Pompey. Juba I of Numidia picked the losing side and ended up dead after Caesar's forces defeated those in Africa supporting Pompey.

Suddenly, the Romans had their hands on vast new territories. It wasn't the end of local rulers, but it was the beginning of the end. Juba II, son of Juba I, made something of a comeback with the support of Augustus, Rome's first emperor. Juba II, though, found himself transferred to Mauretania, and in AD 40 his line came to an end when Caligula had his son, Ptolemy, murdered.

However, the Romans had had a few other difficulties in Numidia during this time. A Numidian called Tacfarinas led a long guerrilla war against Rome, which caused the Romans huge problems, lasted almost a decade, and ended only when the Romans managed to ambush Tacfarinas and kill him.

Roman control was limited to the northern part of what is now modern Algeria, but Roman troops did occasionally venture farther south. Under African emperor Septimius Severus, Roman troops established an outpost at Castellum Dimmidi, but this was abandoned just forty years later. In the last part of the fourth century, a rebellion under local leader Firmus was crushed by Count Theodosius.

In the fifth century, the Germanic Vandals invaded and occupied Roman Numidia.

However, the Roman period was not the last time Italian troops invaded Algeria. The Genoese in the Middle Ages took a keen interest in Algeria, and, for example, besieged Bejaïa in 1136. In another instance, Roger II of Sicily captured land in eastern Algeria in the twelfth century, where he built a series of Norman outposts that were dubbed rather grandly the Kingdom of Africa. And Italian troops formed a significant part of Charles V's disastrous attempt to capture Algiers in 1541. Italians also took part in the war against the Barbary pirates, with Neapolitan ships forming part of the Spanish, Neapolitan, Portuguese, and Maltese fleet that bombarded Algiers in July 1784. In the 1620s, Ali Bitshnin (aka Ali Piccinino), an Italian renegade and convert to Islam, became a prominent pirate prince in Algiers. He even financed the construction of a mosque in the Bab El Oued district of Algiers, which stands to this day.

Algeria eventually came under French control, and Italian soldiers in the French Foreign Legion played a significant role in making that happen. For example, on June 26, 1835, Italian legionnaires held off attackers in bitter fighting against the forces of local leader Kader. And Francesco Zolla, the Venetian father of author Émile Zola, served as an officer in the legion during the conquest of Algeria. Italians also immigrated in significant numbers to French Algeria.

During World War II, Algeria came under French Vichy control, and when Allied forces invaded in 1942, many Italian Americans fought bravely there. Italian Special Forces also sent paratroopers and frogmen into Algeria on sabotage missions intended to slow the Allied advance. And the Regia Aeronautica (Italian Air Force) conducted raids into Algeria, including those by Italian four-engined Piaggio P.108 bombers, based in Sardinia. The Regia Marina (Italian Navy) was also active in the waters off Algeria.

ANDORRA

HANNIBAL CROSSED THE PYRENEES SLIGHTLY TO THE WEST of what is now the tiny Pyrenean state of Andorra. In the late third century BC after Hannibal's withdrawal from Italy, and in the early second century after his final defeat, the Romans expanded their power inland from the strip they controlled along Spain's Mediterranean coast. Then in the late second century, after its victory over Carthage, Rome cemented its control of the area to the north of the Pyrenees. In 118 BC, Narbonne was made into a Roman colony near the Mediterranean end of the Pyrenees, at the junction of the Via Aquitania heading west to Toulouse and the Via Domitia heading south to Spain.

The Romans controlled what is now Andorra and the surrounding region until the early fifth century AD, when tribes that had invaded Gaul from beyond the Rhine crossed into Spain.

And that's pretty much it on Italian military involvement with Andorra. Italian soldiers have been in roughly the same regions of Andorra, such as Carlo Bianco, Conte di Saint-Jorioz, who fought in the Carlist Wars in northern Spain; with the Spanish troops who accepted the Basque surrender during the Spanish Civil War; and Napoleon, who at one time was a coruler of Andorra and invaded the Iberian peninsula with some

Italian forces. Otherwise, not much has happened with any Italians on the military front inside Andorra since the Romans.

ANGOLA

QUITE A BIG COUNTRY, but not, frankly, one that's seen a lot of armed Italians in its time.

Italians probably played a role in the original Portuguese exploration of the area. And Genoese merchants working for the Spanish, like the Grillo family, would send ships to what is now Angola in search of slaves.

In terms of early descriptions of the area, seventeenth-century Italian Capuchin missionaries, like Giovanni Antonio Cavazzi and António da Gaeta, played a key role.

In 1905, Victor Emmanuel III wrote himself into local history by arbitrating a dispute over the boundaries of British and Portuguese control, thus establishing a line that still divides Angola and Zambia.

In 2013, a Framework Agreement on Cooperation in the Defense Sector between Italy and Angola was signed; and in February 2014 the Italian Navy's 30th Naval Group with the aircraft carrier *Cavour* called in at Luanda.

ANTIGUA AND BARBUDA

WELL, THE FIRST EUROPEAN TO ENCOUNTER ANTIGUA was none other than a certain Genoese guy we're going to meet again a number of times. Yep, it's Christopher Columbus. He turned up in 1493 and apparently named the island after the church of Santa Maria de la Antigua in Seville, Spain.

About four hundred and fifty years later, armed Italians operated in the waters of Antigua and Barbuda during World War II, when the islands, as part of the British Empire, were enemy territory.

The Italian submarine *Morosini* attacked the Dutch tanker *Oscilla* 145 miles or so off Antigua on March 16, 1942, sinking it with torpedoes and gunfire. Four of the tanker's fifty-one crew members were killed during the sinking. In August 1942, the *Morosini* itself was lost somewhere in the Atlantic off the French coast while returning to base.

Recently Giorgio Armani landed in Antigua, where he built a home.

ARGENTINA

FROM THE START OF EUROPEAN CONTACT WITH THIS AREA, Italians have had major involvement with Argentina, and today half or more Argentines have Italian ancestry.

In 1527, Anglo-Italian explorer Sebastian Cabot (*Sebastiano Caboto*), working at the time for the Spanish crown, established a fort at Sancti Spiritu on the Paraná River. It was the first Spanish settlement in what is now Argentina, but it didn't have a great future. Two years later, the locals burned it down.

However, plenty of Italians would soon head to Argentina to stay, with large numbers moving there particularly in the nineteenth and twentieth centuries.

Giuseppe Garibaldi himself, although based in Uruguay then, spent time on Argentine soil during his campaigns in a conflict that involved civil wars in both Uruguay and Argentina. In 1845, for instance, his troops sacked Gualeguaychú just across the border from Uruguay.

Italians also made a major contribution to the Argentine armed forces. National figure General Belgrano, one of the fathers of Argentine independence and basically the designer of its flag, had an Italian father. His career included a variety of combat on Argentine soil; for instance, his decisive victory over royalist forces at the Battle of Salta in 1813. An Argentine naval cruiser named the *General Belgrano* was sunk by the Royal Navy in the Falklands War in 1982.

Another Italian Argentine officer was Italian-born Colonel Nicolas Levalle who, among other things, led troops against large numbers of indigenous warriors at Paraguil and defeated them, which eventually extended state control across all of what is now Argentina.

In 1865, the Italian South American Naval Division established a base at Montevideo in Uruguay. One of its early missions was to send the corvette *Ardita*, ready for combat, to Buenos Aires on an emergency mission to sort out grievances over Italian sailors that had been arrested and an Italian ship that had been seized by the local authorities. After the arrival of the *Ardita*, the Argentinian authorities changed their position and released both sailors and ship.

And Italians helped develop the Argentine Navy near the end of the nineteenth century, supplying ships including one called, yes, *General Garibaldi*.

In the twentieth century, Italians continued to be major figures in both military and political circles (as well as, of course, in a wide variety of other areas of life).

The great-grandfather of Juan Perón himself came from Sardinia; and Perón studied in Italy during Mussolini's rule and had some respect for Mussolini's politics. During the 1930s, Italian fascist holiday camps for Italian Argentine children were set up in Argentina.

Perón was toppled in 1955 by a coup led by Italian Argentine Lieutenant General Eduardo Lonardi. In 1958, Italian Argentine Arturo Frondizi was elected president, but also fell to a coup in 1962. Jose Maria Guido then came to power, to be followed by Italian Argentine president Arturo Umberto Illia. Yet another Italian Argentine, Raúl Alberto Lastiri, was president in 1973, and then Perón returned. In 1982, Italian Argentine General and President Leopoldo Galtieri invaded the Falklands (Malvinas), claimed by Argentina.

We can't, of course, end this chapter without mentioning the most famous Italian Argentine of them all. No, not Lionel Messi, although he is Italian Argentine, but, yes, Pope Francis himself.

Since World War II, Italy and Argentina have signed various agreements on defense cooperation.

ARMENIA

CONFUSINGLY, THE MODERN COUNTRY CALLED ARMENIA is much smaller than the Kingdom of Armenia was when the Romans encountered it.

For much of the Roman period, Armenia was the site of battles for power and influence between the Roman Empire and, first, the Parthians, and then the Sassanians.

Rome's great enemy, Hannibal, is said to have arrived in Armenia in the period after his defeat by Rome in his homeland, and he supposedly helped establish or reestablish the great city of Artaxata.

In 68 BC the forces of Lucullus, in pursuit of Mithridates of Pontus, invaded what is now modern-day Armenia and beat the forces of King

Tigranes before retreating. Mark Antony passed by here on his disastrous Parthian campaign. In AD 59, Gnaeus Domitius Corbulo was invading the area again and destroying Artaxata. In 114, Emperor Trajan took Artaxata again and this time made Armenia a Roman province. It didn't last. In 118, the next emperor, Hadrian, gave up the province and reinstalled an Armenian king. In the 160s, the Romans were invading again, this time under Marcus Statius Priscus. More fighting in the region would follow, including a disastrous expedition by the army of Severus Alexander in the early third century.

The battle between east and west for control of the area would continue under the Byzantine Empire. Roger de Flor, an Italian condottiero from Brindisi (1267–1305), was dispatched by a Byzantine emperor to fight in Armenia.

In the chaotic period after World War I, an Italian Military Mission was planned for Azerbaijan, Georgia, and Armenia to investigate the situation there, and it was the intention to send Italian troops to occupy the area with a view to settling its future. However, just days before the troops were supposed to depart, a new Italian government abandoned the idea of sending an occupation force and just sent the Military Mission instead.

Recently, Armenian troops have served within the Italian contingent of the United Nations Interim Force in Lebanon (UNIFIL).

AUSTRALIA

A BIG COUNTRY WITH PLENTY OF AUSTRALIANS of Italian ancestry there now, but not a country with which Italy has had the most military involvement.

Some people have suggested that the great Italian explorer Andrea Corsali, although he didn't make it to Australia itself, may have been vaguely aware of its existence as early as 1515. A letter he wrote refers to a continental land in the vicinity of New Guinea. Could this have been Australia?

Eventually, the Dutch and then the British did the most to open up Australia to Europeans. In 1770, British Captain Cook on board HMS *Endeavour* charted the east coast of Australia and named the bay they had first landed in as Botany Bay. On board with him was an Italian sailor from Venice, Antonio Ponto.

In 1788, the so-called First Fleet arrived at Botany Bay to found the colony that would eventually lead to British control of all of Australia. But in 1793, an expedition led by another Italian turned up. The Spanish expedition, led by Italian Alessandro Malaspina, stopped at the British settlement of Port Jackson for a time before continuing its voyage. In some sense, Malaspina was on a reconnaissance mission, later warning the Spanish authorities of the threat the new English settlers posed to Spanish interests in the Pacific.

Some of the early prisoners sent by the British to Australia as colonists were Italian. And some of those were determined to escape. In 1814, a bunch of prisoners, including Italians, built a boat in order to escape from Tasmania, only to be stopped before they could put their plan into action.

The Italian Navy dropped in a few times during the nineteenth century. For instance, in 1873 the corvette *Vettor Pisani* arrived in Sydney during its voyage of exploration in the Pacific.

But increasingly, Italians moved to Australia in order to settle there. For instance, about three hundred Italians from the Veneto were conned by the marquis De Rays, who led a disastrous expedition to Papua, New Guinea. Many ended up in Australia, and some of them founded a settlement there called New Italy.

At least some of the new Italian immigrants witnessed military action in Australia. The Eureka Rebellion of 1854, in which miners clashed with British troops, is a key point in Australian history, and Italians were there. In particular, Raffaello Carboni from Urbino—who had already taken part in fighting in Italy alongside Mazzini and Garibaldi before arriving in the Ballarat goldfields in 1853 and joining the miners' central committee— wrote the main eyewitness account of the rebellion.

Other Italians served in the Australian military. For instance, Thomas Henry Fiaschi, born in Florence, had an extraordinary career in military medicine. Having moved to Australia, in 1891 he became honorary surgeon captain in the New South Wales Lancers. He then served with the Italian Army in Ethiopia in 1896 and was decorated for his services. He was made major and commanded the New South Wales 1st Field Hospital during the Boer War, even taking the surrender of General Cronje's forces in 1900 and winning the Distinguished Service Order (DSO) for bravery. Then, in 1915 during World War I, he commanded the 3rd Australian General Hospital on the island of Lemnos during the Dardanelles Campaign; and in 1916 he went to work as a surgeon at a military hospital in Schio, Italy.

Giuseppe Garibaldi II, the grandson of the famous Italian patriot, was born in Melbourne. He later led a French Foreign Legion unit in World War I and opposed Mussolini.

World War II saw the arrival of significant numbers of Italian prisoners of war in Australia (as well as the arrival of significant numbers of Italian Americans among the US forces sent to that country).

Today almost a million Australians have Italian ancestry. Among famous Italian Australians are singer Natalie Imbruglia, rugby star David Campese, and former Australian deputy prime minister Anthony Albanese.

AUSTRIA

A USTRIA AND ITALY SHARE A BORDER, and they also share a lot of violent history with many invasions back and forth. My own great-grandfather (CRK), Consul General Thomas Tileston Wells, went so far as to describe Austria as the "hereditary enemy of Italy." (See Appendix, *An Adventure in 1914*, Thomas Tileston Wells.)

The Romans took control of Austria in different stages.

The western part of what is now Austria consisted of a part of the Raetia region. Tiberius and Drusus seized this in 15 BC. The central chunk of modern-day Austria was part of the Noricum region, and the east of Austria was part of the Pannonia region. In 16 BC, the Noricans and Pannonians launched an attack on Roman-controlled Istria to the south. They were defeated by Publius Silius Nerva, and in the aftermath of the defeat the Romans took control of Noricum. Shortly afterward, they took control of Pannonia as well. The north of what is now Austria, beyond the Danube, remained largely beyond Roman control, except for occasional incursions into it.

In AD 121, the philosopher-emperor Marcus Aurelius died in Vindobona, what is today Vienna.

In the fifth century, Rome lost control of Noricum to peoples crossing into the empire, but Italians did fight in Austria again. And strong dynastic links developed between Austria and parts of Italy, particularly under the Hapsburgs. Large numbers of Italians served in or alongside the Austrian Army. For example, during the Austro-Turkish War of 1663–1664, Italian Imperial General Raimondo Montecuccoli saved Austria from Turkish invasion with victory at the Battle of Saint Gotthard.

During the Napoleonic Wars, Italian generals in the Austrian Army included Federico Vincenzo Ferreri, Baron Bianchi and Duke of Casalanza, who had a lengthy military career and fought in a large number of battles right up until 1815, when Napoleon was defeated and exiled. But Italians weren't just fighting for Austria during the Napoleonic Wars; they were also fighting in other armies, including those of the French emperor, who had Italian heritage himself. For example, at the Battle of Aspern-Essling in Austria in May 1809, Napoleon was defeated but his forces were saved from worse disaster by the generalship of Marshal Andrea Massena (born in Nice when it was under Sardinian control). Napoleon rewarded Massena by making him Prince of Essling. Italian troops also played a major role in Napoleon's decisive victory over the Austrians at the Battle of Wagram in July 1809.

The nineteenth century, however, saw increasing conflict between Italy and Austria as the Italians fought to free northern Italy from Austrian control.

In 1859, General Giuseppe Garibaldi commanded the Italian mountain troops (*Cacciatori delle Alpi*) and fought against Austrians in northern Italy. Garibaldi's forces won a series of small victories near the shores of Lake Como and managed to tie down about 11,000 Austrian troops. The general earned the nickname *Rote Teufel* (red devil) with the Austrians. Garibaldi thus helped allow the rest of the Piedmontese Army and Napoleon III's French Army to defeat the Austrians, notably at the battle of Solferino.

The First World War saw bitter fighting between Italians and Austro-Hungarian forces. At the end of the war, as Austrian resistance collapsed, Italian forces advanced into what is still Austrian territory today. Almost two thousand Italian troops were stationed in and around Innsbruck and hundreds more were posted in Vienna to help ensure compliance with armistice terms.

AZERBAIJAN

WHAT IS NOW AZERBAIJAN was on the edge of the Roman world, but Roman soldiers did reach this territory.

For instance, Pompey's campaigning took him into the region, and Mark Antony's disastrous campaign against the Parthians may have taken him across the border into what is now Azerbaijan. An inscription from the reign of Domitian in the late first century AD records the presence of the troops of Legio XII Fulminata south of Baku. In the early second century, Trajan's forces temporarily pushed Roman control farther east. Generally, the Romans fought to exert influence over the area, first in competition with Parthians and then Sassanian Persians. In 233, the army of Roman emperor Severus Alexander was destroyed in what is now Azerbaijan by Sassanian forces.

In the chaotic period after World War I, an Italian Military Mission was planned for Azerbaijan, Georgia, and Armenia, to investigate the situation there, and it was the intention to send Italian troops to occupy the area with a view to settling its future. However, just days before the troops were supposed to depart, a new Italian government abandoned the idea of sending an occupation force and just sent the Military Mission instead.

THE BAHAMAS

I N 1492, ON A DAY THAT WOULD CHANGE THE WORLD FOREVER, a certain Genoese named Christopher Columbus landed in the New World on an island he would name San Salvador. And because of the shallow seas around them — the *baja mar* — the islands became the Bahamas. It wasn't, however, a great day for the local inhabitants, known as Lucayans. Many of them were taken to Hispaniola for forced labor, and many more died of disease.

In 1499–1500, it was Florentine Amerigo Vespucci's turn to sail around the Bahamas. He also seized Lucayans and took some of them across the Atlantic to Europe.

During World War II, when the Bahamas (as part of the British Empire) were enemy territory, Italian sailors once again invaded the seas off the Bahamas. In March 1942, the Italian submarine *Enrico Tazzoli* (named after a nineteenth-century priest who was executed for planning an insurrection against the Austrians in Italy) made its first mission to the region. Under the control of Commander Carlo Conte Fecia di Cossato, the submarine carried out three attacks near the Bahamas. On March 11, the *Tazzoli* attacked the Panamanian-registered Greek freighter *Cygnet* with torpedo and gunfire about five miles from San Salvador and sank it. All thirty crew members were rescued. Two days later, in nearby waters, it sank the British freighter *Daytonian* with torpedoes and gunfire. One crewman was killed, but after the *Tazzoli* asked if the remaining crew were all right, the other fifty-seven were rescued the following day. And on May 15, the submarine sank the British tanker *Athelqueen*, again with torpedo and gunfire. Three crewmen later died on a reef, but forty-six other crew members survived. A collision with the tanker during the attack forced the *Tazzoli* to abandon its mission and return to base in France for repairs and refitting.

BAHRAIN

THE CLASSICAL WORLD SEEMS to have had a little more contact with Bahrain than with some other areas in the Persian Gulf.

Nearchus, a naval commander of Alexander the Great, seems to have visited Bahrain in the third century BC. A man who ruled Bahrain in the second century BC had a wife with a Greek name, Thalassia, who is mentioned in an inscription found in Bahrain; and some of the items from the Al-Maqsha necropolis show Greek or Roman influence.

In more recent years, Italian warships have called in on Bahrain. For instance, the Italian Navy has played part in Maritime Security Operations (MSO) in the Gulf with Task Force 152, which has its headquarters at Manama in Bahrain.

However, one incident in particular is worth focusing on in this chapter: the audacious Italian bombing of Bahrain in 1940. Italy declared war on Britain on June 10, 1940. At that time, Bahrain was a British Protectorate. On October 10, 1940, Italian SM.82 bombers took off from an Italian air base on the Mediterranean island of Rhodes. They flew over Vichy French-controlled Syria, where one plane detached from the formation near Damascus, which then continued on to Kuwait and eventually reached Bahrain. Their target was the oil facilities there, which the planes still in formation bombed. The lone detached bomber hit Dahran, thirty miles to the west in Saudi Arabia. Then the detachment successfully flew across Saudi Arabia and the Red Sea to land at an Italian air base at Massawa, Eritrea. The actual damage from the bombing was not large, but the ability to launch raids at such a long distance so early in the war was a spectacular news story.

BANGLADESH

T RADERS FROM THE ROMAN EMPIRE were probably at least aware of the coast of Bangladesh; and Italian traders like Niccolò de' Conti in the fifteenth century and Cesare Federici in the sixteenth century would also visit the area. The Portuguese played a major role in opening it up to the west in the sixteenth century.

BARBADOS

C HRISTOPHER COLUMBUS PASSED CLOSE BY BARBADOS, and he's not the only armed Italian to do so.

During World War II, when Barbados (as part of the British Empire) was enemy territory, the Italian Marconi-class submarine *Luigi Torelli* was active in the seas off Barbados under the command of Capitano di Corvetta Antonio De Giacomo. The *Torelli* was named after a participant in the Five Days of Milan—a rebellion against the Austrians in 1848—who raised the Italian tricolor flag on top of Milan Cathedral. On February 19 or 20, 1942, some distance to the east of Barbados, the *Torelli* torpedoed and sank the British refrigerated cargo liner *Scottish Star*, which was carrying a two-thousand-ton cargo that included whisky. Four men died in the sinking, but sixty-nine were rescued. Then, after sinking another vessel farther south, on March 11 the same submarine tried to attack the British armed freighter *Orari* just east of Barbados. It couldn't get in position in time. On March 31, it returned to its base in Bordeaux on the French Atlantic coast.

The *Torelli*, however, had plenty more time at sea ahead of it, and it ended up in Japan before being scuttled by the US Navy. We'll tell more of its story in other chapters.

BELARUS

W HAT'S THE LARGEST LANDLOCKED COUNTRY IN EUROPE? The Czech Republic? Hungary? No, it's the huge country of Belarus.

In the sixteenth century, Bona Sforza, from Milan's powerful Sforza family, was the wife of Sigismund I the Old. She played a powerful role in the Grand Duchy of Lithuania, which included extensive lands in what is now Belarus.

This territory was too far to the east for the Romans to reach, but, yes, Italian troops have invaded the land now within its borders.

In 1812, Napoleon set off to invade Russia. Napoleon was, of course, born on Corsica before he went on to become the best-known figure in French military history. But he came from a family with minor Italian noble connections; and he was born on the island in 1769, just a year after it changed from Genoese control to French control. France and Genoa had signed a deal handing Corsica over to the French until Genoa repaid a loan. Napoleon's surname, originally Buonaparte (now commonly spelled as Bonaparte), is pure Italian, as are those of his parents, Carlo Buonaparte and Letizia Ramolino. His first name comes from the Italian for "Lion of Naples." The Buonaparte family had strong connections to San Miniato in Tuscany, where you can today find the Piazza Buonaparte. When he invaded Russia, Napoleon took substantial numbers of Italian troops with him, particularly those in IV Corps commanded by his stepson, Prince Eugène de Beauharnais (yes, Josephine's son), Viceroy of Italy and Prince of Venice. Napoleon also included some Neapolitan troops led by Joachim Murat, King of Naples. Italian commanders such as General Lecchi, Italian Guard commander, would play a major role in the campaign on Napoleon's side; and at least one was involved on the Russian side: the marquis Paulucci.

On June 24, 1812, Napoleon's Grande Armée crossed the Nieman River, and his troops were soon in action in what is now Belarus. Marshal Louis-Nicolas Davout's troops entered Minsk unopposed in early July, but Napoleon's forces weren't going to cross what is now Belarus on their path to Moscow without a fight. Both Prince Eugène and Murat took part in the Battle of Ostrovno on July 25, from which the Russians managed to retreat in good order. IV Corps was involved in further fighting with the Russians on July 26 and 27 in the Battle of Vitebsk. Once again, Napoleon forced the Russian forces to retreat, but he failed once more to score any kind of major victory. It was a sign of things to come. The Russians retreated again and again, using scorched earth tactics and luring the Grande Armée farther and farther east into what is still Russia today, making the French supply lines longer and longer.

After the indecisive Battle of Borodino and the burning of Moscow in September, by October, and with winter fast approaching, Napoleon was left with little option but to order what was left of the Grande Armée to retreat. Ahead lay the appalling suffering of the retreat from Moscow. The route took the army once again though what is now Belarus. And Italian troops were, once again, extensively involved in fighting. At the Battle of Berezina, the men of Prince Eugène's IV Corps, what was left of them, managed to cross the Berezina River despite desperate Russian attempts to prevent the escape of Napoleon's soldiers.

Italian troops paid a heavy price for their bravery in the campaign. They suffered horrific losses. Out of the approximately 27,000 Italians who started the campaign, only about 1,000 were left at the end.

A small number of Italian units were operational in the Baltic region late in World War II (see Latvia), but it's hard to tell to what extent they may have been active in Belarus.

BELGIUM

B ELGIUM IS NAMED AFTER THE BELGIC PEOPLES of the region, first described by, yes, an Italian, Julius Caesar himself.

In 57 BC Caesar advanced into what is now Belgium after attacking the Nervii tribe. In 53 BC, after Ambiorix, king of the Eburones, destroyed a Roman legion, Caesar retaliated by ruthlessly destroying the Eburones.

In AD 69 and 70, the great Batavian Revolt affected parts of what is now Belgium, and other fighting during assorted Roman civil wars followed. Then in the late Roman period, the area became increasingly vulnerable to incursions by people from beyond the empire's borders.

That was not the last time Italians would fight in what is now Belgium.

Italians formed a major component of the Spanish armies that fought the Eighty Years' War from 1558–1648, as the Netherlands fought to free itself from Spanish control. A number of key commanders on the Spanish side were Italian. In the late sixteenth century, for instance, Alessandro Farnese, Duke of Parma, reconquered, at a key point in the war, much of what is now Belgium. And in the early seventeenth century, Genoese aristocrat Ambrosio Spinola, Marquis of the Balbases and Duke of Sesto, was another major commander on the Spanish side.

Napoleon, the French emperor with Italian roots, controlled what is now Belgium for most of his time in power. The battle of Waterloo, fought in Belgium in June 1815, was the final defeat for the King of Italy, as well as for the emperor of the French.

During the Battle of Britain in September 1940, the Corpo Aereo Italiano (the Italian Air Corps) was sent to Belgium to take part in the Luftwaffe's Battle of Britain, Germany's attempt to make an invasion of Britain possible.

On the Allied side, Italian Americans saw heavy fighting in Belgium in the months after D-Day. For example, on September 4, 1944, machine gunner Gino J. Merli showed heroic bravery when his position near Sars-la-Bruyère came under heavy German attack. He was awarded the Congressional Medal of Honor as a result.

The Belgians owe another major cultural debt to Italy. No Columbus would have meant no Belgian chocolate!

Belgium is a founding member of NATO, along with Italy.

BELIZE

GENOESE CHRISTOPHER COLUMBUS was in the vicinity of Belize in 1502 when he visited the Gulf of Honduras on his fourth voyage.

The Spanish and British competed for colonial control of Belize, with the British eventually winning.

Generally speaking, Italian military involvement in Belize has been minimal. However, in the early eighteenth century, an Italian engineer did build the Spanish fort at San Felipe de Bacalar in Mexico near the border with Belize, in order to prevent the British settlers in Belize from expanding their territory.

BENIN

BENIN IS A SMALL COUNTRY that has seen little in the way of Italian military involvement.

The Portuguese built a small fort at Ouidah in Benin, and Italians were active in Ouidah.

Oddly enough, the Portuguese fort of São João Baptista de Ajudá was still a Portuguese enclave in the twentieth century, despite being surrounded first by French colonial Dahomey (Benin's previous name) and then by independent Dahomey; and despite having only five registered inhabitants in 1921 and only two by the time it was annexed by Dahomey in 1961.

When the annexation forces invaded the fort in 1961, its two defenders tried to set fire to it before they were captured.

BHUTAN

I TALY HAS NOT HAD MUCH MILITARY INVOLVEMENT, if any, with Bhutan. Reinhold Messner is one of several distinguished Italian mountain climbers who has "conquered" peaks in Bhutan.

BOLIVIA

A S ELSEWHERE IN SOUTH AMERICA, Italians played a key role in developing and maintaining Spanish colonial rule in Bolivia.

The enormously rich silver mines of Potosi in what is now Bolivia played a huge role in the Spanish, and indeed the entire European, economy from the late sixteenth century into the seventeenth century. And Italians were part of the operation to exploit the mines and were among the estimated 40,000 non-Spanish Europeans recorded there in 1611.

From 1716 to 1720, for instance, Bolivia—or Upper Peru, as it was known then—was ruled in part by an Italian, Carmine Nicolao Caracciolo, 5th Prince of Santo Buono. Many Italians would follow Caracciolo, moving to Bolivia in the nineteenth century.

During that time, Italians were among Bolivia's enemies and potential enemies. For instance, the famous Peruvian soldier Francisco Bolognesi commanded a cavalry regiment during a period of tension between Peru and Bolivia in the 1850s. But one of Bolivia's most well-known figures of the period was also of Italian ancestry.

Hilarión Daza Groselle was born in 1840. His father was called Groselli, and the family came from Piedmont. Groselle joined the military, and in 1876 he seized power in Bolivia in a coup. It did not, however, end well for him. In 1879, he got embroiled in the War of the Pacific, allying with Peru against Chile. The result of the war for Bolivia was the loss of a vast territory to Chile. From the battlefront at Tacna, Groselle fled into exile, including a period of time in Italy. In 1894, he returned to Bolivia but was murdered at the train station in Uyuni.

Paraguay received extensive Italian assistance during the Chaco War against Bolivia in the 1930s. After the war, Colonel David Toro Ruilova's regime asked for an Italian Military Mission, which set up two military academies in the country.

BOSNIA AND HERZEGOVINA

THE ROMANS ARRIVED IN WHAT IS NOW BOSNIA AND HERZEGOVINA during the Illyrian Wars (see Albania and Montenegro). Having said that, Roman control of the area was thrown into question by the massive Illyrian Revolt that started in AD 6. Key in this revolt were a people called the Daesitiates who occupied territory in what is now central Bosnia. The fighting lasted until AD 9 and sucked in vast numbers of Roman troops before the revolt was finally crushed.

The area saw various Roman armies on the move during civil wars, and it also was invaded by more Italian soldiers during the Middle Ages and later.

For example, in the late seventeenth century, Venice mounted some major military operations in what is now Bosnia and Herzegovina. During the Morean War, Venetian forces advanced from coastal territory they already held and took a number of towns, including Čitluk. They threatened Mostar, as they had in 1652 and as they would again in 1717. Italian soldiers also attacked from the north. In 1689, while campaigning against the Turks, Italian Imperial General Piccolomini advanced through Bosnia.

When Yugoslavia was occupied during World War II, Italian troops were generally deployed elsewhere from Bosnia and Herzegovina, but Italian troops did, for instance, occupy Mostar at one stage.

A member of the Italian royal family, Prince Aimone of Savoy-Aosta, Duke of Aosta, became sort of King of Croatia and Prince of Bosnia and Herzegovina. He refused to serve as king in a real sense because of a dispute over the Italian annexation of Dalmatia.

During the Bosnian War, Italian aircraft participated in Operation Deny Flight, enforcing a no-fly zone over Bosnia; and on the conclusion of the Bosnian War in 1995, Italian troops entered Bosnia as part of Implementation Force (IFOR) and subsequently formed part of Stabilization Force (SFOR) there.

Botswana

Not a country that's had much, if any, invading by Italians.
On the other hand, troops from what was then the British-controlled territory of Bechuanaland did invade Italy during World War II. For instance, in 1944 they played a role in the bitter battle for Monte Cassino.

Brazil

Italians have been involved with the amazing country of Brazil pretty much from the start of any European involvement with the area.

Florentine explorer Amerigo Vespucci may have been the first European to reach Brazil. In 1500, Pedro Álvares Cabral claimed the region for Portugal; and in 1501, Vespucci was on an expedition to chart the coastline of this territory that was new to Europeans. The expedition he was on traveled along a significant chunk of the coastline of Brazil.

Pope Alexander VI's Treaty of Tordesillas, signed in 1494, carved up South America into Spanish and Portuguese spheres. In a sense, the father of Cesare and Lucretia Borgia was also, therefore, the father of Brazil. In 1608, however, an Italian-sponsored expedition explored the coastline along Brazil's most northern point with a view toward settlement (see Suriname). A Genoese attempt to create a trading enterprise aimed at exploiting Brazil ended in disaster, but nevertheless, many Italians soon moved there. Italian immigration increased greatly in the nineteenth century, particularly in the last decades; and even more Italians arrived in the twentieth century. Almost one in five Brazilians has Italian ancestry.

One Italian who invaded Brazil in the nineteenth century was Giuseppe Garibaldi himself. In 1839, Garibaldi joined rebels in southern Brazil fighting to set up a separate state in Rio Grande do Sul. Garibaldi conducted a variety of naval operations in support of the rebels, including fighting in Imbituba Bay; and was caught up in various land battles, such as at Forquilhas. Today, a town in Rio Grande do Sul mainly inhabited by Brazilians of Italian descent is called, yes, Garibaldi. It was not all fighting for Garibaldi, though. While in Brazil, he met and married his first wife, Anita Ribeiro da Silva.

In the early nineteenth century Italian ships, including ships of the Sardinian Navy, were sent to Brazilian waters to protect Italian interests. In 1865, Italy's South American Naval Division established a base at Montevideo in Uruguay.

Italians played a major role in Brazilian politics and the military, as well as a wide variety of other aspects of Brazilian life. For instance, a number of Brazilian presidents have had Italian ancestry.

In the 1930s, Brazilian leader Getulio Vargas adopted some policies that were similar to Mussolini's. Mussolini himself saw Brazil as a potential bridgehead for Italian influence in South America and planned to use Italian aircraft sales to the Brazilian Air Force to help expand that influence. The Integralist movement in Brazil, which emerged in 1932, had many similarities to Italian fascism and some Italian support. It tried to seize power in a coup in 1938, but failed and subsequently collapsed.

At the beginning of World War II, Brazil initially remained neutral. However, after the attack on Pearl Harbor, its neutrality started to change as America increased its military links with Brazil.

During the war Italian submarines conducted extensive operations in the waters off Brazil. For instance, just between April 8 and 12, 1942, the *Calvi* sank three ships off the Brazilian coast: the American tanker the *Eugene V. R. Thayer*, the Norwegian *Balkis*, and the Panamanian tanker *Ben Brush*. In July 1942, the *Calvi* itself was depth charged to the surface by HMS *Lulworth* and then hit by gunfire until the crew was forced to abandon ship. A subsequent explosion sank the submarine.

And it wasn't just that Axis submarines were operating in the waters of Brazil. They were also attacking Brazilian merchant ships. On February 25, 1942, the Italian submarine *Leonardo da Vinci* sank the Brazilian ship SS *Cadebelo*. On May 18, the Italian submarine *Barbarigo* torpedoed the Brazilian ship *Comandante Lyra*, although the ship did not actually sink.

On August 22, 1942, Brazil declared war on Germany and Italy, and eventually, Brazilian troops invaded Italy. The first troops of the Brazilian Expeditionary Force arrived in Naples in 1944. Subsequently, the force saw extensive action during the fighting as the Allies advanced in northern Italy.

In the postwar period, examples of cooperation between Italy and Brazil on military matters include the development of the Italian-Brazilian AMX tactical fighter.

Italian influence in Brazil persists. Brazilians, for example, say *ciao* for good-bye.

BRUNEI

ITALIANS HAVEN'T HAD AS MUCH INVOLVEMENT with Brunei as other European nations have, but they did have some of the earliest.

In the summer of 1521, *Victoria*, the flagship of Ferdinand Magellan's round-the-world expedition (minus Magellan, who was already dead) arrived at Brunei, making the crew the first Europeans to set foot on Brunei. Among those on the expedition who had made it that far was Antonio Pigafetta from Vicenza, who would later write a fascinating account of life in Brunei. They were taken on elephants to see the sultan, who lived in an impressive city of 25,000 homes or families. Apart from the palace and the homes of the most important families, Pigafetta noted that the people lived in wooden houses built on piles in the sea and then moved into boats at high tide. To a man who knew Venice well, he must have found some of this very familiar. He also described the sultan's cannons, and the nobles and secretaries that surrounded the sultan in his palace. At some stage the expedition encountered Brunei war junks and temporarily captured them, before finding out they were part of a fleet returning from southern Borneo.

In 1870, an expedition aboard the Italian navy corvette *Principessa Clotilde*, under the command of Carlo Racchia, headed for Borneo and territory controlled by the Sultan of Brunei, in what is now Malaysia. They planned to establish a penal colony there, but opposition from the United States, the United Kingdom, and the Netherlands prevented the plan from being put into operation.

BULGARIA

WHEN THE ROMANS OCCUPIED MACEDONIA during the second century BC, they found the Thracians to their north. The next century was not always an easy one for the relationship between Rome and the Thracians. Rome tried to exercise lordship over assorted Thracian royals, who struggled among themselves for control of the Thracians. Finally, in AD 46, after Rhoemetalces III, King of the Thracians, had been murdered by some of the locals, possibly by his own wife, the Romans took over the area and made it a Roman province. This included most of what is today the modern country of Bulgaria.

Meanwhile, Roman power had been expanding elsewhere into modern-day Bulgaria, including places like Varna—which was called Odessus then, in the province of Moesia—and eventually the Danube frontier. This area, running along much of the current Bulgarian-Romanian border, would become one of the Roman Empire's most significant frontiers, particularly before Trajan's invasion of Dacia, and again after Dacia was abandoned by Rome in the third century.

Major figures from Thrace in Roman history include, of course, Spartacus and Maximinus Thrax, a third-century Roman emperor (235–238).

In 376, Goths displaced by the movement of the Huns to the north sought permission to cross the Danube and settle within the empire. Seeing them as new potential defenders of the Danube frontier, Emperor Valens agreed, and the Goths entered what is now northern Bulgaria. The treatment they received at the hands of local officials, however, soon caused the Goths to rebel. That led to the major Roman defeat in August 378 at the Battle of Adrianople in what is now the European part of Turkey, and in which Valens himself was killed.

More peoples from beyond the imperial borders followed the Goths, including, eventually, the Bulgars, who threatened Byzantium itself.

During the Middle Ages armed Italians would return to Bulgaria.

In 1366, Amadeus VI of the House of Savoy (which would eventually provide Italy with a royal family) invaded Bulgaria. He was supposed to be on a crusade against the Turks, and he did achieve some success against them before turning his attention to attacking the Bulgars on behalf of the Byzantines. He attacked and captured a number of coastal towns in Bulgaria, including Nesebar and Emona, before laying siege to Varna.

And more crusaders followed. Italian ships on the Danube took part in the Crusade of Nicopolis in an attempt to halt the advance of Ottoman Turks into Europe. This, however, resulted in a massive defeat of the crusaders at the hands of the Ottoman Turks, at the Battle of Nicopolis on September 25, 1396. In another example, Italians were deeply involved in the run-up to the Battle of Varna in 1444. Another crusader army once again confronted the Turks, with Genoese and Venetian ships in support in the Black Sea. The crusaders again suffered a terrible defeat, setting the scene for the Fall of Constantinople in 1453, less than ten years later.

Bulgaria was on the losing side in World War I, and Italian troops were part of the victorious Allied force that occupied the country for a period after the war.

In October 1930, with Mussolini present, Princess Giovanna, daughter of King Victor Emmanuel III, married Tsar Boris III of Bulgaria. Boris died under suspicious circumstances in 1943 (he had just visited Hitler), but Giovanna's son Simeon went on to become, briefly, the last tsar of Bulgaria until the Communist takeover became complete.

Bulgaria joined NATO in 2004.

BURKINA FASO

I T IS POSSIBLE THAT TRADERS FROM ROMAN NORTH AFRICA traveled as far south as parts of Burkina Faso. Recent analysis of copper-based objects found at Kissi in northern Burkina Faso, which date from between the first century BC and the ninth century AD, suggests that material in them is derived from ores from North Africa and the Mediterranean.

In the 1980s, Italian SIAI-Marchetti SF.260 aircraft of the Burkina Faso Air Force took part in the Agacher Strip War against Mali.

BURMA

T HE ROMANS SEEM TO HAVE BEEN AWARE of Burma as a land that could be reached by traveling across the sea east from India.

Ancient Sanskrit and Buddhist texts refer to Burma as the Golden Land, and Greek and Roman texts refer to a land in the area called Chryse (*golden* in Greek). And Ptolemy describes a sea voyage that could be made by traveling east from Paloura, in Ganjam, India, to a city called Sada, probably in Burma.

In the Middle Ages, even before the Portuguese and Italians opened up the sea route to India around the Cape of Good Hope, Italians became involved with Burma.

Marco Polo may or may not have actually visited the great Burmese city of Pagan, but he does describe it and Burma in his accounts of his travels. In the mid-fifteenth century Niccoló de' Conti does seem to have visited Arakan in Burma on his travels, and then later again in the same century. And in the very late fifteenth century, just as the sea route was opening up, Genoese Girolamo da Santo Stefano, having traveled via the Red Sea, Aden, and India, arrived with his traveling companion Adorno in the Burmese port of Pegu, only to find himself stuck there due to a war. It was too much for Adorno, who died and was buried there.

When the Portuguese did arrive on the scene in Burma, some Italians were probably involved too.

Certainly, in the nineteenth century, as they tried to decide how to respond to threats from European colonial powers and others, Burmese rulers took a significant interest in links to Italy.

Also in the nineteenth century, after the Burmese had fought a series of wars against Britain, King Mindon Min resolved to update his national infrastructure and his armed forces. He turned to Westerners, including Italians, to help. The Italians helped develop factories, train the armed forces, and build fortifications along the Irrawaddy River.

In 1871, the Italian Navy corvette *Principessa Clotilde* arrived in Rangoon to establish official links, and the Burmese actively sought official Italian involvement in their country as a counter to British and French pressure. A deal was signed providing for Italy to supply arms and technicians.

Italian officers who played a major role with the Burmese armed forces were Captain Barberis, a military tactician; Comotto, who had served as an Italian naval officer; Molinari, a military engineer; army officer Arriti de Perruca; and engineer Fedrici from La Spezia. And Italian activity was not restricted to training, but on occasion included accompanying the Burmese troops on operations.

Then the third Anglo-Burmese War broke out. On November 14, 1885, Camotto and Molonari were on board the king's boat when they encountered British naval forces on board two ships, the *Kathleen* and the *Irawaddy*. While firing at the Burmese shore batteries, the British naval force also used their guns to clear the decks of the Burmese ship, and the Italian officers were captured.

The British took control of Burma, but the Japanese invaded and occupied most of it during World War II. Italian Americans would play a valuable role in forcing the Japanese back out. For instance, the famous Merrill's Marauders included a number of Italian Americans.

BURUNDI

A COUNTRY THAT ITALIANS haven't had that much to do with militarily. A military man from an old Italian family, Georg Leo Graf von Caprivi de Caprera de Montecuccoli, was German chancellor in 1890 and made a deal with Britain that, among many other measures, allotted Burundi—as far as Britain was concerned—to the German sphere of influence. Shortly afterward, it did, indeed, come under German control.

Apparently, the Burundi Air Force operates one Italian aircraft, a SIAI-Marchetti SF .260W.

CAMBODIA

ROMAN LINKS WITH CAMBODIA were not extensive, but Roman coins have been found at Oc Eo in Vietnam; and the ancient Khmer site of Angkor Borei clearly had strong links to Oc Eo, probably by a canal network.

In the Middle Ages Italian explorers, including the monk Odoricus Mattiuzzi, made it to Cambodia.

The French Foreign Legion, founded in 1831, has had its share of Italian nationals. The Legion served in Cambodia in the French colonial era and, more recently, on peacekeeping duty in 1992.

During the Vietnam War, President Nixon launched an "incursion" into Cambodia, and the country was heavily bombed. Some Italian Americans fought in Cambodia with the US forces.

Between 1992 and 1993, Italian personnel took part in the UNTAC (United Nations Transitional Authority in Cambodia) mission.

CAMEROON

It seems unlikely that many Romans made it as far as Cameroon. It has been suggested that the story of the Carthaginian explorer Hanno seeing a mountain with flames coming from the top is a reference to Mount Cameroon. However, other explanations suggest Hanno's fiery mountain was far to the west and closer to known areas of Carthaginian exploration.

It is also possible that Romans made it as far as the Lake Chad area, and a small part of the shoreline of Lake Chad is located in Cameroon.

The Portuguese were the first Europeans definitely to reach the coast of Cameroon, naming the Wouri River the Rio dos Camarões, the river of prawns.

A military man from an old Italian family, Georg Leo Graf von Caprivi de Caprera de Montecuccoli, was head of the German Navy from 1884 to 1888 and German chancellor from 1890 to 1894. During this time, Germany was imposing colonial rule on the area that would become today's state of Cameroon.

Italian antifascist Ettore Toneatti was among the Free French forces that landed in Cameroon on January 1, 1941.

CANADA

I TALIANS MAY NOT HAVE ACTUALLY INVADED CANADA, but you will find more Italian restaurants in Canada than there are Canadian restaurants in Italy.

Italians did, however, play a major part right from the start in the European "invasion" of what is now Canada. We tend to think of Britain and France as the major European powers in Canada, but it was Italians who laid the foundations for British and French power in Canada.

In 1497, Giovanni Caboto (aka John Cabot), born in Italy but working for the English, arrived and claimed the Newfoundland region for England, the first European definitely to reach the North American mainland since the Vikings. He was followed in 1527 by another Italian, Giovanni Verrazano, who explored more of Canada on behalf of the French.

Italian involvement with the invasion of Canada didn't stop there. Italians played a significant role as the British and French pushed farther into Canada and settled it. For instance, Italians were present in the Carignan-Salières Regiment sent to Canada in 1665 to counter attacks by the Iroquois. And two Italian brothers, Enrico and Alphonse de Tonti, played a significant part in the French colonial project in the Great Lakes area in the late seventeenth and early eighteenth centuries. Alphonse was, for example, at one stage governor of Frontenac.

And during the War of 1812, Italians served in the British Army in Canada, in the de Meuron and de Watteville's Swiss mercenary regiments.

The Italian diaspora represented a peaceful invasion of North America from the fifteenth century on. From 1876 to 1942, about 126,000 Italians immigrated to Canada.

Guy Lombardo (1902-1977), the leader of the Royal Canadians, was a distinguished Italian Canadian who sold well over 100 million records.

During the First World War, Italians and Canadians were allied against the Central Powers, and Italian immigrants served in the Canadian forces sent to fight in Europe.

When Mussolini declared war on Britain on June 10, 1940, Canada, as part of the Commonwealth, was at war with Italy. This created problems for the Italian Canadian community. Thirty-one thousand Italian Canadians were immediately designated as enemy aliens, and some six hundred were imprisoned during the war.

Some Italian submarines did operate in the North Atlantic but mainly far to the east of Canada. They were, however, attempting to sink Canadian ships. For example, on March 14, 1943, off the African coast, an Italian submarine fired two torpedoes into the transatlantic steamer *Empress of Canada*, sinking it. On board were thousands of British soldiers and, in addition, hundreds of Italian prisoners of war.

During World War II, it was really the Canadians who invaded Italy, not vice versa. On July 10, 1943, the 1st Canadian Infantry Division and the 1st Canadian Army Tank Brigade were among the first to wade ashore in the invasion of Sicily. Canadians also had fought in North Africa, where they helped capture thousands of Axis soldiers in 1942. Later, also in 1943, they would land and fight on the Italian peninsula.

Over 92,000 Canadians served during the Italian campaign in World War II, and over 5,200 were killed. After Mussolini's arrest, many Italians fought alongside Canadian troops against the Axis forces.

In 1949, Italy and Canada became founding members of NATO. Since then, Italians and Canadians have served in peacekeeping missions around the globe. Both have sent forces to the recent conflict in Afghanistan.

Today there are over one and a half million Italian Canadians living in Canada. The singer Michael Bublé "invades" concert halls around the world and is one of the most famous Italian Canadians alive today.

CAPE VERDE

I T IS POSSIBLE THAT THE ROMANS WERE AWARE of the Cape Verde islands, although that's hard to prove.

What is definite, though, is that in the fifteenth century Italians did invade the Cape Verde islands. Or at least landed on them, since they seem to have had no permanent human residents prior to the arrival of Italians and Portuguese in the second half of that century.

The question of exactly who first reached all the Cape Verde islands and how is a matter of some debate, but Italians, in the pay of the Portuguese, as well as Portuguese explorers themselves were definitely involved. Alvise da Ca' da Mosto from Venice, along with Antoniotto Usodimare from Genoa, and others probably reached the Cape Verde islands during a voyage of exploration along the African coast in 1456. But a voyage that included Antonio de Noli, also from Genoa, made it to the Cape Verde islands in 1460 or 1462 and covered new ground (plus presumably new sea). And it was de Noli who became the first governor ruling the islands.

Plenty more Italians followed them to the islands, including, of course, another man from Genoa, a certain Christopher Columbus.

The royal Italian warship *Staffetta* called in on its long cruise around Africa in 1887–1888.

During World War II, Italian submarines operated extensively in the waters off Cape Verde, and an Italian destroyer called *Antonio da Noli* served in the same conflict. It hit a mine off Corsica and sank in September 1943.

CENTRAL AFRICAN REPUBLIC

I T IS UNLIKELY THAT THE ROMANS GOT THIS FAR SOUTH, although trans-Saharan trade routes may have linked the area with Roman-controlled territory far to the north. The expedition of Julius Maternus, which took him on a four-month journey south from Libya, is supposed to have reached far enough across the Sahara to bring him to the land of Agisymba, in an area where the rhinoceros lived, but this was probably somewhere in the region of Lake Chad.

Italian explorer Gaetano Casati, approaching the area from the east along the Bahr el Ghazal basin, did, however, reach the vicinity in the late 1880s. Shortly afterward, an Italian explorer in the service of France, Pietro Paolo Savorgnan di Brazzà (after whom Brazzaville, capital of the Republic of the Congo, was named), was governor with authority over assorted areas, including some territory in what is now the Central African Republic. In 1892, he appointed Victor Liotard (great name) commandant of Upper Ubangi.

The Central African Republic has had difficult times, and Italian armed forces have played some role in trying to help alleviate different troubles. For instance, in December 2013, Italian Air Force and UN personnel operating in Brindisi started a humanitarian airlift to Bangui, the capital of the Central African Republic. And in the summer of 2014, an Italian military contingent from the 8th Parachute Assault Engineer Regiment "Folgore" and other units were deployed to Bangui as part of EU multinational forces aimed at helping stabilize the country after the recent violent turmoil there.

CHAD

I T'S NOT ENTIRELY CLEAR WHETHER ANY ROMANS ever marched into Chad. Roman artifacts have been found in southern Libya, showing extensive links between the Garamantes people there and the Roman Empire.

Assorted Roman expeditions in this region did penetrate far to the south of the territory they permanently controlled in the north. For instance, an expedition south from Libya under Septimius Flaccus lasted some months and ended up in the middle of the "Aethiopians." Unless the expedition was far off course, this presumably refers to black people; and Flaccus may have reached as far south as the Tibesti Mountains, which are mainly located in northern Chad. And, as mentioned in the previous chapter, an expedition under Julius Maternus did get as far as the land of Agisymba, where the expedition encountered rhinoceroses. This may well have been in the region of Lake Chad, and if so, their route could have taken them through Chad.

Italy did try to get control of a big chunk of Chad during the fascist period. The 1935 Franco-Italian Agreement would have pushed the border of Italian-controlled Libya a lot farther south into what is now Chad, giving Italy control of the so-called Aouzou Strip. In the end, the agreement was never fully implemented. The dispute over exactly who owned this area led to war between Libya, under Colonel Gadhafi, and Chad, until the International Court of Justice determined in 1994 that the area belonged to Chad.

During World War II, after Chad declared for the Free French, the border became a war zone. It was a war zone remote from the main fighting and difficult to operate in, but this did not prevent some hostilities across the border. For example, in January 1942, an Axis team in a daring venture set out to bomb the Allied air base at Fort Lamy (now N'Djamena) in Chad. The air base was a vital point on the route that took Allied aircraft, which had been ferried from America, across Africa to the Middle East.

A Luftwaffe Heinkel 111 and an Italian Savoia set out from Hun in southern Libya and established a temporary base at Campo Uno, also in southern Libya. From there the Heinkel, navigated by Italian Major Roberto Vimercati Sanseverino, flew south over Lake Chad and bombed the air base at Fort Lamy, doing considerable damage to aircraft and fuel supplies before returning to Italian-controlled territory. The bomber couldn't locate Campo Uno again and had to land in the desert; but after supplies were dropped to them, the crew managed to return safely.

Italy sent a number of personnel to assist with the European Union's EUFOR Chad, which from 2008–2009 helped develop the expertise of Chadian security forces.

CHILE

Yes, it's a long distance from Italy. In fact, parts of Chile are about as far as you can get from Italy in South America, but armed Italians have played a major role in Chile, right from the start of the European presence there.

Genoese explorer Giovanni Battista Pastene played a particularly significant role during Spanish expansion into what is now Chile. In the 1540s, he was sent by the Spanish crown to explore southern Chile, and in 1544 was ordered to try to reach the Straits of Magellan. He didn't make it, but in the process he did reach the mouth of the Bío-Bío River and nearby Talcahuano Bay. And in 1550, he played a major role in supporting a Spanish military campaign in the Bío-Bío region. He became regidor of Santiago on regular occasions and eventually mayor. He was also the first governor of Valparaiso. Later Italian immigrants named the modern Chilean town of Capitán Pastene after him.

Pastene wasn't by any means the only Italian involved in the early Spanish attempts to impose colonial control. For instance, Italian military engineer Battista Antonelli was commissioned in 1581 to build a fortress on the shores of the Straits of Magellan. In the end, the attempt to create a colony called Rey Don Felipe turned into a bit of a disaster. Actually, quite a big disaster.

Lots more Italians arrived in the nineteenth century, and many famous Chileans have had Italian ancestry. For instance, two presidents of Chile, Arturo Alessandri and Jorge Alessandri, both came from an Italian family originally from Tuscany; and Salvador Allende's wife, Hortensia Bussi, was Italian Chilean. Arturo Dell'Oro was born in Chile but served with distinction and bravery in the Italian Air Force in the First World War. He was killed in combat in 1917; the airport at Belluno as well as the military airport at Pisa are named after him.

And a son of an Italian immigrant became one of Peru's most famous soldiers. Francisco Bolognesi played a major role in building up the Peruvian Army. He was killed in 1880, heroically defending the then Peruvian port of Arica against attacking Chilean forces during the War of the Pacific. Arica eventually fell and is now within Chile's borders.

In the late nineteenth century, the Italian Navy took quite an interest in Chile. For example, in 1867, the corvette *Magenta* passed through the Straits of Magellan on a voyage of exploration. In 1882, the corvette *Caracciolo* explored extensively around the Magellan straits and the Patagonian canals. In the same year, the corvette *Vettor Pisani* arrived, exploring from Moraleda Canal through Darwin Canal, giving Italian names to lands that did not yet have any. Such names included Puerto Italiano, Monte Italia, and even Monte Vesuvio.

CHINA

IN AD 166, ROMANS CLAIMING TO BE DELEGATES from Marcus Aurelius seem to have arrived at Rinan in Vietnam before traveling to the Chinese court.

Marco Polo and his uncles, Venetian traders, launched a commercial invasion of China in the thirteenth century that foreshadows twenty-first century Italian investment in China. Marco Polo spent seventeen years at the court of Kublai Khan, who ruled China at the time. In 1295, after a twenty-five-year absence, he returned to his native Venice rich with precious stones and even more precious stories.

Marco Polo wasn't the only Italian to make it to China in the Middle Ages. For instance, Florentine Giovanni de' Marignolli traveled there in the fourteenth century. And in the early sixteenth century, Rafael Perestrello, a Portuguese explorer from an old Italian Piacenza family and a cousin of the wife of Columbus, broke new ground by sailing to China shortly after the route to the east through the Cape of Good Hope opened.

In 1898, the Kingdom of Italy sought an imperial outpost on Chinese soil. Rome sent warships and landed marines at San Mun Bay, demanding that it become an Italian port and coaling station for the Italian Navy. During the 1900 Boxer rebellion, the Kingdom of Italy joined the eight-nation alliance that fought against the anti-imperialist movement. A detachment of Italian cruisers was dispatched to Beijing. An Italian expeditionary force of nearly 2,000 men landed.

From 1901 until 1947, Italy had a small 151-acre colony on the coast of northeastern China in Tientsin. Among other sites, the Italians also garrisoned a fort at Shan Hai Kwan.

During the Allied Intervention in Siberia in 1918 and 1919, Italian troops made use of facilities inside China, using them, for instance, for training the Legione Redenta that was formed from freed Italian prisoners of war.

Italian adventurer Amleto Vespa fought first for a Chinese warlord in the 1920s, and then for the Japanese in the 1930s.

Forces from Imperial Japan—which allied with Italy from 1940 until 1943—occupied the Italian concession during much of World War II.

Puccini's *Turandot*, unfinished at his death in 1924, represents the most famous opera to be set in China and is a significant Italian cultural invasion. In the opera, Ping, Pang, and Pong are the three principal ministers to the emperor. The opera was banned by the Chinese Communist regime as a decadent anti-Chinese work of art for many years. Its first Chinese performance took place in 1990 at the Shanghai Opera House. *Turandot* has now become one of the most popular productions in China's many opera houses.

In recent years, Italian merchants, following in the footsteps of Marco Polo, have taken a keen interest in the commercial potential of China. Sales of Italian wine have grown rapidly in China.

Ferrari has been selling its cars in China for more than twenty years.

In April of 2012, the Italian luxury fashion designer, Brunello Cucinelli, raised over $200 million in an IPO. Proceeds were deployed in China, where they opened new stores in Hong Kong and Shanghai.

At the same time, Italy has become a popular tourist destination for the Chinese, who have done a reverse Marco Polo—quaffing Brunello, shopping, and seeing the historic sites.

COLOMBIA

WELL, THE COUNTRY IS NAMED AFTER CHRISTOPHER COLUMBUS, and he did come pretty close to it on his fourth voyage. And Genoese explorer Giovanni Battista Pastene explored the coast of Colombia a few decades later.

Italians played key roles in the Spanish colonial administration of the area. For instance, Battista Antonelli from Gatteo in Romagna was the military engineer responsible for building the San Felipe de Barajas Castle, the San Sebastián de Pastelillo Fort, and the San Fernando Fort at Cartagena.

Other Italians have also had a major involvement with the country. Early nineteenth century soldier, revolutionary, and cartographer Agustin Codazzi is one example. Carlo Castelli is another example.

Castelli was born at San Sebastiano Po near Turin and fought in the Napoleonic Wars with revolutionary fervor. In 1814, though, he headed for South America and was soon fighting for the independence armies in the Cauca Valley in what is now Colombia. It wasn't a huge success on that occasion, but in 1816, Castelli met Simon Bolivar himself and went on to have a long military and political career in South America, some of it taking place in Colombia. For instance, he played a significant role at the Battle of El Santuario in 1829; and in August 1830, Castelli led a pro-Bolivarian rebellion. After victory at the Battle of Funza on August 27, 1830, he marched into Bogota, the capital of Colombia, and took control. The region of Antioquia became his power base. In November 1830, he managed to capture his archrival Cordova and take him to Medellin. Castelli almost had him shot there and then, but instead decided to go through the proper legal process. In March 1831, Cordova escaped, and the war was on again. This time, after a number of skirmishes, it was Castelli's turn to end up in prison. He was sentenced to death for treason but managed to avoid execution after international pleas on his behalf.

Armed Italians returned to the vicinity of the Cauca Valley later in the nineteenth century. At the center of the crisis was one Ernesto Cerruti, born in Turin in 1844. He became an officer in the Italian Army before moving to South America and the Colombian port of Buenaventura. Cerruti got himself involved in a number of enterprises, including arms dealing. When a rebellion occurred, he was accused of helping arm and finance the rebels, and his property was confiscated. An Italian warship, the cruiser *Flavio Gioia*, was sent to support the demands of the Italian government for redress. Could it be war between Italy and Colombia? The dispute was first referred to the King of Spain and eventually to US President Grover Cleveland, who ruled in favor of Italy. Still, it caused a serious rift between Italy and Colombia that took years to mend.

The composer of the music of the Colombian national anthem was Italian. Oreste Sindici was born in Ceccano in the Province of Frosinone and studied in Rome before moving to Colombia. And one of the most famous Colombians today is, of course, Shakira. She has some Italian ancestry from her mother, Nidia Ripoll.

THE COMORO ISLANDS

THE PORTUGUESE TOOK AN EARLY INTEREST in these islands in the Indian Ocean, and it's possible Italians may have been involved in that effort.

In 1936, as tension mounted between Italy and France, there was a secret Italian attempt to reconnoiter the Comoros to prepare for a war that would match Italian and French naval power in the Indian Ocean.

COSTA RICA

ON SEPTEMBER 18, 1502, Genoese Christopher Columbus turned up, to be followed by other Italians as the Spanish imposed colonial control on the area.

One person of Italian descent who played a huge role in the wars and politics of Central America in the early nineteenth century was Francisco Morazán, whose grandfather had been Corsican. Morazán was, from 1830–1839, president of the Federal Republic of Central America. Having fled into exile after defeat in battle in 1840, in 1842 he invaded Costa

Rica in an attempt to take over the government there. In April of that year, he landed with about five hundred men and five ships at Caldera in Costa Rica. After negotiating with the military forces opposing him, he entered San José and took power. But Morazán did not have long ahead of him in power in Costa Rica. In September, a rebellion broke out. After bitter fighting, Morazán was eventually captured and put in front of a firing squad. Allegedly, he gave the order to shoot.

Italians were among the nationalities that immigrated to Costa Rica in the nineteenth century. Giovanni Leggero, who had taken part in the Defense of the Roman Republic in 1848, moved to Costa Rica and ended up losing an arm in fighting against William Walker's forces (see Nicaragua).

Still, as the Second World War erupted, tensions rose between Italy and Costa Rica. In April 1941, for instance, Italian and German sailors in a Costa Rican harbor learned that the Costa Rican government was about to seize their ships, and the ships were set on fire instead.

And after the attack on Pearl Harbor, Costa Rica declared war on Germany and Italy on December 8—two days before the United States.

The war did not end close contact between Italy and Costa Rica. For instance, Vito Giulio Cesar and Ugo Sansonetti, sons of an Italian admiral, established a community of Italians known as San Vito de Java in the south of the country.

CROATIA

W HEN THE ROMANS FIRST ENCOUNTERED the territory that is now Croatia, they found it inhabited by a number of different peoples, and the history of their conquest of the area reflects that diversity. For instance, in the Istrian Peninsula in the northwest of what is now Croatia, they clashed with a people called, not surprisingly, the Istri or Histri.

The first clashes took place in the late third century BC. They culminated in the early second century BC with a number of Roman advances into Histrian territory, ending in an attack on the Histrian king Epaulon in his capital at Nesactium. Epaulon committed suicide when he realized the Histri could no longer hold the city against the attacking Romans.

In the south of what is now Croatia, the Romans fought with the peoples there during the Illyrian Wars in the late third and early second centuries BC, including clashes on the Croatian islands of Hvar and Vis. Finally, in 168 BC the Romans scored a major and decisive victory over the Illyrians.

Along with fighting for the central coastal territory, the Romans fought a number of conflicts against the Dalmatae in the last two centuries BC. And to the north of the Dalmatae, Roman control and influence spread gradually over the Liburnians at around the same time. Conquest of the interior and east of what is now Croatia took longer; and a number of Roman civil wars erupted throughout the territory.

The Middle Ages saw plenty of Italian action in the area as well.

For example, in Istria, which had been at one stage a sort of border between Frankish territory and the peoples to the east, as well as an area where the Patriarchs of Aquileia had great influence, Venice eventually began to exercise considerable control. It had dominated much of Istria's western coastline since the ninth century, and in 1267, it took control of a lot more.

Farther south, Venice also took charge of Dalmatia.

On Ascension Day 998, Pietro II Orseolo, Doge of Venice, assumed the title Duke of the Dalmatians. Venice would maintain control of much of Dalmatia until the Napoleonic period. Venice had authority over a lot of Croatian islands; while on the mainland, its control was focused on the three major cities of Zara/Zadar, Spalato/Split, and Ragusa/Dubrovnik, until Dubrovnik became independent. Fighting between Venetian and Ottoman forces took place in Dalmatia. For example, during the Cretan War of 1645–1669, the Ottomans attacked in the region, capturing several islands and the key inland fortress of Novigrad. The Venetian forces counterattacked, retaking territory—including Novigrad—and pushing as far inland as Knin, which they held briefly. And again during the Morean War (1684–1699), Venetian and Ottoman forces clashed in what is now Croatian territory, and once again the Venetians took Knin.

Other figures with Italian links were also active in the area. For example, in the late fourteenth century, Charles of Durazzo, King of Naples, also became ruler of Slavonia, Dalmatia, and Croatia, as well as eventually Hungary. His son, Ladislaus of Naples, ended up selling his Dalmatian interests to Venice. Pipo of Ozora also campaigned in Croatia.

The Venetians lost control of their Croatian territories in 1797, although the Napoleonic Kingdom of Italy briefly continued Italian political control in the area before the Austrian Empire became the dominant force.

In 1866, it was suggested that Garibaldi invade Dalmatia, but instead he chose to advance into the Trentino.

However, Italian troops did arrive in force again at the end of World War I, and Italy took control of Istria again. And the Fiume incident saw Italian poet Gabriele D'Annunzio seize the port of Fiume in 1919, before Italy annexed it in 1922. Farther south, after clashes between Italian troops and other forces in a number of areas, the Italians ended up in control of Zadar again and the island of Lastovo.

During the years between the wars, Mussolini gave some assistance to exiled Croatian Ustasha leaders who wanted to separate Croatia from Yugoslavia.

And in 1941, Italian troops invaded Yugoslavia, moving into Dalmatia. Italy annexed parts of Dalmatia, while a separate Croatian state was established with the Ustasha government. A member of the Italian royal family, Prince Aimone of Savoy-Aosta, Duke of Aosta, became (officially) King of Croatia and Prince of Bosnia and Herzegovina.

After the Italian armistice with the Allies in 1943, some Italians ended up fighting alongside Yugoslav partisans against the Germans. For instance, the Partisan Battalion Pino Budicin operated mainly in Istria, and a number of Italians operated in Partisan units named after Garibaldi.

Over the centuries, Dalmatian Italians and Istrian Italians had become a sizeable community. Some fled after 1943, but Dalmatian Italian and Istrian Italian communities still remain in Croatia today.

Croatia joined NATO in 2009.

CUBA

CUBA IS BY FAR THE LARGEST ISLAND in the Caribbean. So perhaps it should come as no surprise that when Columbus, hoping to find his way to the riches of Asia, approached its coastline on October 24, 1492, he mistook it for a continent.

He named the island *Isla Juana*, after the Spanish prince of Asturias. Columbus seemed to be enchanted by Cuba, pronouncing it the "sweetest and fairest" of lands. He was, however, disappointed not to discover gold on the island and soon moved on to Hispaniola (see Haiti and Dominican Republic).

In addition to Columbus, other Italians played a significant role in establishing and maintaining Spanish rule in Cuba. For example, Italian military engineer Battista Antonelli designed the spectacular El Morro fortress for Havana.

In 1605, Mantua, Cuba, was founded by shipwrecked Italian sailors.

Cuba was under Spanish rule for many centuries. The Spanish-American War of 1898 ended that. An Italian American from New York State, Frank O. Fournia, won the Medal of Honor for rescuing wounded soldiers while serving in the US Army in Cuba during this war.

Cuba became a major sugar producer in the early twentieth century. It is the mere addition of sugar that distinguishes an authentic café cubano from a traditional Italian espresso. This popular drink might even be classified as a sweet Cuban invasion of Italy!

Cuba and Italy both eventually joined the Allied cause in World War I.

Immediately after Pearl Harbor, Cuba joined the Allies and declared war on fascist Italy. Some Italian Cubans were arrested and imprisoned during the war. A small but efficient Cuban Navy patrolled the waters off Cuba, hunting German and Italian submarines. Italian submarines such as the *Leonardo da Vinci* and the *Enrico Tazzoli* retraced the path of Columbus, hunting for merchant ships in the waters off Cuba. Even Ernest Hemingway, who had served in Italy in World War I, took his fishing boat *Pilar* out hunting for Axis submarines.

The famous mobster Lucky Luciano was born in Sicily in 1897. During World War II, while a prisoner at Sing Sing, he provided intelligence information on his native land to the US Navy prior to the July 1943 invasion of Sicily. His sentence was commuted by the governor of New York in 1946 on the condition that he would be deported to Italy. He was, but in October of 1946, he moved to Cuba, where he helped to organize a mob takeover of the island nation. Luciano and Meyer Lanksy sealed a deal with the Batista regime one night in 1946 at the Hotel Nacional. Frank Sinatra provided the entertainment. Havana would be transformed into a Caribbean Las Vegas.

An Italian-born entrepreneur, Amadeo Barletta, was the publisher of *El Mundo,* one of the largest Cuban newspapers in the 1950s.

Fidel Castro led the Cuban Revolution that would sweep Batista and the Mafia from power in Cuba. Later, the CIA hired the Mafia to assassinate Castro, but with no success.

In 1961, Italian-built 105mm howitzers were used at the Bay of Pigs by Castro's forces against the American-supported invaders.

A visitor to Havana today might stumble upon the Napoleon Museum, which houses one of the finest collections of Napoleonic memorabilia in the world. This museum, dedicated to the former King of Italy and founded in 1961, was once the home of Orestes Ferrara, an Italian Cuban who had been ambassador to the United States.

CYPRUS

I N 58 BC, ROME NEEDED MONEY and needed it badly. Julius Caesar had exhausted the treasury with his consular schemes in the previous year, and a plebeian tribune, Publius Clodius Pulcher, knew that additional ambitious public spending would need new sources of funds. He reckoned he had the answer. The rich island of Cyprus looked ripe for exploitation, so in 58 BC he got a law passed that allowed Rome to seize Cyprus from Ptolemy, who was ruling it at the time. Accusations of piracy in the area may have been a pretext, and Ptolemy killed himself shortly afterward, so the Romans moved in unopposed.

However, they lost the island again, sort of, a few years later when Mark Antony, in a romantic gesture, gave it to Cleopatra. However, by the end of 31 BC, she had no further use for it, since she was dead, and Roman rule resumed.

Military involvement with the island was minimal during the Roman period, except for the tragic events of AD 116, when a Jewish revolt in Salamis was ruthlessly crushed.

The island eventually became part of the Byzantine Empire and suffered Arab invasions. And then the crusaders arrived.

Among the Italian crusaders who spent time on the island was one Richard Filangieri. Richard was the son of the Lord of Nocera and a member of the Neapolitan aristocracy. He was also a commander of troops in the service of the Italian-born Holy Roman emperor Frederick II. Frederick's forces were caught in a grim battle with the forces of the powerful Ibelin family (who some have suggested also had Italian roots) for control of territory in Cyprus and the Holy Land. In 1232, Filangieri's forces clashed with Ibelin forces at the Battle of Agridi in Cyprus. Filangieri ended up fleeing to Kyrenia. The city was besieged by land and then eventually from the sea, by the Genoese. Filiangieri, however, did manage to escape the debacle before his fellow Italians fully closed the trap on him and Kyrenia.

But a battle for control of Cyprus between Genoa and Venice had yet to be decided. In 1292, a Venetian fleet attacked Genoese targets in Cyprus. After a fight between Venetians and Genoese after the coronation of Peter II of Cyprus, a Genoese expeditionary force invaded the island in 1372. The Genoese captured Peter, attacked Nicosia, and took Famagusta, which they hung onto for almost a century. Genoa had the upper hand in Cyprus.

Italian merchant families became more and more powerful in Cyprus during the fourteenth century. Among them was the powerful Cornaro family from Venice, which had produced several doges. In 1472, Caterina Cornaro was installed on Cyprus as the queen of James II of Cyprus, also known as James the Bastard. James actually had managed to throw the Genoese out of Famagusta, but Venice was another matter. By August 1474, with both her new husband and their young son dead, Caterina was queen of Cyprus on her own. It didn't last. In 1489, she sold the island to Venice, which is where she died in 1510.

Venice would not stay in control of Cyprus for long. A massive Ottoman-Turkish invasion force landed on Cyprus in 1570. Nicosia fell after a siege and bitter fighting. Kyrenia surrendered, and only Famagusta was left. On August 1, 1571, after a siege of many months, the garrison, out of supplies, surrendered too.

It was not, however, to be the end of Italian dreams of controlling Cyprus. For instance, in 1607, Ferdinand I of Tuscany planned to seize Cyprus and the Holy Land. His fleet did attack Famagusta but failed to take it, and he gave up. And in 1633, Victor Amadeus I of Savoy, after receiving an appeal from a Greek priest seeking his help in liberating Cyprus from the Turks, declared himself King of Cyprus, even though he wasn't.

During World War II, Italian soldiers returned to Cyprus. Or rather, Italian air crews bombed the island, by now under British control, on a number of occasions. The first Italian air raid targeted Cyprus on September 22, 1940. In the following months, a number of raids would hit a variety of targets on the island, including Paphos, Nicosia, Larnaca, and Famagusta. At the time, British forces on Cyprus feared an Axis attempt to seize the island similar to the operation against Crete, but such an attack never came.

A planned commando raid by paratroopers and frogmen of the X Arditi Regiment in January 1943 was cancelled.

Italian forces have been to Cyprus since World War II. For instance, the Italian Navy has evacuated European civilians to there from Lebanon at times of crisis in that country. And in 2005, Italy sent a number of

Carabinieri officers to take part in UNFICYP, the United Nations Peacekeeping Force in Cyprus.

CZECH REPUBLIC

Y ES, THE CZECH REPUBLIC has had Italians fighting on its soil.
Generally speaking, Roman invasion of the territory now known as the Czech Republic was a near miss.

In 9 BC, Roman legions under Nero Claudius Drusus won a victory over the Marcomanni somewhere in the Elbe River region. The result was to push the Marcomanni eastward into a region then occupied by a tribe called the Boii, from whom Bohemia would get its name. A Marcomannic chief called Maroboduus carved out a territory for himself, and Roman merchants traveled to him to sell him goods. But the Roman military had other ideas. They were targeting his land and had a large-scale invasion force ready to go, only to have to cancel the operation when a rebellion in Pannonia in AD 6 rather urgently called their attention elsewhere.

And if the Romans hadn't had such a nasty shock at the Battle of the *Teutoburger Wald* in AD 9, when Arminius and his Germans wiped out three legions, then the Roman advance at that stage, or shortly after, might well have pushed deep into what is now the Czech Republic. Instead, they seem to have settled for a deal in which the Marcomanni had a kind of client status.

This wasn't the end of it, though. Other near misses were to come, the most significant of which was the attack on the Marcomanni in the late second century by philosopher-emperor Marcus Aurelius. To be fair to Marcus Aurelius, the Marcomanni seem to have started it that time. They invaded the empire and made it as far as Aquileia in Italy before they were stopped.

In 172, the forces of Marcus Aurelius struck north, into the lands of the Marcomanni. Then in 173, they hit another tribe, the Qadi. But at that stage, the emperor was distracted by a rebellion in the east; and in 177, the tribes rebelled. Marcus Aurelius began another campaign against the enemy a year later. The Romans were victorious and plans were afoot to create a new province, but by 180 Marcus Aurelius was dead. His successor, Commodus, having no interest in the campaign, made peace and gave up the newly conquered territories. But traces of temporary Roman camps in northeastern Moravia do suggest a substantial Roman invasion of what is now the Czech Republic, even if it didn't last.

Many Italian soldiers were to follow their footsteps.

For example, during the Hussite Wars, the famous Florentine condottiero Filippo Scolari played a key role in the imperial forces attacking Bohemia to crush the uprising. He was, however, nearing the end of a spectacular career, and it was not his finest campaign. He took part in the Battle of Vitkov Hill in 1420, was in the inconclusive Battle of Kutna Hora in 1421, but lost to the Hussites at the Battle of Německý Brod in 1422. He did have success in another campaign in Serbia before finally dying in 1426.

The seventeenth century was another period of major activity by Italian soldiers in what is now the Czech Republic as large parts of Europe were torn apart by the Thirty Years War. For instance, Florentine Ottavio Piccolomini, sent by the Grand Duke of Tuscany to help the imperial forces, fought alongside the forces of the Catholic League as captain of a cavalry regiment and had great success at the Battle of White Mountain outside Prague in 1620. Another Italian officer, Matteo Galasso, also led a unit in the invasion of Bohemia in 1620, and by 1625 was a colonel in his own regiment. Another Italian, Carlo Spinelli, led thousands of Neapolitan troops first to Austria and then to the Battle at White Mountain. Later in the war, the famous Raimondo Montecuccoli would also fight in what is now Czech territory, saving Brno from siege in 1645.

In fact, in the period after 1634, Italians began to own significant chunks of land in what is now the Czech Republic. For instance, the Piccolomini family acquired an estate at Náchod, the Colloredo picked one up at Opočno, and the Collalto family got one at Brtnice.

The end of the eighteenth and beginning of the nineteenth centuries was another time of major military activity by Italians in what is now the Czech Republic. And they were there in a number of different armies. Yegor Gavrilovich Zuccato, for instance, from an Italian Russian family, was with the Russian Army fighting in Prague in 1799. Italians also served with the Austrian Army in the area. Plenty were with the French forces as well. Troops of the Italian Royal Guard, for example, fought in Napoleon's decisive victory at Austerlitz in 1805.

More Italian troops saw action in Bohemia later in the nineteenth century, such as the Italian troops in the Austrian Army during the Austro-Prussian War. And then we have the twentieth century.

Combat didn't reach the area, then still part of the Austro-Hungarian Empire, during the First World War; but after that, the Italian Army found itself involved in a war on Czech soil.

Late in that war, the Italians armed and trained a volunteer Czechoslovak Legion to fight on the Allied side. After the war ended, and as new nations emerged from the old Austro-Hungarian Empire, Italian troops accompanied the Czechoslovak Legionaries to the new Czechoslovakia. The border between the new Czechoslovakia and the new Poland was an area of some dispute. Italy and France sided with Czechoslovakia; and on January 23, 1919, the Czechoslovak Army, with Italian and French support, attacked the Poles. After bitter Polish resistance and eventual pressure from the Allies for the Czechs to halt their advance—the front line came to rest along the Vistula—an armistice was signed on January 30.

Mussolini publicly supported Hitler in the 1938 dismemberment and eventual annexation of Czechoslovakia.

The Czech Republic joined NATO in 1999.

DEMOCRATIC REPUBLIC OF THE CONGO

THIS IS THE CONGO COUNTRY that used to be a Belgian colony. Italians played a significant role in early Portuguese exploration of the African coast, and in the mid-nineteenth century, other Italians ventured into the area from the other direction, from Sudan and the Nile. One of them, Giovanni Miani, died in 1872 at Nangazizi in what is now the Democratic Republic of the Congo.

And in December 1885, Italian naval officer Giacomo Bove, funded by the Italian Foreign Ministry, set off with Enrico Stassano and Captain Guiseppe Fabrello of the Italian infantry to investigate expanding Italian trade and influence in the area that now forms part of the Democratic Republic of the Congo. It turned out that the possibilities weren't great because other Europeans had already firmly established themselves there.

In the late nineteenth century, the King of Italy did, however, get to determine a characteristic part of the border of what would become the Democratic Republic of the Congo, when he adjudicated in a territorial dispute between Belgium and Britain and helped create the protruding Congo Pedicle.

In September 1942, the Italian submarine *Alpino Bagnolini* was in position off the mouth of the Congo; it failed to sink anything there before moving farther west.

The Italian military returned to the area in the chaotic years following the country's independence from Belgium. In November 1961, thirteen Italian Air Force crewmen serving with the United Nations, including a number of World War II veterans, were tragically killed in the Kindu massacre after being falsely accused of supporting Katangese secessionists. A memorial to the murdered airmen stands outside Leonardo da Vinci-Fiumicino Airport.

Some Italians also fought as mercenaries in the Congo.

In 2006, Italian troops were part of the EUFOR RD Congo Mission, assisting the United Nations during the elections there.

DENMARK

O F ALL THE SCANDINAVIAN COUNTRIES, Denmark is the closest to what was the Roman Empire. Perhaps not surprisingly, therefore, it also has rather more marked concentrations of Roman artifacts than in the other Scandinavian countries. Some of these no doubt arrived along trade routes, but it's also been argued that some were brought to Denmark by men returning there after fighting in or alongside the Roman Army. It's even possible that some were taken there by Roman soldiers or naval personnel. Unlike with the other Scandinavian countries, we do know from historical sources that at least one Roman military expedition either reached the seas off Denmark or came very close to them. Pliny the Elder describes how in the reign of Augustus, a fleet sailed up the north coast as far as the promontory of the Cimbri and learned about an enormous sea beyond it. The promontory of the Cimbri seems to be Jutland, most of which now lies inside Denmark, and the sea beyond it is the Baltic. The work of classical geographers also shows that they knew Jutland was a peninsula, suggesting a familiarity with what is now Danish territory.

Italians have on occasion invaded Denmark. For instance, during the Second Northern War of 1655-1660, Raimondo, Count of Montecuccoli, as a field marshal in the Hapsburgs' Imperial Army, found himself in Denmark fighting invading Swedes. Between 1658 and 1659, among other activities, he pushed the Swedes out of Jutland and landed on the Danish islands of Fyn and Als, capturing those as well.

As members of NATO, both modern Italy and Denmark have assorted military links.

DJIBOUTI

T HE COAST OF DJIBOUTI FORMS MOST OF ONE HALF of the straits at the mouth of the Red Sea, the Bab-el-Mandeb. This area was well known to Roman merchants who made the voyage through the Red Sea, either to trade at local ports or to pass into the Indian Ocean. And the Roman Empire even seems to have had some military presence in the region. An inscription from one of the Farasan Islands, lying to the north in the Red Sea, records that in AD 144, during the reign of Antoninus Pius, troops of the Legio II Traiana Fortis and its auxiliaries built a fortified camp on the island. They did so under the command of one Avitus, who is identified as the prefect of both that area and of the Pontus Herculis, the Straits of Hercules, the Roman name for the Red Sea straits. It may well be that Avitus controlled ships operating in the Red Sea down to the straits rather than exercising too much direct control over any of the shoreline as far south as Djibouti, but it's interesting, nonetheless.

Italian traders continued to travel through the Bab-el-Mandeb in the Middle Ages, and Italian mercenaries fighting for the Egyptians in the late nineteenth century operated not far from Djibouti when battling the Ethiopians, but it was during the twentieth century that Italy took the most intense interest in Djibouti.

In the scramble to divide up East Africa among the European powers in the nineteenth century, Italy ended up with Eritrea to the north of Djibouti and Italian Somalia to the south of British Djibouti and British Somaliland. When the Italians occupied Ethiopia as well in 1936, Djibouti, or French Somaliland as it was then known, became a prime target for future Italian expansion. And the Second World War was not far distant.

In 1938, the Italians already had moved troops into French-controlled territory in the area, and clashes occurred on the ground as the Italian and French governments argued over the interpretation of the 1897 Franco-Ethiopian agreement that had defined the border. Late that same year, Italian foreign minister Galeazzo Ciano made an aggressive speech demanding that France cede Djibouti to Italy, and crowds in Rome angrily demonstrated in favor of Italian control of the territory. As war clouds gathered, the Italian Navy made plans to seize Djibouti in the event of war breaking out with France and Britain.

When war was declared in September 1939, Italy stayed out at first, but in June 1940, as German tanks raced through France, Mussolini declared war on France, and Italian operations against French Somaliland began. Italian ground forces advanced along a strategic rail route and clashed with the French defenders at Ali Sabieh. Meanwhile, the Italian Navy was active in the Red Sea and the Italian Air Force was active in the skies over French Somaliland. For instance, on June 21 they bombed Djibouti in the teeth of heavy French antiaircraft fire; and on June 22, they bombed Djibouti's port during the night, followed by waves of aircraft that hit the airfield.

It was not, however, a long war. On June 24, the armistice between Italy and France came into effect as resistance in France crumbled. However, as confusion in French Somaliland persisted about how the armistice was to be implemented there, clashes continued through July. Eventually, a Vichy regime was installed in Djibouti that was friendly to Italy, and the French regime there would end up defending its territory against British forces rather than Italian.

Some Italians served in the 13th Demi-Brigade of the French Foreign Legion, which was based in Djibouti from 1961 until 2011.

In recent years, Italy has had some minor security involvement with the area. For instance, Italian Carabinieri have been stationed in Djibouti to train Somali police forces as part of the MIADIT Somalia operation, and Italian forces deployed on antipirate operations have used facilities in Djibouti.

DOMINICA

O N SUNDAY, NOVEMBER 3, 1493, Genoese Christopher Columbus caught sight of the island and named it Dominica after the Italian word for Sunday.

That may be pretty much it from the point of view of Italians invading Dominica. Piedmontese troops were sent to the neighboring French Caribbean island of Martinique in 1805, but probably too late to be involved in French attacks on Dominica.

An interesting early connection with Dominica is that of an Italian painter who launched a peaceful artistic "invasion" of Dominica in the eighteenth century. Agostino Brunias was born in Rome in about 1730. He moved first to London as a young man and then settled in Roseau in Dominica. He painted mainly scenes of life in Dominica but also painted on other Caribbean islands, leaving a remarkable record of the area at that time. When he died, he was buried at Roseau.

DOMINICAN REPUBLIC

THE DOMINICAN REPUBLIC GAINED ITS INDEPENDENCE from Haiti in 1844, but Italians made their mark on the territory much earlier than that.

One need not look far to find signs of Italian "invasions" in the Dominican Republic. A visitor to La Isabella will find the Casa Almirante, or Admiral's House. This was the first American home of the famous Genoese explorer Christopher Columbus. The palace of Diego Columbus, the oldest son of Columbus, is in the capital of the Dominican Republic, Santo Domingo. Most impressively, the Columbus lighthouse, built in the shape of a cross and completed in 1992, casts incandescent beams from its 102-foot-high perch in Santo Domingo.

Christopher Columbus has become a highly controversial figure in world history. His detractors have denounced him as racist, greedy for gold, a religious fanatic, and too comfortable with slavery. His defenders have pointed to his undoubted courage, his extraordinary seamanship, and his stubborn determination. They have also noted the impossibility of imposing twenty-first-century values onto the fifteenth century and the unfairness of blaming Columbus for all the evils of subsequent European colonialism.

What is indisputable about Columbus is that he changed the world forever. To biologists, he is known as the father of the Columbian Exchange, which may arguably rank as the most consequential Italian invasion in history. As a result of the Columbian Exchange, Europeans received tomatoes, potatoes, cocoa, tobacco, and boatloads of silver from the New World. Spaghetti Bolognese did not exist before Columbus. There was no Swiss chocolate before the introduction of cocoa to Europe. The Spanish, in fact, kept the existence of chocolate a secret for a century after Columbus.

Those living in what became known as the Americas received horses, pigs, the lowly earthworm, and Christian missionaries. Lacking immunities, they also received new diseases, such as the smallpox that eventually ravaged the indigenous population of two continents. It has been estimated that, thirty years after the first arrival of Columbus, over 90 percent of the native population of the island of Hispaniola was killed by enslavement and disease.

Not all exchanges are fair.

Some scientists have gone so far as to claim that Columbus, in a sense, reversed continental drift and restored Pangaea to the world. It seems inarguable to say that, for better or worse, the Genoese sea captain transformed our world, making it a smaller, more connected planet.

Rafael Trujillo, who ruled the Dominican Republic for thirty years, from 1930 until his assassination in 1961, was an admirer of Mussolini and received his first foreign decoration from Il Duce. The British foreign minister to the Dominican Republic went so far as to suggest that Trujillo "viewed himself as a prospective Dominican Mussolini."

In spite of this, the two dictators clashed over tobacco interests in the 1930s, and Mussolini even threatened to dispatch elements of the Italian Navy to the Dominican Republic in 1935 over the Barletta incident.

After the attack on Pearl Harbor in 1941, Trujillo's Dominican Republic joined the Allied side. Italian submarines prowled menacingly in the Caribbean waters surrounding the Dominican Republic until the Italian capitulation of 1943.

The Italian diaspora has had a significant impact on the Dominican Republic. For example, Francisco Gregorio Billini, who was of Italian heritage, served briefly as the twenty-third president of the Dominican Republic in the 1880s. Much more recently, Miss Dominican Republic 2012 was the lovely Dulcita Lieggi, also of Italian stock.

Dominican troops fought briefly alongside Italian forces in the recent war in Iraq.

EAST TIMOR

ITALIANS WERE AMONG THE FIRST EUROPEANS to reach the island of Timor. In January 1522, what was left of the Magellan expedition discovered the island after traveling across the Pacific. Among the members still alive at that stage was Antonio Pigafetta from Vicenza. Pigafetta records the presence of many different types of fruit and of rare woods. The expedition traded iron, nails, red cloth, and vinegar for some of the wood.

And a number of Italians played significant roles in the history of what is now East Timor during the period of European colonialism. One of them, Johan Paravacini, was at the heart of the so-called Contract of Paravacini, a major element in the struggle between the Dutch and Portuguese for control of different parts of the island. The contract would eventually lead to the splitting of the island into West Timor, now part of Indonesia, and East Timor, now independent.

And Italians played a part in East Timor's independence. In 1999, Italian military personnel took part in Operation Warden launched by INTERFET, the International Force for East Timor, in the aftermath of the vote for independence. The international force landed rapidly in East Timor to help deal with violence and chaos after the referendum vote for independence. The amphibious assault ship *San Giusto* from Italy was part of this operation, and units of Italian marines and Italian paratroopers also served in East Timor.

ECUADOR

I T'S A LONG, LONG DISTANCE FROM ITALY, but yes, Italians have had some military involvement with this country. Quite a lot, actually.

For a start, Genoese explorer Giovanni Battista Pastene explored the coast of Ecuador in the sixteenth century while in the service of the Spanish (becoming pretty much the first European to do so). Other Italians followed in his footsteps as Spanish control spread across the area. In the 1540s, Gonzalo Pizarro, Governor of Quito, led a short-lived rebellion against the new viceroy of Peru. Italians are named among the rebels, including Baptista Calvo from Genoa and Francisco Bonifacio from Savoy.

In the nineteenth century, the Italian community in Ecuador grew, until Italians formed the largest foreign community in Ecuador's biggest city, Guayaquil. And Italians inevitably got involved to some extent in Ecuador's turbulent political and military history of that time.

In the 1880s, the Italian Navy corvette *Vettor Pisani* was active in Ecuadorian waters. It had a scientific purpose, but it was also there to show the Italian flag and did manage to get just a little bit involved in a civil war in Ecuador. The *Vettor Pisani* visited the Galapagos Islands, part of Ecuador, for scientific purposes, but it was on the Ecuadorian mainland where the corvette got closer to the action. The corvette put in at Guayaquil, and there the Italian commander, Palumbo, attempted to mediate between President Ignacio de Veintemilla and General Eloy Alfaro and to ensure the safety of Italian and other civilians. After General Alfaro's forces finally took Guayaquil, Palumbo tried to prevent looting and evacuated some vulnerable civilians to Paita, Peru.

But it was in the period after World War I that Italy had perhaps the most military influence on Ecuador. In 1922, an Italian Military Mission was sent to Ecuador. Italians were to help reorganize the army and, most significantly, help establish an Ecuadoran air force. General Alessandro Pirzio Biroli, who would later be more widely known for his actions in the Balkans, was at one stage head of that mission in Ecuador.

Italian military links remained strong until 1940 when, with the entry of Italy into World War II on the German side, the last Italian military advisors were withdrawn.

However, Ecuador wasn't the only country in the region that received Italian military assistance at that time; and in 1941, Italian-supplied bombers and Italian-trained paratroopers played a major role in Peru's rapid victory in the war between it and Ecuador.

Many Italian Ecuadorians have become famous in their country. For instance, an Italian Ecuadorian, Cosme Renella Barbatto, learned to fly in Italy after World War I and became, basically, the first Ecuadorian pilot. The Ecuadorian Air Force now has a training school named after him.

EGYPT

Yes, the land of, among many others, Cleopatra.
Rome had already been involved in Egypt for some time before it took the final step of taking over. For already in the second century BC, Rome was interfering in the internecine squabbling during Egypt's Ptolemaic dynasty.

This trend increased in the next century. For instance, in 55 BC, a friend of Pompey restored Ptolemy XII Auletes to the throne of Egypt after the king had been forced to flee. And then in 48 BC, Julius Caesar, in pursuit of Pompey, turned up in Egypt. When he arrived, Caesar was presented with Pompey's head, but seeing this as an unfitting end for the great Roman, Caesar had his killers killed.

While in Egypt, Caesar got involved with both an Egyptian civil war and, of course, more famously with Cleopatra, who was fighting her brother. Caesar supported Cleopatra and was eventually triumphant at the Battle of the Nile in 47 BC.

After Caesar's assassination, Mark Antony followed in Caesar's sandal-steps with Cleopatra; and it was only after the defeat of the lovers' forces by Octavian's troops at Actium in 31 BC that Rome, in 30 BC, took direct control of Egypt.

Assorted combat in Egypt would follow: for example, against Jewish rebels in the early second century AD; against Queen Zenobia in the third century AD (her capital at Palmyra was captured in 2015 by ISIS); and then later in the same century, against the usurper Domitius Domitianus. But basically, the Byzantine Empire would inherit Egypt.

Armed Italians returned to Egypt in force during the Middle Ages. A Venetian fleet, for instance, raided the Egyptian coast in 1124. Italian crusaders played a significant part in the Fifth Crusade's disastrous attempt to invade Egypt in the thirteenth century. Genoese and Venetian ships were in the Christian fleet that captured Alexandria in 1365. And after fighting a Catalan fleet in Alexandria and losing, the Genoese went on to attack Damietta in Egypt in 1412 and to raid other parts of the Egyptian coast.

At the end of the eighteenth century, Napoleon, a French general with Italian heritage and with Italian troops in his army, invaded Egypt. Britain had Italians in Egypt too at this time. They fought on its side in Edward Dillon's Regiment of Foot, which had been raised in northern Italy in 1795.

Italian soldiers played a major role in the Egyptian Army in the nineteenth century as well. Gaetano Casati, Romolo Gessi, and Giacomo Messedaglia, for example, served as commanders over a long period in the Egyptian Army, and Maria Federigo Pasha became an admiral in the Egyptian Navy.

Verdi's *Aida* premiered in Cairo on Christmas Eve, 1871.

In 1882, under pressure from a rebellion in Egypt, Britain offered Italy joint control in return for Italian military support, but Italy turned the offer down. Britain would remain the dominant European power in Egypt, so when Italy declared war on Britain in 1940, an Italian invasion of Egypt from neighbouring Italian-controlled Libya became a real possibility.

In September 1940, Italian troops did invade Egypt from Libya. However, a British counteroffensive forced Italian troops back into Libya. After the arrival of the Afrika Korps, however, Axis troops proceeded to force British forces back. A period of fighting in Cyrenaica and around the Egyptian border ensued before the Axis forces were finally able to capture Tobruk, in eastern Libya, and once again press across the border into Egypt.

The Axis offensive, however, ground to a halt with the British victory at El Alamein in late 1942; and as Allied superiority in supplies began to have a decisive effect, the Axis forces were thrown into retreat in a series of actions across Libya and into Tunisia.

On December 19, 1941, six Italian Navy divers using manned torpedoes conducted a daring raid on Alexandria's harbor, in which they successfully put the *Valiant* and *Queen Elizabeth* out of operation. Lieutenants de la Penne and Bianchi were awarded gold medals for gallantry for having affixed limpet mines to the hulls of these two Royal Navy battleships. For a brief time, the Italian Navy was probably in a stronger strategic position than Britain in the Mediterranean, or *Mare Nostrum*.

In the period since World War II, Italian soldiers have been in Egypt again as part of assorted international forces. In the 1980s, for instance, Italian minesweepers were sent to the Gulf of Aqaba and to the waters south of Suez.

EL SALVADOR

ITALIANS PLAYED A ROLE IN THE SPANISH colonial occupation of El Salvador, as they did with other places in the region.

One person of Italian descent who was greatly involved in the wars and politics of Central America in the early nineteenth century was Francisco Morazán, whose grandfather was Corsican. In 1827, Morazán, after fleeing from Honduras to La Union in El Salvador, raised a small army—including troops from El Salvador—and returned to Honduras to seize power after victory at the Battle of La Trinidad. In 1828, though, it was Morazán's turn to invade El Salvador with an army that again included Salvadoran volunteers. After extensive clashes, including fighting around San Miguel, Morazán's forces eventually entered San Salvador in triumph in October. From 1830–1839, Morazán was president of the Federal Republic of Central America. After losing that position, he became chief of state of El Salvador. In September 1839, he defeated invading forces at the Battle of San Pedro Perulapán, but after defeat at Guatemala City in March 1840, Morazán fled from El Salvador into exile. In 1841, he returned to El Salvador to prepare the invasion of Costa Rica that led to his death. Today El Salvador has a regional department called Morazán.

As with other countries in the area, the nineteenth century saw Italian immigration into El Salvador.

From 1931 until 1944, El Salvador was ruled by Maximiliano Hernández Martinez, who admired Mussolini. Martinez supported German and Italian intervention in the Spanish Civil War, and he received military assistance from Mussolini's Italy. For instance, Italians assisted with training the Salvadoran Air Force.

Nevertheless, this did not prevent El Salvador from taking America's side in World War II. In December 1941, after the Japanese attack on Pearl Harbor, El Salvador declared war on Italy as well as the other Axis powers.

Italy contributed Carabinieri to ONUSAL, the United Nations Observer Mission in San Salvador.

EQUATORIAL GUINEA

IT SEEMS UNLIKELY THE ROMANS KNEW ANYTHING about Equatorial Guinea, even of Bioko Island (formerly Fernando Po), which played such a large role in European exploration of Africa's west coast. The voyage of the Carthaginian explorer Hanno has given rise to endless speculation, as experts try to match his recorded details to actual known geography. One suggestion would terminate his outward voyage in the region of Mount Cameroon and Bioko, but most interpretations tend to place his terminus far to the west of that.

Italians played a significant role in early Portuguese exploration of the African coast, and it was the Portuguese who were the first Europeans to settle Bioko (hence the name Fernando Po, after the Portuguese explorer Fernão do Pó).

In December 1885, Italian naval officer Giacomo Bove, funded by the Italian Foreign Ministry, set off along with Enrico Stassano and Captain Guiseppe Fabrello to investigate the possibilities for expanding Italian trade and influence in the area. They dropped in on Fernando Po (by then under Spanish colonial control) before pressing on to the Congo. They decided the possibilities weren't that great since other Europeans had by that time firmly established themselves there.

At least one notable military action involving Italians did take place on Fernando Po during World War II, although in this instance, it was Italians being invaded rather than doing the invading.

In other chapters, we explore the operations of Italian submarines off the African coast. In 1941, British authorities were concerned about reports that German and Italian submarines were receiving assistance in their sea campaigns from shore-based resources. In the search for these resources, British investigators came across three Axis ships—two German and the Italian *Duchessa d'Aosta* anchored in the then neutral territory of Fernando Po. The *Duchessa d'Aosta* was regarded as particularly suspicious because of its radio transmitter and fears that it could be carrying arms and ammunition. Any open British action against the three ships risked severely antagonizing the Spanish government at a time when the British were desperate to keep Franco from joining the war on the Axis side. So in January 1942, a British commando team was sent in in Operation Postmaster. Italian and German officers were lured off their ships, and two tugs transported the commandos into the harbor. After blowing the anchor chains with explosives, the tugs towed the ships out to sea and into international waters. They were intercepted by the Royal Navy to establish the official British version of the ships being legally captured.

ERITREA

THE ROMANS WERE VERY FAMILIAR with the coastline of Eritrea.
      It was an area well known to Roman merchants who made the voyage through the Red Sea, either to trade at local ports or to pass into the Indian Ocean. The port of Adulis was located on the coast of what is now Eritrea; and Pliny describes the locals bringing ivory, rhinoceros horn, hippopotamus skins, apes, tortoiseshell, and slaves there to sell. The Roman Empire even seems to have had some kind of military presence in the region, as recorded by inscriptions on the Farasan Islands on the other side of the Red Sea.

      However, it was in the nineteenth century that Italians took a serious interest in the region militarily. The opening of the Suez Canal increased Italian awareness of land to the south. Soon after, an Italian shipping company, the Rubattino Shipping Company, bought some land on the Eritrean coast around the Bay of Assab to allow coaling of its ships. Then in 1885, the Italian government, with the support of Britain, which was keen to prevent any expansion of French influence in the area, took control of the Eritrean port of Massawa. General Oreste Baratieri expanded Italian control inland, but Italian attempts to push into Ethiopia ended in disaster (from Italy's point of view) at the Battle of Adowa (or Adwa) in 1896 (see Ethiopia).

During World War II, Eritrea became a key strategic area for Italy. For example, the Italian Red Sea Flotilla had a base at Massawa.

However, in January 1941, British forces invaded Eritrea. The key battle took place at Keren and lasted throughout February and March. Italian troops fought with enormous tenacity and bravery to halt the British advance, but finally were forced to surrender. The capital, Asmara, fell on April 1. Before Massawa fell, many of the Italian ships managed to escape and the dock facilities were destroyed. Assab held out until June before being captured.

However, it was not the end of Italian military operations in Eritrea. Italian military personnel continued to fight a guerrilla campaign against the British there. In one instance, Captain Francesco de Martini managed to escape to Yemen after conducting sabotage, and then in the summer of 1942 he returned to Eritrea to conduct more attacks until he was finally captured.

Italy contributed military personnel to UNMEE, the United Nations Missions in Ethiopia and Eritrea, which was launched in 2000 and ended in 2008.

ESTONIA

E STONIA IS THE MOST NORTHERN of the trio of the Baltic Republics. It's a long distance from Rome. Roman coins and artifacts, probably connected with merchants dealing in amber, do turn up in Estonia, but not in great quantities.

However, when the Swedish Army under the French general Pontus de la Gardie took Narva in Estonia in 1581, an assault by Italian mercenaries proved decisive.

And after he had helped drive out Napoleon's forces from Russia and the Baltic region in 1812, Italian Filippo Paulucci was made governor general of, among other territories, Estland, the Governorate of Estonia within the Russian Empire.

General Marietti was the Italian member of the Allied Commission in the Baltic States that helped end the violent chaos in the area after World War I and organized the evacuation of German troops.

In October 1942, however, during World War II, Italian MAS torpedo boats that had been fighting the Soviets on Lake Ladoga were stationed at Tallinn in Estonia.

Typhoon fighters from the Italian Air Force were deployed to Estonia in January 2015, where they have intercepted Russian planes over the Baltic.

ETHIOPIA

T HE ROMANS WERE AWARE OF the Kingdom of Aksum, which occupied much of what is now Ethiopia, and traded with it. Ivory, in particular, was something Aksum had that the Romans valued.

In the nineteenth century, Italian explorers began investigating parts of Ethiopia. For instance, in 1878 an expedition led by Pellegrino Matteucci visited Ethiopia. And the expansion of Italian colonial control on the Eritrean and Somali coasts set the scene for Italian attempts to invade Ethiopia as well.

Italian forces clashed with the Ethiopians in 1887, and then in 1895 the first Italo-Ethiopian war erupted. The Italians launched a full-scale invasion of Ethiopia with the intention of occupying it. It proved to be, for the Italians, a disastrous decision. On March 1, 1896, at Adowa, an Italian force attacked an Ethiopian force five times larger than itself. In the fighting that followed, a third of the Italian force was killed and three thousand soldiers were taken prisoner. The Italian government promptly abandoned its attempt to invade Ethiopia.

Most of the "Italian" forces were made up of ascaris; that is, local soldiers who served in European colonial armies. Their officers were Italian. Many ascaris who were taken prisoner after the battle paid a terrible price; limbs were amputated before they were released from captivity. Some genital mutilation (castration) of the Italian-led forces, of both the dead and the wounded, also occurred. This was a relatively common practice in that part of the world at the time.

After accounts of the battle were published, many Italian Americans wanted to form a volunteer force to avenge Adwa and defend Italian honor. Forty members of the Italia Club in Chicago stepped forward. Donations were raised in many Italian-American communities for the Italian Red Cross.

In Italy, the defeat prompted different reactions. It brought down the Crispi government. Some students at the University of Rome demonstrated in the streets and shouted "Viva Menelik" (the Ethiopian king) in what may have been one of the first anticolonial demonstrations.

Fascist propaganda would later play up the heroic sacrifice of the sons of Italy in Africa. Mussolini's 1935 invasion of Ethiopia was designed in part to avenge their humiliation at Adwa. A huge statue of Il Duce was later erected on the battlefield.

In October 1935, a vast Italian Army with extensive armored and air support advanced into Ethiopia in the second Italo-Ethiopian war. They reached Adwa and captured Aksum. The Ethiopians retaliated with a Christmas offensive. But in 1936, the Italians continued to press forward. The Italian forces had vast superiority in armaments and won a series of encounters, including the Battle of Enderta, the Battle of Shire, and the decisive Battle of Lake Ashenge. On May 5, 1936, Italian forces entered the Ethiopian capital of Addis Ababa. However, Ethiopian resistance had not ended in substantial parts of the country, and a bitter guerrilla war followed before Italy took full control. Mussolini ordered the use of poison gas, delivered via artillery and by air, against Ethiopian forces. General Graziani declared brutally, "The Duce will have Ethiopia, with or without the Ethiopians."

In 1938, Giovanni Ruazzi, winner of a Gold Medal of Valor, was killed while flying over Ethiopia with the Italian Air Force. A statue of him can be found today in San Cassiano in the Dolomites.

Full Italian control of Ethiopia would not last long. In June 1940, Italy declared war on Britain, and after early Italian successes in east Africa, Britain retaliated.

In January 1941, British and Ethiopian troops crossed into Italian-held Ethiopia. Addis Ababa was recaptured in April 1941, and Emperor Haile Selassie had returned to his capital by May. Also in May, Prince Amedeo, Duke of Aosta and commander in chief in Ethiopia, fought to defend entrenched Italian positions at Amba Alagi before he had to surrender. In July, General Gazzera also surrendered after being forced to abandon Jimma; and in November 1941, Italian forces made their last stand in the area at the Battle of Gondar.

As in Eritrea and Somalia, however, Italian resistance fighters continued to wage a guerrilla war after the end of main combat operations. However, support for this war declined after the Axis defeat at El Alamein in the autumn of 1942.

In recent decades, Italian personnel have taken part in a number of international efforts in the region, including UNMEE, the United Nations Mission in Ethiopia and Eritrea.

FIJI

ELL, ITALIANS HAVEN'T HAD A HUGE amount of military involvement
with Fiji, but they have had a little. A Spanish naval expedition
led by Italian naval officer Alessandro Malaspina did reach Fiji in the late
eighteenth century during its voyage of exploration in the Pacific.

He wasn't the only Italian naval officer to visit Fiji. The corvette
Garibaldi arrived in Fiji's waters in 1873. In the 1880s, the corvette
Carraciolo called in on its circumnavigation of the globe, as did the *Etna*
in the next decade. In 1904, the Italian cruiser *Liguria* arrived with the
Duke d'Abruzzi, then a captain in the Italian Navy, on board.

FINLAND

VEN THIS FAR NORTH, ROMAN COINS have been found, although this is
probably due to the long reach of trade routes that led to Rome rather
than the presence of many Romans.

In the early nineteenth century, however, one Italian military
commander was definitely active here. Carlucci (see Latvia, Lithuania)
was at that point serving with the Russian Army.

Operatic baritone Eugenio Giraldoni, famous for creating the role of
Baron Scarpia in Puccini's *Tosca*, was another Italian who definitely made
it to Finland. In fact, he died there after moving there to teach.

In 1939, the Soviet Union attacked Finland. The Italian government
was one of many governments that sympathized with the plight of the Finns,
and the Italians tried to send a consignment of aircraft and other weapons
to help the Finns resist the Soviet onslaught. The effort was impeded by
Hitler, who at that point had a Nonaggression Pact with the Soviet Union.
A small number of Italian volunteers joined the Finnish forces in actual
fighting, and one Italian pilot died while flying with the Finns.

Military links were renewed after the German invasion of the Soviet
Union in 1941. And this time, the Italian Navy played a significant role. In
the spring of 1942, the XII Squadriglia MAS (Mezzi d'Assalto) was assigned
to assist the Finns and Germans in attempts to disrupt Soviet supply lines
that ran across Lake Ladoga to besieged Leningrad. Four torpedo boats
were taken from Italy by rail to the Baltic coast, across the sea to Helsinki,

and finally by road to the lake. The Italian crews saw action on a number of occasions and managed to sink a Russian merchant ship and a gunboat. In autumn, the lake froze and the unit was reassigned, first to Estonia and then to the Mediterranean, leaving their vessels behind for the Finns.

FRANCE

I TALY HAS INVADED FRANCE MANY TIMES and deeply influenced her over thousands of years. France has returned the favor. Julius Caesar declared that, "All Gaul is divided into three parts." Much later, three famous Frenchmen would play a decisive role in creating the modern Italian state. More on that anon.

Even before the Romans, the Etruscans established themselves in Corsica in the sixth century BC, after an Etruscan and Carthaginian fleet clashed with a Greek Phocean fleet at the Battle of Alalia in the second half of the sixth century BC. The Greeks actually won the battle but lost so much of their fleet, they ended up abandoning Corsica to the Etruscans.

But it was, of course, the Romans who first launched a major Italian invasion of what is now mainland France. The area known as Provence gets its name from being a province of the Roman Empire. Romans introduced the secrets of viticulture to the Gauls.

From an early time, the Romans had regularly clashed with the Gauls in Italy; and during the Second Punic War, Hannibal used Gaul as a route to invade Italy as well. In the second century BC, Rome began to invade Gaul with serious intent. At first, a major Roman priority was developing a land route to the territories it controlled in Spain.

In 121 BC, Roman forces under Quintus Fabius Maximus Allobrogicus achieved a major victory over the Allobroges and Arverni, Celtic tribes in southeastern Gaul. The Greek Phocean colony of Massalia (Marseilles) was sympathetic to Rome and allowed Roman plans to progress. The Roman colony at what is now Narbonne in southwestern Gaul was founded in 118 BC as a key point on the Via Domitia, the road that ran through southern Gaul and linked Spain to Italy.

More Roman campaigns in Gaul followed, particularly those conducted by Julius Caesar. Between 58 BC and 51 BC, Caesar established Roman rule over almost all of what is France today. He smashed the Helvetii at the Battle of Bibracte in 58 BC, and then clashed with the Suebi under Ariovistus, defeating them. In 57 BC, he headed north to campaign against the Belgae. Despite heavy fighting, he eventually triumphed. He then moved across Gaul to attack the Veneti in what is now Brittany, before returning to the east. In 55 and 54 BC, he launched his expeditions to Britain, but in 53 BC, Ambiorix and the Eburones rose in revolt. Caesar ruthlessly crushed them. However, a year later, Vercingetorix, chieftain of the Arverni, launched a much more serious rebellion against Caesar, which prompted other tribes to rise against him too. Caesar suffered a defeat at the Battle of Gergovia, but eventually a Roman victory in the Battle of Alesia proved decisive, ending the rebellion and cementing Roman rule. In 46 BC, Caesar established a Roman colony in Arles.

The wars had brought great devastation to Gaul, and further fighting followed under Augustus. For instance, Agrippa, a Roman general, crushed an Aquitanian revolt, and Rome completed its conquest of the east.

However, plenty of fighting continued throughout the Roman period. Much of it involved Roman civil wars, such as those during the period of the Gallic Empire in the third century, when Gaul became part of a separate empire that split from the main empire. However, Gaul also saw major invasions by people from beyond the empire's borders. And in the fifth century, full-scale invasions brought about the end of Roman power throughout Gaul.

However, in the Middle Ages, armies from Italy invaded France again. Italian mercenaries were regularly used by French kings.

When Catherine de Medici launched a matrimonial "invasion" of France in 1533 by marrying Henry II, her chefs introduced Italian sauces to French kitchens. The French would later export their gastronomy to the world as classic French cooking.

Some territories that are now controlled by France were once under long-term Italian control. Corsica is one, for it was under either Pisan or Genoese control until Genoa finally sold the island to France in the eighteenth century. The area around Nice was, for substantial periods, controlled by the Dukes of Savoy, and then by the Kingdom of Piedmont-Sardinia before it was ceded to France in 1860.

Italian troops and generals played a major role in Spanish and imperial armies that invaded France in the sixteenth and seventeenth centuries. Savoy's forces also fought in southern France.

The Revolutionary and Napoleonic Wars also saw extensive movements of soldiers between France and Italy. During the Franco-Prussian War of 1870-1871, Garibaldi led the volunteer Army of the Vosges, fighting on the French side against the invading forces.

The three famous Frenchmen (though all had Italian links) that played roles in creating modern Italy were Napoleon (a man as noted elsewhere with a strong Italian heritage), his nephew Napoleon III, and Giuseppe Garibaldi. Yes, Garibaldi, one of the most famous Italians of all, was actually born in French territory.

General Napoleon fought his initial battles for Revolutionary France in northern Italy (Marengo, Rivoli, Lodi, etc.). He won many victories over Austrian armies that had been the overlords of northern Italy for many years. After becoming emperor of France, Napoleon also crowned himself King of Italy at the Duomo in Milan in 1805. His stepson, Eugène Beauharnais, became Viceroy of Italy.

Italy was a source of funds and of manpower for Napoleon's ambitions. Over 165,000 Italians, representing 2 percent of their total population, fought for Napoleon's empire from 1802 to 1815. Many of Napoleon's family members also had close connections to Italy. His sister Elisa was Grand Duchess of Tuscany, based in Lucca; another sister, Caroline, became Queen of Naples. His brother Lucien retired to Italy and took up archaeology at Cicero's estate at Tusculum.

Napoleon had a healthy respect for his Italian soldiers, writing in 1809: "The troops of the Kingdom of Italy covered themselves with glory … since the Romans, no period has been so glorious for Italian arms."

In the 1850s, the wily Count Cavour of Piedmont sought to win Napoleon III's support for the cause of Italian unity. He even dispatched his beautiful cousin, the Countess of Castiglione, to Paris, where she soon became the emperor's mistress. French forces defeated the Austrians at the battles of Magenta and Solferino in 1859, giving Piedmont control of northern Italy.

On July 4, 1807, Giuseppe Garibaldi, the unifier of modern Italy, was born in Nice. The future general was, therefore, born a French citizen and a subject of Napoleon's empire. Nice was transferred to the House of Savoy by the Congress of Vienna in 1815. Much later, Garibaldi would fall out with Cavour when the latter bargained away Garibaldi's hometown. Cavour gave it back to Napoleon III's France in exchange for territorial concessions in northern Italy, for Piedmont and the Kingdom of Savoy.

After the fall of Napoleon III as a result of the Franco-Prussian War, General Garibaldi returned to France to fight his final campaign, leading his Army of the Vosges against the Prussians in 1870. He was an ardent revolutionary, inspired by the spirit of 1789, who rallied to the cause of the French Republic. His international brigade of irregulars included Poles, Englishmen, Spaniards, Irishmen, Frenchmen, and many Italians.

In 1831, King Louis-Philippe created the French Foreign Legion, whose current motto is "Legio Patria Nostra" (the Legion is our home). Many Italians have served France faithfully while in the legion, fighting around the world.

At the beginning of World War I, even before Italy had entered the war on the Allied side, some Italians joined the Allies against the Central Powers. From August 1914 until April 1915, 4,913 Italians, led by Australian-born Giuseppe Garibaldi II (Peppino), joined the French Foreign Legion to fight for France. When Italy entered the war, however, the Italian members of the legion returned to Italy to join the Italian Army. Later in the war, troops from the Italian Army also served in France. They played a role in halting the German advance at the Second Battle of the Marne in 1918, and then took part in the Allied counteroffensive that followed.

In the Second World War, however, France and Italy were initially on opposite sides. On June 10, 1940, Mussolini declared war on France. Italian troops made determined attempts to advance into France but faced just as determined French resistance. The Italian invaders did manage to take some ground, including the French port of Menton, before the French government, facing total defeat at the hands of German forces in the north, signed an armistice with Italy on the twenty-fourth of June. As a result of the armistice, Italy occupied small pockets of territory along the French-Italian border and annexed some of it. However, in November 1942, when the Germans decided that Vichy France should be occupied, Italian forces hugely extended their area of occupation to include locations like Toulon and the island of Corsica. After Italy's armistice with the Allies in September 1943, German troops moved in to occupy the areas previously held by Italy. On Corsica, though, the arrival of German troops led to an uprising by local resistance units. Many Italian troops chose to fight alongside the resistance fighters against the Germans. Free French forces also landed on the island. In October, the Germans withdrew, and the island was fully liberated.

During World War II, Italian submarines were based at Bordeaux, from where they left on missions to attack Allied shipping in the Atlantic and Caribbean. Some were even sent from Bordeaux on blockade-running missions to Japan.

In both World War I and World War II, Italian Americans fought bravely in France. For example, on September 29, 1918, Michael Valente distinguished himself in an attack on the Hindenburg Line near Ronssoy and was later awarded the Medal of Honor. In World War II, Arthur F.

DeFranzo also won the Medal of Honor. On June 10, 1944, he led an attack on German positions near Vaudubon in Normandy before dying of his wounds. And Vito R. Bertoldo won the Medal of Honor for his actions on January 9, 1945, when at Hatten in eastern France, he covered the withdrawal of US forces as the Germans counterattacked.

Italy and France are NATO members whose troops have recently served alongside each other in Afghanistan.

GABON

PIETRO PAOLO SAVORGNAN DI BRAZZÀ is better known these days for his involvement with the area now known as the Republic of the Congo (its capital, Brazzaville, is named after him). But he also had a lot to do with Gabon.

Brazzà was Italian born, in January 1852, but ended up in the French Navy. In 1872, he arrived in Gabon on a ship that was on an antislavery mission. Soon, he was exploring inland, up the Gabon and Ogooué Rivers. In the end, Brazzà played a significant role in extending French influence across what is now Gabon before moving on to the Congo.

During the 2006 EUFOR mission to the Democratic Republic of Congo, Italian airmen who were part of the mission made use of the Libreville International Airport in Gabon as a base. Fifty men from the 46th Air Brigade Pisa landed there with a C-130J aircraft on July 17.

GAMBIA

HANNO, THE CARTHAGINIAN EXPLORER, appears in several of our African chapters. He wasn't Roman, obviously, but the Romans were at least aware of his voyage along the west coast of Africa. It is generally accepted that Hanno made it at least as far south as Gambia, so it is not impossible that Roman ships did too.

Certainly when the Portuguese started to explore the Atlantic coast of Africa in the fifteenth century, Italians were a major part of the effort. In 1455, the Venetian Alvise da Ca' da Mosto headed south toward unknown territory. En route, he teamed up with a Genoese explorer Antoniotto Usodimare and eventually they reached the mouth of the Gambia River.

They sailed up the river, only to be attacked by the locals and forced to retreat. The following year, Ca' da Mosto returned. This time, he sailed farther up the river and spent time meeting and trading with the locals.

The Portuguese were the first Europeans to develop links with Gambia. However, they sold their trade enterprise in the area to England in 1588.

During World War II, Italian submarines operated in the waters off Gambia. During the same war, in December 1941, the Italian destroyer *Alvise da Mosto* was sunk by British forces in the central Mediterranean while it was escorting an oil tanker. In June 1942, the Italian destroyer *Usodimare* was accidentally sunk by an Italian submarine off the Tunisian coast.

GEORGIA

I N THE FIRST CENTURY BC, MITHRIDATES OF PONTUS took control of much of what is now the country of Georgia, then called the Kingdom of Colchis. When the Romans defeated him, they became a major force in the region.

Not all went smoothly from then on. Julius Caesar ended up fighting a successor to (and son of) Mithridates, Pharnaces II, at Zela in what is now Turkey. That was the victory that Caesar summed up with "Veni, vidi, vici" (I came, I saw, I conquered). In AD 62, Polemon II of Pontus gave up control of the last bit of Pontus that Rome hadn't already grabbed, and of Colchis too, and Nero grabbed it for Rome.

Roman control of the northern and inland parts of the territory was less secure and less long-lived than the southern and coastal bit. And from the third century AD, Sassanid-Persian influence would put increasing pressure on Roman, and subsequently Byzantine, influence. Along the coast in the far south of what is now Georgia, however, Rome established a firm presence at places like Batumi and Gonio.

In the Middle Ages, the Genoese followed the Romans to Georgia with trading colonies at a number of places along the Georgian coast, including some that had been Roman sites before, like Pitsunda and Gonio.

More Italians arrived later in Georgia, like Filippo Paulucci, born in Modena, who came in 1807. Serving in the Russian Army, he won a major victory at the Battle of Akhalkalaki in 1810 in Georgia.

And in another example, in the chaotic period after World War I, an Italian Military Mission was planned for Azerbaijan, Georgia, and Armenia to investigate the situation there, and it was the intention to send Italian troops to occupy the area with a view to settling its future. However, just days before the troops were supposed to depart, a new Italian government abandoned the idea of sending an occupation force and instead just sent the Military Mission.

Recently, Italy has contributed to EUMM, the European Union Monitoring Mission in Georgia, established in 2008, to help prevent any resumption of conflict with Russia and pro-Russian forces in the area.

GERMANY

THE ROMANS NEVER OCCUPIED ALL OF WHAT IS NOW GERMANY, but they did occupy much of the country in a variety of different campaigns. Some Roman reverses in Germany shook the foundations of the Roman Empire.

Caesar's campaigns in Gaul saw him clash with assorted German tribes. Subsequently, in 39 and 38 BC, Agrippa campaigned in the Rhine region, an action that would lead to the founding of what is now Cologne.

In 16 BC, however, Roman forces under Marcus Lollius suffered a significant defeat on the east bank of the Rhine at the hands of the Sugambri, and a Roman legion actually lost its eagle.

After the defeat, though, Drusus and Tiberius campaigned successfully in the region. In 15 BC, they took control of Raetia, a region that covered much of what is now the south of Germany. In 11 BC, Drusus achieved a victory over the Sugambri at the Battle of the Lupia River. Further successful campaigning in Germany followed, and Roman forces pushed deeper and deeper into northern Germany. Lucius Domitius Ahenobarbus crossed the Elbe, and in AD 4, Tiberius launched another campaign in the area. A Roman fleet escorted him to the mouth of the Elbe, from where he advanced along the river some distance.

However, Publius Quinctilius Varus suffered a crushing defeat at the Battle of the *Teutoburger Wald* in AD 9, in which three Roman legions were destroyed. Emperor Augustus was so distressed by this setback, he hit his head against a door, muttering, "Quinctilius Varus, return my legions to me." In the aftermath of the defeat, both Tiberius and Germanicus campaigned against the Germans with some success, but the drive into northern Germany was abandoned and the Rhine became a key part of the imperial border.

Tacitus, a Roman historian and wine snob, dismisses beer, sniffing that for drink, Germans "used the liquid distilled from barley or wheat," which after fermentation gives it "a certain resemblance to wine."*

In the later first century and the second century, further Roman advances were made into the area between the Rhine and Danube frontiers, and Rome occupied a vulnerable triangle of land there.

Roman Germany saw extensive fighting during its existence, including conflict during Roman civil wars. Additionally, in the third, fourth, and fifth centuries, there was much fighting against invasions by peoples from beyond the imperial frontier. The triangle of land between the Rhine and the Danube was abandoned in the late third century; and in the fifth century, Roman power in Germany came to an end.

However, Italian soldiers invaded Germany again after the fall of Rome. For example, Italian mercenaries fought in Germany, and people like Italian-born Emperor Frederick II were part of the Holy Roman Empire's structure. Italian generals and troops were prominent among the forces fighting in Germany during the Thirty Years War. Ottavio Piccolomini, for instance, played a major role in the Battle of Lützen in 1632 (in which the Swedish king Gustavus Adolphus was killed). Piccolomini went on to be involved in the plot against Wallenstein of Bohemia; and in his long military career, he played a key role in the imperial victory in the Battle of Nördlingen in 1634. Another key Italian military figure in Germany at that time was Raimondo Montecuccoli, also present (and wounded) at Lützen in 1632, and at Nördlingen in 1634.

During the Napoleonic Wars, Italian troops were among the forces of the French emperor fighting on German soil, such as at the Battle of Leipzig in 1813.

In the 1930s, Mussolini and Hitler forged the Pact of Steel, crucially binding the fates of Italy and Germany. During World War II, various Italian military units made use of assorted facilities in Germany. Many Italians were also subjected to forced labor in Germany.

During the same war, Italian Americans fought with great bravery during the Allied invasion of the country. For instance, Peter J. Dalessandro was awarded the Medal of Honor for his heroic attempts to hold off a German attack near Kalterherberg, Germany, on December 22, 1944. And Mike Colalillo was awarded the same medal for his actions on April 7, 1945, near Untergriesheim, Germany, for heroism during an attack on German positions.

West Germany joined NATO in 1955, and the united Germany is a key NATO member today, alongside Italy.

* Tacitus, *Germania*, trans. from the Latin by Hutton, Peterson, et al. (Boston: Loeb Classical Library, 1970), 167.

GHANA

I TALIANS HAVE HAD A LITTLE ARMED INVOLVEMENT with the territory that is now Ghana.

It's possible that some ships from the Mediterranean passed by Ghana in the pre-Christian period.

What is now Ghana eventually became a British colonial possession, but it was the Portuguese who were the first Europeans to explore its coast. And among the Portuguese were some Italians. In 1482, they built a fort at São Jorge da Mina. Columbus spent at least a little time there before he set off across the Atlantic to change history. São Jorge da Mina was taken over by the Dutch in 1632 and by the British in 1872.

Recent military links between Italy and Ghana have included the arrival in 2014 of the 30th Naval Group of the Italian Navy.

GREECE

G REEKS, OF COURSE, INVADED SICILY and the Italian mainland long before Rome invaded Greece. In fact, the first Italians to invade Greece were almost certainly fighters from the Greek colonies in Sicily who were getting involved in wars on mainland Greece and in the Greek islands. For instance, in 372 BC, Iphicrates attacked and captured a fleet of ten Syracusan triremes sent to Corcyra (Corfu) to help the Spartans based there.

The Roman invasion of Greece was not a quick and simple matter.

In the late third century BC, Roman troops were involved in the First Macedonian War. In this, Rome teamed up with Attalus I of Pergamum and the Greek Aetolian League to fight Philip V of Macedon, who was himself allied with Rome's great enemy, Carthage. The war wasn't exactly the most major Roman invasion of Greek soil, but Roman forces did land on some Greek islands, like Corfu, which would see a lot more Italian invasions later.

The First Macedonian War ended in 205 BC, and by 200 BC, the Second Macedonian War was on. In 197 BC, a Roman army with Aetolian allies smashed Philip V's army at the Battle of Cynoscephalae, but at this stage the Romans did not have a huge interest in taking control of all of Greece.

During the Roman-Seleucid War of 192–188 BC, Roman forces fought in Greece yet again. This time they clashed with the Seleucid Empire from the east, which had allied with the Aetolian League and sent forces to Greece. However, in 191 BC, a Roman army clashed with a Seleucid army at Thermopylae and decisively defeated it.

The Third Macedonian War broke out in 171 BC. By now, Philip V was dead, so it was his son Perseus who led Macedon's forces against Rome. He had an early success at the Battle of Callinicus but lost decisively at the Battle of Pydna in Greece in 168 BC. And this time, the Romans decided they were going to get more extensively involved in Greece. They split the Kingdom of Macedon into four client republics. They also sacked the territory of Epirus in 167 BC, part of which is in Greece.

However, this was not the end of fighting in Greece. In 150 BC, the Fourth Macedonian War began. This time, a guy called Andriscus was attempting to reestablish a Macedonian kingdom. Instead, the Romans defeated the forces opposing them in 148 BC at the second Battle of Pydna. Then in 146 BC, the Achaean League went to war with Rome. Rome smashed the forces of the League; and in the same year that it destroyed Carthage, it destroyed Corinth too. It then established firm Roman control in Greece.

However, Rome's long path to conquering all of Greece was not finished yet. During his first war with Rome (88–84 BC), Mithridates the Great (see Turkey) invaded Greece, and many Greeks rebelled against Rome and sided with him.

In 87 BC, the Roman general Sulla landed in Greece from the west with a Roman army. He blockaded Athens in a bitter siege, defeated one of Mithridates's armies at the Battle of Chaeronea in 86 BC, and again at the Battle of Orchomenos in 85 BC.

Plenty more Roman combat in Greece would follow. Greece would also see extensive fighting during later Roman civil wars, including decisive battles like the Battle of Philippi and the Battle of Actium.

In AD 67, Emperor Nero led a cultural invasion of Greece. It was a grand tour, actually. He competed as a thespian, and naturally won, at festivals in Olympia, Delphi, Isthmia, and other towns. His love of all things Greek made him deeply unpopular with many Romans. Much later,

Shakespeare, who appreciated actors, would describe Nero as "an angler in the lake of darkness."

Many more Italians would follow in Roman footsteps, invading Greece and its islands in the Middle Ages. For instance, Bohemond of Taranto, later one of the leaders of the First Crusade, led a campaign against Byzantine forces in northern Greece in the late eleventh century. He penetrated as far as Larissa in northwestern Greece, which he besieged but failed to take. Boniface I, Marquis of Montferrat, was one of the leaders of the Fourth Crusade. After the crusaders sacked Constantinople, he occupied the throne of the Kingdom of Thessalonica, one of the states temporarily carved out of the Byzantine Empire. The kingdom lasted only twenty years. The Genoese seized Rhodes in 1248 and held it until it was recaptured by the Empire of Nicaea. The Principality of Achaea, whose rulers also had extensive Italian connections, did last into the fifteenth century, as did other smaller units, like the Duchy of the Archipelago, established by Venetian Marco Sanudo. And in the late fourteenth century and through much of the fifteenth century, the Florentine family Acciaioli ran the Duchy of Athens.

Venice was, of course, also building its own Greek empire. It took control of various places, including the Greek islands of Euboea, Corfu, the Ionian Islands, and, of course, Crete.

And then the arrival of Ottoman power in the region in the fifteenth and sixteenth centuries set the scene for some fierce fighting.

For example, the first Ottoman-Venetian War was fought from 1463–1479 in the Peloponnese and in the Aegean, and the Venetians eventually lost control of Euboea. The two sides clashed again in that area between 1499 and 1503. And again in Greece between 1537 and 1539. The Ottomans failed to take Corfu, but Venice did lose key possessions like Nauplion. Venice and the Ottomans were at war again between 1570 and 1573. In 1571, a Christian fleet including a high percentage of Italian ships smashed a Turkish fleet at the Battle of Lepanto in the Gulf of Patras. One hundred and seventy Turkish galleys were sunk or captured and fifteen thousand Christian slaves were freed. And in the Cretan War of 1645–1669, the Venetians fought the Ottomans over Crete. The fighting was fierce and prolonged, and in the end the Ottomans took the island.

In 1684, Venice retaliated. In the Morea War of 1684–1699, Venetians invaded Greece and occupied the Peloponnese, the Morea. Their success, however, was short-lived. Venice and the Ottomans were at war yet again in 1714, and this time the Ottomans retook the Peloponnese. In 1715, the Venetians even lost their last few outposts around Crete, like Spinalonga, which they had previously managed to hold. The Venetians did, however, manage to defeat a massive Ottoman invasion of Corfu, although they eventually lost the island to the French at the end of the nineteenth century.

In 1897, Italian forces returned to Crete as part of the international force that briefly occupied the island after the departure of Ottoman troops. During the Italo-Turkish War of 1911–1912, Italy once again invaded and occupied Greek islands. In 1912, Italian forces occupied Rhodes and a number of other Aegean islands previously held by the Turks.

Italian troops fought on Greek soil again during World War I. An Italian expeditionary force fought on the Salonika front in northern Greece, and Italian troops from Albania occupied border areas inside Greece.

In 1923, a dispute over the killing of four Italian League of Nations workers saw the return of Italian troops to Corfu. Italy bombarded part of the island and landed marines there before withdrawing as part of a deal.

However, Mussolini had ideas of rebuilding an Italian empire in the Greek islands, and in October 1940, Italian troops based in Albania advanced across the border into Greece. The invasion was not a success. The Greeks counterattacked and, in turn, advanced into Albanian territory. An Italian counterattack followed in the spring of 1941. Then in April, German troops attacked Greece as well. The fresh onslaught rapidly destroyed organized resistance by the Greek Army, and on April 27, 1941, Athens fell. In June, German paratroopers launched a daring assault on Crete; and as part of the Axis invasion, Italian troops landed in the eastern part of the island. Following the invasion, Italian forces occupied most of Greece.

In March of 1941, the HMS *York*, a heavy cruiser, was sunk by Italian E-boats of the X Flottiglia MAS off the Bay of Suda in Crete.

The Italian armistice with the Allies in the autumn of 1943 saw events like the massacre of the men of the Italian Acqui Division on Cephalonia by German troops, and some Italians ended up fighting in Greek partisan units.

Italy and Greece have for a long time both been members of NATO.

GRENADA

CHRISTOPHER COLUMBUS SIGHTED GRENADA on his third voyage in 1498, the first European to do so. He named the island Concepción but doesn't seem to have done much more.

Aside from that, Italian military involvement with Grenada has been limited.

In World War II, Italian submarines operated in waters not far from Grenada, at a time when Grenada was part of the British Empire and, therefore, was enemy territory.

Italian Americans took part in the US invasion of Grenada in 1983.

GUATEMALA

THIS IS ONE OF THOSE PLACES that Columbus didn't reach.

One person of Italian descent who did, however, played a huge role in the wars and politics of Central America in the early nineteenth century. This was Francisco Morazán, whose grandfather was Corsican. In January 1829, Morazán invaded Guatemala. Despite one of his divisions being defeated at Mixco in February, Morazán gradually attracted more support from local Guatemalans, including the people of Antigua. After a victory for Morazán's forces at San Miguelito, Guatemala's chief of state surrendered in April of 1829. From 1830–1839, Morazán was president of the Federal Republic of Central America. A rebellion led by Rafael Carrera from Mataquescuintla, Guatemala, would lead to defeat at Guatemala City in March 1840, and exile for Morazán.

In 1905, the Italian cruiser *Umbria* was involved in some serious destruction in Puerto de San José. Not intentionally, however. The cruiser fired a salute. Guatemalan artillery fired a salute in reply. Somewhere in the middle of it all, the roof of the commander's residence was set on fire. Italian marines stormed ashore to help put it out.

Jorge Ubico, President of Guatemala from 1931 to 1944, had fascist links. His government was the first to recognize Franco's government in Spain, and Ubico admired Mussolini. This did not, however, stop Guatemala from taking America's side in World War II and declaring war on Italy in December 1941.

Italy contributed a Carabinieri contingent to the MINUGUA (United Nations Verification Mission in Guatemala) in 1997.

Among famous Guatemalans of Italian descent are Monsignor Juan José Gerardi Conedera, bishop and human rights defender, and opera singer Aida Doninelli. Dante Nannini Sandoval was born in Guatemala City in 1888. He became a pioneer of flying in Guatemala before joining the Italian armed forces in September 1915. During World War I, he shot down one balloon and three aircraft.

GUINEA

OST OF THE COUNTRY IS FARTHER SOUTH than Guinea-Bissau and came under French colonial rule rather than Portuguese. Italians have had a little involvement with this country.

Italian explorers Ca' da Mosto and Antoniotto Usodimare may not have made it quite this far south, but other Italians in the late fifteenth century and the early colonial period did.

And a man with Italian heritage played a significant role in extending French control across the area in the late nineteenth century. Joseph-Simon Gallieni, whose father was an Italian-born officer, rose to prominence in the French Army, pushing French control inland across various parts of West Africa. One of the areas to which he sent expeditions was the Fouta Djallon Highlands of central Guinea.

During World War II, Italian submarines were in action off the coast of Guinea. For example, on January 14, 1941, the Italian submarine *Commandante Cappellini*, under the control of Commander Todaro, attacked the British liner *Eumaeus*. A gun battle ensued in which three of the submarine's crew were killed before the British crew ran out of ammunition for their 4.7 inch gun. In the end, though, the *Cappellini* torpedoed and sank the *Eumaeus*, and twenty-three of the Britons on board died; sixty-three were rescued. Before the *Cappellini* could escape, it was bombed by a Walrus amphibious aircraft from Freetown, a hundred and fifty miles away. Badly damaged, the *Cappellini* was forced to stop in the Spanish Canaries temporarily, but it did finally make it to Bordeaux.

GUINEA-BISSAU

NOTHER CHAPTER FEATURING THE DUO of Venetian Alvise da Ca' da Mosto and Genoese Antoniotto Usodimare. In 1456, on their second voyage and after spending time up the Gambia River, the pair cruised down the African coast as far as Cape Roxo, where Senegal now meets Guinea-Bissau. Then they headed farther south, exploring parts of what is now the coast of Guinea-Bissau, including the vast estuary near what is now the capital, Bissau.

Portugal eventually became the European colonial power in the country.

During World War II, Italian submarines operated in the seas off Guinea-Bissau. For instance, on May 7, 1941, the Italian submarine *Enrico Tazzoli,* under the command of Fecia di Cossato, sank the Norwegian freighter *Fernlane* off the coast. The thirty-five members of the crew were all eventually rescued.

GUYANA

G UYANA'S COLONIAL HISTORY WAS MOST CLOSELY TIED with the Netherlands and Britain, so this really isn't going to be a big chapter.

However, Christopher Columbus did sail along what is now the coast of Guyana in 1498. He was followed by Florentine Amerigo Vespucci, shortly after calling in at the mouth of the Essequibo River.

And in the seventeenth century, the region was almost the site of a Tuscan colony. English captain Robert Thornton was sent by Fernando I of Tuscany to explore the possibilities of setting up an Italian colony on the north coast of South America. Thornton did make it to the area and explored territory, mainly in what is now French Guiana, but the plans for the colony never came to anything.

From 1913 until 1922, Cecil Clementi, grandson of Italian musician Muzio Clementi, was colonial secretary in charge of what was then British Guiana.

Italian submarines operated in the waters off Guyana during World War II at a time when British Guiana was part of the British Empire and hostile territory.

HAITI

O N DECEMBER 4, 1492, COLUMBUS CHANCED upon the island of Hispaniola. After noticing the natives wearing gold earrings, he found a quantity of gold, which would encourage his financial backers (mostly Italian bankers) to support his subsequent voyages. It was on this island that he would attempt to found a Spanish settlement, and he would return to Hispaniola in all three of his subsequent voyages. The large indigenous population (Taino) introduced Columbus to pineapples, tobacco, chili pods, canoes, and even the hammock—an innovation that would transform the lives of sailors. He left a garrison on the island and sailed back to Spain. When he returned in 1493, he found that the garrison had been overrun, all the troops massacred by the natives.

Subsequent waves of Spanish colonists would bring infectious diseases that would wipe out about 90 percent of the Taino population within thirty years of Columbus's first arrival.

Haiti would later become a French colony that catered to the European sweet tooth with sugar plantations that were worked by slaves brought from Africa, laboring in horrendous conditions. Toussaint L'Ouverture led a slave rebellion against the French planters.

In the early nineteenth century, Italian soldier Carlo Castelli, after fighting with proindependence armies in New Granada, was forced to escape to Haiti. In 1816, the Haitian president introduced him to Simon Bolivar, whose cause he then joined.

As we noted in *America Invades*, US Marines first landed on Haiti in 1817. Italian Americans serving in the US armed forces have participated in many subsequent American interventions in Haiti.

Bancroft Gherardi, from Louisiana, was the first Italian American admiral in the US Navy. Admiral Gherardi led a US fleet that intervened in a Haitian civil war in 1888–9.

Italian submarines hunted for merchant shipping in waters off Haiti during World War II.

In 2010, after a massive earthquake hit Haiti, about nine hundred Italian military personnel were used in Operation White Crane to assist.

Today, the Italian Haitian community numbers around a hundred thousand, including the half-Haitian, half-Italian supermodel Claudia Cedro.

HONDURAS

A MERIGO VESPUCCI MAY HAVE SAILED along the Honduras coast on a 1497–8 voyage, but we're on slightly firmer ground with the man from Genoa.

Yep, score another one for Columbus. On July 30, 1502, on his fourth voyage, he arrived at the Bay Islands; and on August 14, 1502, he went ashore on the mainland on Honduras in the vicinity of what is now

Trujillo. He also gave the country its name—Honduras—derived from the deep water in the area.

Other Italians followed in his footsteps as the Spanish bloodily imposed colonial rule, including Genoese Giovanni Battista Pastene en route for the Pacific and his journey of exploration along South America's Pacific Coast.

One person of Italian descent who played a huge role in the wars and politics of Central America in the early nineteenth century was Francisco Morazán, of Corsican descent. Francisco was born in 1792 in Tegucigalpa, now the capital of Honduras, and he rose to be head of state in Honduras, leading his troops to victory at the Battle of La Trinidad on November 11, 1827. From 1830–1839, he was president of the Federal Republic of Central America. Today, the Tegucigalpa department is called Francisco Morazán.

As with other countries in the region, the nineteenth century saw a fair amount of Italian immigration into Honduras. For instance, the Sicilian-born Vaccaro brothers were the founders of Standard Fruit Company (now Dole) that exported bananas from Honduras to New Orleans.

In December 1941, following the attack on Pearl Harbor, Honduras declared war on Italy.

More recently, Roberto Micheletti has been a prominent politician in Honduras. His father came from Bergamo, Italy.

HUNGARY

TOWARD THE END OF THE FIRST CENTURY BC, the Romans arrived in force in the western part of what is now Hungary. They soon fortified the southern bank of the Danube where it flows through the land, including building such major sites as Aquincum, near what is Budapest today.

In the early second century AD, Trajan's invasion of Dacia brought a small amount of eastern Hungary into the empire as well, though the Romans only hung onto that for little more than a century and a half, until Emperor Aurelian decided that crises elsewhere in the empire meant he had to let something go.

And the situation was not always peaceful in western Hungary either. For instance, in the fourth century, the activities of the Sarmatians prompted Emperor Constantine to campaign in the area.

Eventually, though, various peoples from across the Danube arrived in the part of Hungary that the Romans had held since the late first century BC; for instance, the Huns, the Avars, and, of course, the Magyars.

Italians were a large factor in medieval Hungary. They were one of the major immigrant groups into the country. Italian merchants played a leading role in trade there, and Italian knights, military men, and aristocrats had significant involvement as well.

For example, assorted kings of Hungary had major Italian links. And a particularly important character on the military front was Filippo di Stefano Scolari, Pipo of Ozora, a Florentine condottiero who became one of the great military commanders of late medieval Hungary.

The influence of Italian soldiers in Hungary continued after the Middle Ages as Christian armies clashed with the Ottomans.

For example, when war broke out between Emperor Rudolf II and the Turks in 1593, many Italian troops and Italian commanders headed to Hungary to fight.

Italian Raimondo Montecuccoli, a general in the forces of the Holy Roman Empire, invaded Ottoman-occupied Hungary during the Austro-Turkish War of 1663–1664. Piedmontese troops were among those in his army. He was victorious at the vital Battle of Saint Gotthard in the far west of Hungary on August 1, 1664, when the Ottoman Army was seriously mauled and forced to retreat.

And Bologna-born Luigi Marsili was one of the Italians taking part in the operation to capture Buda from the Turks in 1686. Later, he was put in charge of mapping the new border between the imperial territories and lands still held by the Ottomans.

Italians played a major role in Austrian and Austro-Hungarian armies in the eighteenth, nineteenth, and twentieth centuries.

The Italian Military Cemetery in Budapest holds the graves of 1,500 Italians from First World War prisoner of war camps.

Italian military personnel played assorted roles in Hungary after World War I, including involving themselves politically in Hungary's argument with Romania; and as members of the Allied military commission based at Sopron, charged with considering the question of the border between Hungary and Austria.

Hungary joined NATO in 1999.

ICELAND

D ID THE ROMANS EVER REACH ICELAND? Good question.
The first European settlement in Iceland is traditionally said to
have been carried out by Vikings in the ninth century, though it is possible
that Irish monks settled there some time before then and were pushed out
by the Vikings. So how did third-century Roman coins wind up in Iceland?
Admittedly, only a few have been found, but it's still a fascinating question.
The Greek explorer Pytheas referred to an island called Thule, and other
classical writers also referred to this island. Different writers, however,
say different things about it, suggesting they are not all referring to the
same place. Some references, like those describing it as north of Britain,
close to the frozen sea, and where it is permanent night in midwinter and
permanent day in midsummer, could refer to Iceland. Other references,
such as descriptions of inhabitants, seem more to suggest Scandinavia.
The easiest answer to the mystery of the Roman coins in Iceland is that
some Vikings brought them with them as curios, but so far we can't prove
the Romans didn't reach Iceland before them.

Christopher Columbus may have visited Iceland before going on to
make his rather more famous westward voyage into the Atlantic.

In 1933, however, Iceland was to play enthusiastic host to an
"invasion" of a squadron of twenty-four Italian Savoia-Marchetti seaplanes
arriving from Northern Ireland. It was the beginning of putting Iceland
on the international transatlantic air routes, and it's still regarded today in
Iceland as an important event.

During World War II, Iceland was occupied by Allied troops, and
Italian submarines operated in the waters to the south of the island. On
December 27, 1940, the *Enrico Tazzoli*, under Captain Vittore Raccanelli,
torpedoed the British freighter *Ardanbhan* south of Iceland. All the crew
died. And on February 24, 1941, the *Michele Bianchi*, under Captain
Adalberto Giovannini, torpedoed a ship in a similar area. Despite some
confusion over the identity of the ship, it seems likely it was the British
freighter *Huntingdon*. All the crew were rescued. The *Bianchi*, though,
was sunk in the Atlantic just a few months later by a British submarine. All
crew was lost.

Italian military forces have definitely reached Iceland since then.
Iceland is a NATO member, which has led to assorted military links. For
instance, in the summer of 2010, six Italian Air Force Eurofighter Typhoons

with supporting aircraft were based in Iceland for over a month, taking charge of NATO's Icelandic Air Policing operation. This is an operation that patrols Icelandic airspace to make up for the fact that Iceland does not itself maintain an air force.

INDIA

THE ROMANS WERE, OF COURSE, well aware of India. Extensive trade links existed between the Roman Empire and India, with plenty of ships making the journey across the Indian Ocean from the Red Sea, particularly to India's west coast. India is often mentioned in Roman texts, and large numbers of Roman coins have been found in India. Trajan, when he reached the Persian Gulf with his army, is supposed to have looked with longing at ships headed for India and wished he could have followed them.

He didn't. Nor did any other Roman emperor or his forces, but it is possible that Roman mercenaries fought in India. Tamil sources describe kings employing guards they describe as Yavanas. *Yavana* is a word that seems to have originally meant Greek (from Ionian) but was then applied to all Westerners. That included Roman traders and some of their products. So it is quite possible that these Yavana were either Greek or Roman veterans. Many kings of many nations have employed foreigners as their personal bodyguards precisely because they are detached from local politics and local loyalties, apart from to their employer.

Italians returned to India in the Middle Ages. Niccolò de' Conti, for instance, traveled to India in the fifteenth century, as did Girolamo da Santo Stefano.

But it was the Portuguese exploration of the sea route around the Cape of Good Hope that would really open up India to the west, and Italians played a significant part in that. For one thing, they helped finance the exploration. The 4th Portuguese Armada to India in 1502 included two ships captained by Italians, Thomaz de Carmona, or Cremona, and Giovanni Buonagrazia.

In addition, as the sea route around Africa was being opened up, Italian mercenaries were already in action in India. Vasco da Gama found Italian mercenaries serving on the Malabar Coast, and two of his men jumped ship to join them.

More Italian mercenaries were to follow them to the region. General Ventura, for instance, is recorded to have commanded troops east of Jammu.

In 1798, Napoleon hoped to invade India when he set off for Egypt; and in the twentieth century, Mussolini had plans for India. Mussolini established an Indian unit that included former Indian prisoners of war. The Italians gave assistance to some anti-British activists, like Mohammad Iqbal Shedai and Sardar Ajit Singh. The Italians set up Radio Himalaya to broadcast to the region during World War II.

Italian soldiers were sent to the area after World War II as part of UNMOGIP, the United Nations Military Observer Group based along the ceasefire line between India and Pakistan in the State of Jammu and Kashmir.

One of India's most influential politicians in recent years has been Italian-born Sonia Gandhi.

INDONESIA

NOT AN AREA YOU USUALLY THINK OF as having had much Italian historical involvement, but it has had some.

For a start, trade routes probably linked the Roman Empire to the area. The description of the region by the geographer Ptolemy suggests that he was aware of a route that Indian ships took to reach Borneo, an island now divided between the countries of Malaysia and Indonesia. And Rouletted Ware (a pottery produced from about 500 BC to AD 200), which seems to have originated in India, has been found as far west as Berenike in Egypt and as far east as Bali in Indonesia, suggesting some of the spectacular long-distance links in operation even at this early stage.

Niccolò de' Conti, from Chioggia in the province of Venice, seems to have spent time on Java in the mid-fifteenth century; and Genoese merchant Girolamo da Santo Stefano had made it to Sumatra by 1497 and used the name Sumatra. And certainly when the Portuguese opened up the sea route from Europe to the East at the very end of the fifteenth century and the beginning of the sixteenth century, Italians played a significant role. As early as 1510, for instance, Florentine merchant Girolamo Sernigi sent four of his ships to the straits of Malacca between Malaysia and Indonesia. The local Portuguese commander dragged them into an attack on Goa and then on Malacca (in Malaysia).

The great Italian explorer of the early sixteenth century, Andrea Corsali, also acquired knowledge of the area at about the same time, describing Sumatra and New Guinea.

Not long after, Genoese Leon Pancaldo (born in Savona) and Antonio Pigafetta, from Vicenza, also turned up in the area, having arrived with Ferdinand Magellan from the opposite direction after they rounded Cape Horn and crossed the Pacific. It was getting a bit crowded there!

In the seventeenth century, an attempt to recreate in this area the success of the Dutch East India Company led to ships of the short-lived Genoese East India Company being attacked in the Sunda Strait by the Dutch.

And in the late nineteenth century, as Italy tried to catch up with its European competitors in the race to establish colonies around the world, Italians once again headed for what is now Indonesia. In 1869, the plan was for one Emilio Cerruti to buy the islands of Kei, An, and Batchiane from the local rulers, using Italian government money, and then send in an expeditionary force to take control. The plan never came off, partly due to opposition by other Western powers.

Italian naval forces were in Indonesian waters again during World War II, when the area was occupied by the Japanese. Some Italian submarines made it as far as Japan. The *Reginaldo Guiliani*, with a mixed German and Italian crew, was torpedoed and sunk by the British submarine *Tally-Ho* on February 14, 1944, in the Straits of Malacca, where Girolamo Sernigi's fleet had first arrived over four hundred years earlier.

Italian aircraft took part in humanitarian relief efforts in Indonesia after a tsunami struck.

The Indonesian Navy uses naval guns produced by the Italian company Oto Melara.

IRAN

THE FIRST ITALIANS TO INVADE IRAN may have arrived there with the forces of Alexander the Great.

With such a diverse army as he had, it's certainly possible Italians were among either the actual fighting troops or with Alexander on a noncombat basis.

Alexander's family had connections with Italy. His uncle, Alexander I of Epirus, had led a military expedition to Italy to aid the city of Tarentum; and, coincidentally or not, there is some evidence of Tarentines with Alexander in the east. The writer Athenaeus does refer to Italian entertainers with Alexander at Susa, in what is now Iran: Philistides from Syracuse, a juggler; Alexis from Tarentum, who sang Homer's poetry; and Heracleitus from Tarentum, a singer and lyre player.

And then came the Romans. For much of its history, one of Rome's major adversaries had their heartland in what is now Iran. First it was the Parthians and then their successors, the Sassanids. Much of the fighting between the two powers took place to the west of Iran's borders, but the Romans did make it into what is now Iran.

For instance, Mark Antony's disastrous clash with the Parthians in 36 BC may have taken him into Iran. And certainly Trajan, during his campaigning in the east, invaded what is now Iran, capturing again the city of Susa.

In AD 216, according to historian Herodian, the emperor Caracalla married a Parthian princess. The wedding was never consummated because she and many guests were slaughtered at the wedding feast, prefiguring the Red Wedding in *A Game of Thrones* by over a thousand years. The name of the Parthian princess is, alas, lost to history.

The Middle Ages would again see armed Italians operating in Iranian territory. For example, in 1428, another Italian, Giovanni de Valle from Venice, operating on the Caspian under the orders of the Khan of Darband, attacked ships sailing from Astarabad (now Gorgan) in Iran.

And in the nineteenth century, a number of Italian soldiers had significant involvement in Iran. In particular, Paolo Di Avitabile, born in 1791 in Agerola, played a major role in leading Persian troops. Later in the century, an Italian officer from Naples, Colonel Luigi Pesce, who had gone to Iran to train local troops, would become the first person to photograph the mighty Persian ruins of Persepolis.

In 1988, during the Iran-Iraq War, Italian frigates and minesweepers were sent to the Persian Gulf to defend Italian shipping.

IRAQ

YES, MANY ITALIANS have fought in Iraq.

The first Italians may have arrived in what is now Iraq with Alexander the Great (see Iran).

Certainly the Romans spent plenty of time invading what is now Iraq.

Ctesiphon, a major city and often the capital of both Parthian and Sassanian Empires, the two main enemies of Rome in the east, lies about twenty-two miles south of Baghdad. It was the constant target of Rome's attempts to push east and destroy its main regional competitor.

In AD 116, Trajan on his great campaign to the east thrust deep into what is now Iraq and captured Ctesiphon before continuing south to the Persian Gulf. However, Trajan died in 117 before he could consolidate his gains in the area, and his successor, Hadrian, gave up Ctesiphon again.

However, in 165, the Romans hit Ctesiphon again. This time it was Avidius Cassius who sacked the city, but with his army short of supplies and some his soldiers having caught the plague, he was forced to retreat again.

In 197, the Romans returned. This time it was Emperor Septimius Severus. Once again he sacked Ctesiphon but was unable to capture Hatra. He did, however, establish a long-term Roman presence in northern Iraq, including the fortified post of Singara.

Just a few years later, another Roman army was rampaging across what is now Iraq. The emperor Caracalla—who, among other things, built baths in Rome and assassinated his Parthian bride—sacked Arbela (modern-day Erbil) in 216, close to the site of Alexander the Great's decisive victory over the Persians in the Battle of Gaugamela/Arbela.

Shortly afterward, another emperor, Severus Alexander, set off toward Ctesiphon but didn't make it.

In 244, another Roman emperor, Gordian III, headed again for Ctesiphon but was defeated by the Sassanid Persians at the Battle of Misiche, perhaps located somewhere near modern Fallujah, and ended up dead.

A period of Sassanid expansion westward followed shortly after. But by 283, as the Sassanids were distracted by internal conflict and threats to their empire from the east, another Roman, Emperor Carus, advanced on Ctesiphon. This time, Carus captured Ctesiphon and sacked it. But again, he died shortly after doing so.

In 298, Galerius won a decisive battle over the Sassanids at Satala. He pressed on and captured Ctesiphon yet again. The peace deal finally signed with the Persians was very much in the Romans' favor and lasted some decades.

However, in the fourth century, the Sassanid king Shapur II started advancing again, prompting Emperor Julian II to mount yet another Roman offensive in what is now Iraq. It wasn't a great success. In fact, it was a disaster. Julian won the Battle of Ctesiphon in 363 but didn't manage to take Ctesiphon itself. He was forced to start retreating and shortly afterward was killed in combat. The Roman Army made a hasty peace deal, giving up masses of territory, including most of what they had held in northern Iraq since 197, and then retreated.

Though the Byzantines would return later, this was pretty much the end of Rome's attempts to push east, deep into Iraq.

The crusaders wouldn't even make it as far east as the Romans. For instance, in 1104, a crusader force besieged Harran, near what is now Turkey's border with Syria and not a huge distance from Iraq. However, in the ensuing Battle of Harran, the crusader army, which by that time included Bohemond I, Prince of Taranto and Prince of Antioch, was decisively defeated by the Seljuk Turks, allowing Byzantine and Muslim powers in the region to reestablish their dominance.

However, armed Italians did return to Iraq during World War II. In 1941, the anti-British Rashid Ali al-Gaylani took power in Iraq, and he wanted Axis help against the British forces then in his country. A number of German aircraft were dispatched to Iraq, and eventually a few Italian planes arrived as well. In the end, though, the limited Axis assistance achieved little, and Rashid Ali al-Gaylani fled Iraq as British forces advanced.

And, of course, Italian forces have been in action in Iraq rather more recently.

For example, during the Gulf War to liberate Kuwait from Saddam, Italian Tornadoes (an aircraft developed by the United Kingdom, West Germany, and Italy) operating out of a base in the United Arab Emirates attacked targets inside Iraq. Italian military personnel were also deployed to northern Iraq at this time to assist Kurdish refugees.

And Italy played a major role in the occupation of Iraq. In 2003, the Nasiriyah suicide bombing killed at least twenty-eight people, including seventeen Carabinieri, and injured many more. Italian forces withdrew from Iraq in 2006. They lost more troops there than any other coalition nation, apart from the United States and the United Kingdom.

In 2014, Italy began assisting with operations against ISIS in Iraq.

IRELAND

S EVERAL YEARS AGO, a popular history made the claim that the Irish saved civilization.* They would not have had Western civilization to save, however, if the Romans had not invented so much of it!

Did the Romans ever invade the Emerald Isle?

From the writings of contemporary geographers, it is clear the Romans knew a lot about Ireland; and the fact that a range of Roman objects have been found in Ireland suggests significant trade links.

And the Romans do seem to have given some serious consideration to the possibility of invading Ireland.

According to Roman historian Tacitus, when Agricola advanced into what is now Scotland, he set up a strong garrison on the shore opposite Ireland in order to have troops available to invade Ireland. Agricola apparently reckoned that this would make strategic sense for Rome, and that a force of just one legion and a few auxiliaries would be adequate to conquer Hibernia. Tacitus also records that Agricola extended hospitality to an exiled Hibernian king or prince, with the possible intention of using him in an invasion attempt.

Some have suggested that a promontory fort in Drumanagh, near Dublin, where some Roman material has been found, may represent the site of a Roman incursion into Ireland. Others suggest the Roman material more likely arrived there by trade.

The English king Edward II does seem to have had definite plans to send Italian soldiers to Ireland. In 1317, he recruited one thousand Genoese mercenaries under the command of Antonio de Passagno to fight the Scots in Ireland.

However, on some occasions, Italian troops have definitely fought in Ireland. Italian and Spanish troops, for instance, landed in Ireland to aid the Desmond Rebellion, led by the Earl of Desmond against Queen Elizabeth. However, the six hundred Italians and Spanish who came ashore at Smerwick in 1580 found themselves besieged and forced to surrender by Queen Elizabeth's forces. Those captured were executed and their bodies thrown into the sea.

Many Irish troops have volunteered to fight in Italy on behalf of various popes. The St. Patrick's Battalion, for example, fought against the Garibaldini at the Battle of Spoleto in 1860.

The Irish came very close to altering Italian military history when in 1926 Violet Gibson, an Irishwoman, shot Mussolini three times in a failed assassination attempt in Rome. In the end, she only slightly wounded his nose. She was committed to an insane asylum for the rest of her life but outlived Il Duce, dying in 1956 in the United Kingdom.

Italian submarines operated in waters off the Irish coast during World War II.

* Thomas Cahill, *How the Irish Saved Civilization: The Untold Story of Ireland's Heroic Role From the Fall of Rome to the Rise of Medieval Europe* (New York: Anchor Books, 1996).

ISRAEL

R OMAN POWER SERIOUSLY ARRIVED in what is now the modern state of Israel with Pompey the Great.

Pompey involved himself in a local conflict, which led him to besiege and take Jerusalem in 63 BC. Over the next century, different, and sometimes changing, political arrangements followed for different parts of what is now modern-day Israel, as some became client kingdoms, parts of Roman provinces, or self-governing. A period of instability in the region, accompanied by Parthian intrusion, also occurred during the civil war between Pompey and Caesar and after Caesar's death.

In AD 66, the first Jewish-Roman War broke out. The Roman army of Cestius Gallus suffered a crushing defeat. General Vespasian was then dispatched to the war zone. Years of bitter fighting followed. In 69, Vespasian became emperor, and so it was his son Titus who besieged and captured Jerusalem in 70. However, even this was not the end of the war. Masada did not fall until sometime around 73.

Jewish resistance to Rome continued, though. During the Kitos War of 115–117, which saw Jewish uprisings across a number of areas in the east regions of the Roman Empire, there was fierce fighting in what is now the modern state of Israel. And in 132, the Bar Kokhba Revolt, or the Third Jewish-Roman War, broke out. Again, years of bitter fighting followed until the Romans finally crushed the revolt in 135.

Even that, though, was not the end of Jewish opposition to Rome. For instance, in 351, another Jewish rebellion broke out, and Roman troops were sent in to suppress it.

Italian soldiers returned in large numbers to the area during the Crusades.

Italian naval power was hugely influential on a number of occasions. In 1101, a Genoese fleet helped capture Caesarea and Arsuf. And in 1104, Genoese ships again played a key role in the capture of Acre. After that, Genoa established a major trading colony in the port.

In another example, Italian-born King of Italy and Holy Roman Emperor Frederick II led the Sixth Crusade in 1228. After a bit of negotiation, he managed to secure extra land for the Christians and had himself crowned King of Jerusalem.

In 1607, another Italian monarch, Ferdinand I of Tuscany, had dreams of capturing Cyprus and then continuing on to invade the Holy Land. However, he gave up after his forces failed to take Famagusta in Cyprus.

General Caffarelli, a French general of Italian descent, was with Napoleon at the siege of Acre in 1799. He died of gangrene there after being shot in the arm, and his tomb is still there.

During World War II, Italian airmen were in action over the country. Soon after Italy declared war on Britain in June 1940, the Italian Air Force started bombing targets in what was then the British-controlled Palestine Mandate. The raids hit a number of locations, including Tel Aviv, Haifa, Acre, and Jaffa. A raid on Tel Aviv on September 9, 1940, killed 137 people.

IVORY COAST

THE PORTUGUESE WERE THE FIRST EUROPEANS who definitely explored the Ivory Coast, and among them were Italians.

In November 2004, in Operation Ippocampo during fighting in the country, Italian C-130s flew into Abidjan with Italian soldiers on board as security, to evacuate Italian and other civilians to nearby Accra. Italian Joint Force Headquarters also helped control operations in the Ivory Coast in 2011.

JAMAICA

IT'S ANOTHER ONE FOR Genoa's Christopher Columbus.

On May 5, 1494, on his second voyage to the West Indies, Columbus landed in Jamaica. It was not a good day for the inhabitants of the island. The Spanish would eventually take control of Jamaica and keep it until the English took it from them in 1655.

In 1540, the island was actually given to the Columbus family as a personal estate. They didn't do much to develop it, but we can say that because of this, in some sense, Italians once controlled Jamaica.

In the early eighteenth century, a possibly Italian pirate also ended up on Jamaica, though not in the manner he might have wished. Captain

Matthew Luke (English version of his name) had already captured four British merchant ships when he made a rather bad (from his point of view) mistake. In 1722, he attacked what he thought was another merchant ship, only to find it was, in fact, the HMS *Launceston*. Soon Luke and his crew were prisoners and en route for Jamaica, where forty-one out of fifty-eight of them were hanged.

The Italian warship *Flavio Gioia* called in at Port Royal and Kingston in the late 1880s.

JAPAN

H AS ITALY INVADED JAPAN? The question seems absurd. On further consideration, however, there have been substantial military connections between Italy and Japan over the course of history.

No Roman may ever have reached Japan, but it is possible that some Roman manufactured goods did. Glass beads have been discovered by archaeologists in fifth-century tombs near Kyoto, and analysis has suggested they may have originated in the Roman Empire.

After the Portuguese, with Italian help, opened up the sea route around the Cape of Good Hope, Italian Jesuits helped develop contacts between Europe and Japan, and Italian merchant adventurers could be found in Japanese waters. Florentine Francesco Carletti, for instance, visited Japan in 1597–8.

A period of isolation from European contact followed, but after Commodore Matthew Perry's black ships once again opened up Japan in the 1850s, Italian commercial and political connections with Japan increased dramatically. Formal relations between the two nations were established in 1866. Two cruisers of the Imperial Japanese Navy, *Kasuga* and *Nisshin*, were built in Genoese shipyards. Both ships would participate in the decisive Japanese victory over the Russian Navy at the Battle of Tsushima Strait during the Russo-Japanese War in May 1905.

In the same year, Puccini's *Madame Butterfly*, set in Nagasaki, premiered at La Scala. Many Japanese opera singers, including Tamaki Miura, have played the role of Cio-Cio-San over the years.

Italy and Japan were allied in both world wars of the twentieth century. During the First World War, fourteen Japanese destroyers were sent to the Mediterranean to support the allies, and especially the Italians, in fighting Austrian submarines.

In 1920, two Italian World War I pilots, Arturo Ferrarin and Guido Masiero, flew the eleven thousand miles from Rome to Tokyo for the first time. Both pilots would later be killed during World War II while test piloting aircraft.

In September of 1940, fascist Italy and Japan made up two-thirds of the Tripartite Alliance with Nazi Germany. When the war began going badly for Italy and German enthusiasm for the alliance cooled, Mussolini declared that he was the world's biggest fan of Japan.

The Italian naval defeat at the Battle of Taranto on November 12, 1940, had a profound impact on Japan and the course of World War II. In the space of less than one hour, outdated British biplanes launched from the decks of aircraft carriers managed to put half of the Italian battle fleet out of combat for about six months. Lieutenant Commander Takeshi Naito was an assistant naval attaché based in Berlin at the time. After the battle, he flew to Taranto to inspect the damage inflicted on the Italian fleet. Naito later lectured Admiral Yamamoto's staff on the battle, which played a major role in formulating the Japanese plans for the subsequent attack on Pearl Harbor, which brought the United States into World War II on the Allied side.

The Italian Navy provided some direct assistance to Japan during the war. Great efforts were made to send submarines around the world carrying important material to beat the Allied blockade. It was a hugely dangerous task, but three submarines, the *Cappellini*, *Guiliani*, and the *Torelli*, did actually make their staggering journeys through seas patrolled by Allied warships to the Far East. The *Guiliani* was subsequently sunk, but the *Cappellini* and *Torelli* came first under German control after the Italian armistice with the Allies in 1943 and subsequently under Japanese control after May 1945, with mixed crews until the end of the war. An Italian-made ship was used to strike one of the final Axis blows of World War II when, in August of 1945, the Japanese-manned crew of the *Torelli* shot down an American B-25 bomber. At the end of the war, US forces captured both *Cappellini* and *Torelli* at Kobe in Japan, and they were subsequently sunk off Kobe.

And in 1942, in an epic of wartime flight that followed Ferrarin and Masiero's flight of 1920, a three-engine Italian Savoia-Marchetti SM.75, with important code changes for the Japanese, departed from Rome. It then took off in secret from an air base in German-held Ukraine and flew in the dark over Soviet-held territory until it reached Japanese-held territory in China. From there, it was able to make the rest of its journey to Tokyo. Once it had delivered its cargo, it then safely made the return journey in the same fashion. The round trip was 9,600 miles, and Mussolini greeted them on their return to Rome.

Italian Americans, who represented one in twelve American military personnel in World War II, participated in many invasions of Japanese-held territory in the Pacific. Gunnery Sergeant John Basilone of the US Marine Corps (see Solomon Islands) grew up in Raritan, New Jersey. Basilone had fought earlier on Guadalcanal, where he earned the Medal of Honor (see Solomon Islands). On February 19, 1945, he was killed on the first day of the invasion of the Japanese-held island of Iwo Jima.

Since World War II, Japan and Italy have had assorted military and defense links.

JORDAN

POMPEY CREATED THE ROMAN PROVINCE OF SYRIA in 64 BC. And then in 63 BC, Pompey's officer Scaurus invaded the Kingdom of Nabataea, which occupied much of what is now Jordan. He reached the city of Pella and then withdrew. More Roman soldiers were to follow, in 55 BC, under Gabinius.

The Romans didn't take control of the Nabataean Kingdom at this stage, but they had firmly announced their interest in the area and their determination to exert influence over it. Local rulers essentially became clients of Rome, and the cities of the Decapolis paid money to Rome.

When Rabbel II, the king of Nabataea, died in AD 106, Trajan decided to send in the legions. The invasion does not seem to have taken much time or effort, and thus Roman rule was established over a large part of what is the modern country of Jordan.

The area did see some fighting during the First Jewish-Roman War of AD 66–74, and in the third century the Sassanid Persians were becoming an increasing threat, plus the rebellion of Zenobia briefly threatened Roman rule across the entire region.

The area would, however, eventually pass from Roman rule to Byzantine rule.

Italian soldiers returned to what is now Jordan with the Crusades. The crusaders built a defensive line of castles in Jordan, including those at Shobak and Kerak.

The Italian military has had assorted links with Jordan in recent years. For instance, the Airmobile Brigade Friuli headed to Jordan for Exercise

Eastern Desert 2005, and paratroopers taking part in Exercise Eager Lion were there in 2012.

KAZAKHSTAN

O K, HUGE COUNTRY, but only with tiny Italian military involvement.
    In the thirteenth century, the route of Italian explorer Giovanni Da Pian Del Carpine to the court of the Great Khan, which led him north of the Caspian Sea, took him through what is now Kazakhstan.

In the fourteenth century, Italian pirates were active on the Caspian Sea. In 1374, Genoese Luchino Tarigo sailed from the Black Sea up the River Don. He then took his ship across land to the Volga and sailed it into the Caspian. He turned to piracy, attacking and capturing loads of vessels. His main area of activity on the Caspian seems to have been farther south than Kazakh waters, but he must have been at least within a few miles of Kazakh territory when he entered the Caspian at the mouth of the Volga.

During World War I, Italians from the parts of Italy then under the control of the Austro-Hungarian Empire were taken into the Austro-Hungarian Army. Some of them ended up on the Eastern Front fighting the Russians, and some of them became prisoners of war at a place called Kirsanov.

When the Russian Revolution forced Russia out of the war, the resulting deal signed with the Germans at Brest Litovsk set these prisoners free. But getting home wasn't going to be easy for all of them. Some managed to escape the chaos of revolutionary Russia by heading north to Archangel and taking ships from there. But, as revolution turned into civil war, for some the only route home was to head east along the Trans-Siberian Railway as far as Vladivostok on the Pacific Coast. At the time, this route would have taken some of these Italian soldiers through the key Trans-Siberian rail junction of Petroplavovsk. Petropavlovsk is now Petropavl and is just inside Kazakhstan.

Some freed Italian prisoners were also formed into combat units in Russia, but we'll deal with them in the chapter on Russia. The so-called Savoy Unit formed by Andrea Compattangelo did see action in Samara just north of the Kazakh border.

And during World War II, the extraordinary Rome-to-Tokyo journey conducted in 1942 by a single long-range Italian aircraft flew through what is now Kazakhstan's airspace near Lake Balkhash.

KENYA

I T SEEMS HARD TO BELIEVE THAT ITALIANS have ever invaded Kenya, but, yes, they have.

It's quite possible the Romans were aware of the Kenyan coast from traders who had traveled in that area. An amazing document from the Roman period, the *Periplus of the Erythraean Sea*, shows comprehensive knowledge of the Indian Ocean. In part, the text lists details of the coast south of Somalia until it comes to the southernmost location it describes: a port called Rhapta, where ivory was available in great quantities, far south along the African coast. Then it refers to an area even farther south, where the unexplored ocean bends around toward the west and mixes with the western sea, which seems to suggest at least a secondhand knowledge of the Cape of Good Hope. The exact location of Rhapta is unclear but could well be in Tanzania, to the south of Kenya, which would mean that the Kenyan coast would be even more familiar to the Romans.

The apparent knowledge of the Cape of Good Hope is fascinating, particularly since it wasn't until 1488 that a European ship actually went around it, though coming from the west initially. This was Portuguese Bartolomeu Dias. He was, of course, followed by Vasco da Gama, en route for the rich spice trade of India and beyond. But while da Gama was Portuguese, Italians played a significant role in his expeditions. For instance, on da Gama's 1502 India armada, Thomaz de Carmona (Cremona) and Giovanni Buonagrazia were two Italians who commanded ships. The expedition called in at Malindi, in what is now Kenya, before heading across the Indian Ocean to the subcontinent.

In 1591, the Portuguese built the spectacular Fort Jesus on Mombasa Island according to the design of Milanese military architect Giovanni Battista Cairati.

In the end, the British, though, became the dominant colonial power in Kenya. To the north, Italy invaded Ethiopia in 1935, which meant that on June 10, 1940, when Mussolini declared war on France and Britain, the Kenyan border with Ethiopia was suddenly a war zone.

It wasn't long before the fighting started in earnest. Just three days later, on June 13, three Italian Caproni bombers entered Kenyan airspace and bombed the air base at Wajir. Soon after that, Italian ground troops crossed the border. Bitter fighting ensued before the Italians finally managed to capture Fort Harrington in Moyale, and then they pressed farther south. At its largest extent, the Italian advance into Kenya reached Buna and Dabel, about sixty miles from the border. But supply problems and a need to concentrate on military developments elsewhere prevented any further Italian advance into Kenya. Eventually, the British launched their own campaigns in East Africa; and on July 15, 1941, Moyale was captured by advancing British troops.

As Italian control of East Africa collapsed, the Italian governor general of the area, Prince Amedeo, the Duke of Aosta and a cousin of King Victor Emmanuel III, was given permission by Mussolini to surrender. The prince, educated at Eton and Oxford, accompanied his men into captivity in Kenya and, after dying of disease, was buried there in the Italian War Memorial Church at Nyeri, along with hundreds of other Italian soldiers.

In 2014, the Italian aircraft carrier *Cavour* and her escorts visited Kenya.

KIRIBATI

K IRIBATI IS AN ISLAND NATION in the Pacific.
  In World War II, the Japanese occupied some of the islands, including Tarawa. Italian Americans participated in the bloody battle of Tarawa, which was fought in November 1943. For instance, Sergeant Ugo Mauriello, a marine from New York, was killed on Kiribati on November 20 and buried at sea the next day.

KOSOVO

A S THE ROMANS EXPANDED across the Balkans, their advance brought them to the little land that is now known as Kosovo.

Though the Romans had a major victory over the powerful Illyrian people as early as 168 BC, when Gentius, their king, surrendered, it seems that tribes in the Kosovo area held out longer. It's unclear, therefore, when what is now Kosovo came wholly and thoroughly under Roman rule. It certainly seems to have done so sometime late in the first century BC, although the great Illyrian rebellion of AD 6–9 would temporarily cause a major disruption of Roman power in the region. Still, Roman towns and cities like Ulpiana were built, and the territory eventually came under Byzantine control.

Italian soldiers were in action here again during the Middle Ages. For instance, Constantine Bodin's attempt to seize the Bulgarian throne in 1072, an attempt that focused on Kosovo and surrounding lands, was supported by Italian mercenaries.

In 1689, General Piccolomini, advancing deep into Ottoman territory, led an army of the Holy Roman Empire into Kosovo and surrounding areas. He sparked a major local rebellion against the Ottomans, but contracted the plague and died at Prizren in Kosovo on November 9 of that year.

In the last days of World War I, Italian troops would again invade Kosovo. In October, as German and Austro-Hungarian forces withdrew, Italy's 35th Division captured Prizren and then advanced northward through Kosovo, pursuing the retreating enemy.

And in 1941, Italian troops invaded again. The Germans took the northern part of Kosovo, but once again, Italian troops occupied Prizren, marching into it on April 14, 1941. After the Italian armistice with the allies in September 1943, the Germans occupied the whole of Kosovo.

Italy played a major role in the Kosovo War that began in 1999. Twelve Italian air bases were key in the air campaign, and Italian aircraft were a significant percentage of those conducting the NATO air campaign. The Italian Army participated in the NATO land advance into Kosovo in June 1999, and has played a major role in NATO's operation there.

KUWAIT

K UWAIT WAS CERTAINLY KNOWN TO THE GREEKS in the days of Alexander the Great; and remains of Greek buildings and other items from that period, such as Greek coins, have been found on Falaika Island.

The Romans may have made it to Kuwait too. For instance, in AD 116, after capturing Ctesiphon, the Parthian capital in what is now Iraq, Emperor Trajan took his forces south until he reached the waters of the Persian Gulf. He is said to have looked with longing at those waters and at a ship headed for India, sad that he could not take Roman power there. This must have taken place certainly not far from Kuwait. Trajan also established a short-lived province of Mesopotamia. But by AD 117, Trajan was dead, and his successor would retreat to what he regarded as defendable borders.

Italian aircraft have been on operations over Kuwait on a number of occasions. For instance, during the audacious Italian air raid on Bahrain in 1940, the attackers flew over Kuwait on their way from Rhodes to their target. During the Gulf War to liberate Kuwait from Saddam, Italian Tornadoes operating out of a base in the United Arab Emirates attacked targets inside Kuwait. In the first Italian strike of the war, an Italian Tornado was shot down over Kuwait, and Lieutenant Gianmarco Bellini and Captain Maurizio Cocciolone were captured. Both officers were held by Iraqi forces as POWs until their release, which followed the brief ground campaign to liberate Kuwait. And recently, Italian Tornado fighter-bombers have again been sent to Kuwait, this time to help counter ISIS.

The Italian Navy too has had involvement with Kuwait. For example, during the war between Iraq and Iran when ships, particularly tankers, heading to or from Kuwait were being targeted in the Gulf, the Italian Navy helped protect them. Italian warships were also active in the Gulf during the operations to liberate Kuwait.

The Italian land forces based in Iraq also made use of facilities in Kuwait.

In July 2012, a Memorandum of Agreement on cooperation between Italy and Kuwait in the defense field was signed.

KYRGYZSTAN

I T HAS TO BE SAID THAT, IN GENERAL, the countries in this region have not been areas of major Italian involvement, but Italians have had some significant links with Kyrgyzstan.

In the days of the Silk Road and Giovanni da Pian del Carpine and Marco Polo, it's possible early Italian explorers visited ancient cities in Kyrgyzstan, like Osh, en route to China.

However, to the south of Kyrgyzstan, beyond Tajikistan, is another country, Afghanistan, which has recently led to some more definite Italian involvement in the country.

As part of operations in Afghanistan, in October 2002, the 5th Autonomous Operations Department (5th ROA) of the Italian Air Force was sent to operate C-130s of the 46th Air Brigade in Pisa. It was based at Manas air base in Kyrgystan, about twelve miles from the Kyrgyz capital of Bishkek. On October 22, it operated its first flight to Bagram in Afghanistan.

LAOS

L AOS IS A LANDLOCKED COUNTRY IN SOUTHEAST ASIA that has been called "the land of a million elephants." Some have remarked that its shape resembles that of Italy.

Italian missionary Giovanni-Maria Leria, in the seventeenth century, was one of the first Europeans to visit Laos and live there.

The French colonial experiment in Laos lasted from its acquisition by the French in 1863 until their decisive defeat at Dien Bien Phu in 1954. Some Italians in French Foreign Legion units were based in Laos during this time.

The Ho Chi Minh Trail ran through Laos during the Vietnam War and was bombed heavily during this tragic conflict. In 1971, the United States supported a South Vietnamese offensive into Laotian territory. Italian American soldiers fought with US forces in Laos.

Astonishingly, the decadence of ancient Rome is today celebrated in the Golden Triangle in Laos, where one can find the Kings Roman Casino, built by a Chinese entrepreneur with elaborate classical columns and statues. Rome sells.

LATVIA

A S WITH LITHUANIA, THE DISCOVERY OF ROMAN COINS and artifacts in Latvia point to links between the Roman Empire and the area, which are probably connected by the valuable trade in Baltic amber.

The eighteenth century saw a rather different kind of involvement. Karl Ernst of Courland, a son of the reigning duke, became a good friend of Casanova and visited Venice from what is now Latvia. Casanova himself also traveled to Riga.

In his 1812 attack on the Russian empire, Napoleon launched his main initial thrust through Lithuania, but he also sent troops into Latvia at the same time. A French marshal with the unlikely name of Jacques MacDonald (turns out he was of Scottish Jacobite ancestry), who was in command of the Grande Armée's left wing, was dispatched with tens of thousands of troops to take Riga. He tried to lay siege to it, but in the end failed to capture it.

One Italian was to have more luck than Napoleon in taking control of Riga. Filippo Paulucci, born in 1779 in Modena, had ended up as a commander in the Russian Army. After successes fighting in the Caucasus, on October 29, 1812, he was made military governor of Riga. Later, he was influential in rebuilding the suburbs of Riga that had been burned during the war.

Another significant Italian commander in the area was General Marietti, an Italian member of the Allied Commission in the Baltic States that helped end the violent chaos in the area after World War I and to organize the evacuation of German troops.

In the period after 1943, the Aeronautica Nazionale Repubblicana, the Italian air force that remained allied to the Germans, stationed the 1 Gruppo Aerotrasporti "Trabucchi" at Spilve air base outside Riga to assist the German troops resisting the Soviet advance. By the end of summer 1944, they had been virtually wiped out.

Recently, Italian planes have again been operational in the Baltic area. In January 2015, Italian Air Force planes took over NATO's Air Policing mission in the Baltic States. Italian Eurofighter Typhoon fighter jets had already visited the region to prepare for the mission.

LEBANON

T HE INITIAL ROMAN INVASION isn't a hugely dramatic story. In the aftermath of the war against Mithridates and Tigranes, Pompey decided to wrap up the Seleucid Empire, having Antiochus XIII killed in 64 BC and (apart from that) peacefully taking over what was left of the empire, including what is now Lebanon. Still, a period of instability, accompanied by Parthian intrusions into the region, followed during the civil war between Pompey and Caesar and after Caesar's death.

Italians invaded Lebanon again in the Middle Ages. While primarily focused on the Holy Land, of course, the crusaders took territory in what is now Lebanon as well, and Italians played a major part. Venice, for instance, helped capture the port of Tyre. It received in return, via the Pactum Warmundi of 1123, a privileged position in the city and rights for Venetian merchants. A painting in the Doge's palace in Venice still commemorates the storming of the city. Genoa acquired a colony at Tripoli in what is now Lebanon.

And Italian ships were in action in Lebanese waters again in the early twentieth century. During the Italo-Turkish War, Italian forces feared the Ottoman naval forces at Beirut were a threat to Italian supply lines, which ran through the Suez Canal to Italian colonial territories in East Africa. Consequently, they decided to wipe out the Ottoman force.

On February 24, 1912, two Italian cruisers, *Giuseppe Garibaldi* and *Francesco Ferruccio*, approached Beirut Harbor. When a deadline for surrender expired, they started shelling the Ottoman naval vessels in the harbor. The Ottoman force was destroyed, and a number of Italian shells hit the city as well.

A large Italian contingent, including Bersaglieri and marines from the San Marco regiment, took part in the Multinational Force in Lebanon (MNF) that entered Lebanon in 1982. Their initial goal was to arrange the departure of the PLO. The forces left in 1984, after suicide bombings had killed a large number of American and French troops.

In recent decades, Italian troops have played a significant role in international efforts in Lebanon. They took part in UNOGIL (United Nations Observation Group in Lebanon) in 1958, and have been an important element in UNIFIL (United Nations Interim Force in Lebanon), and with Operation Leonte .

LESOTHO

ANGLO-ITALIAN SIR JOHN CHARLES MOLTENO, first prime minister of the Cape Colony, did have quite a lot to do with Basutoland (as Lesotho was then known). On a number of occasions, he intervened in the region. For instance, when Langalibalele, king of a local tribe, crossed into Basutoland, Molteno promptly sent out the Frontier Armed and Mounted Police, and Langalibale was captured.

Italy itself hasn't invaded Lesotho. However, despite it being one of the smallest countries in Africa, Lesotho has invaded Italy. Well, at least troops from what was then the British colony of Basutoland joined the invading forces in Italy in 1943, and were involved in the bitter fighting around Salerno.

LIBERIA

OK, NOT A COUNTRY THAT ITALIANS have had much to do with militarily, but a few points can be made.

Italian explorer Giacomo Bove called in, in the late nineteenth century, as did the Italian warship *Staffetta* during its cruise along the African coast in 1887–1888. And the Italian Navy was in action in the waters off Liberia during World War II.

In the summer of 1941, the Italian submarine *Tazzoli*, under Fecia di Cossato, was on patrol off the Liberian coast, and on August 19 it torpedoed and sank the Norwegian tanker *Sildra*. All its crew survived.

Liberia itself, despite heavy American influence, did not declare war on Germany until January 1944.

LIBYA

THE COASTAL PART OF WHAT IS NOW WESTERN LIBYA came under Roman control in 146 BC after the Romans destroyed Carthage in the Third Punic War (see Tunisia). The coastal part of eastern Libya came under Roman control in 96 BC after Ptolemy Apion, King of Cyrenaica, left it to Rome in his will. Not the most dramatic of Italian invasions.

Much of the south of what is now Libya was occupied by a powerful people known as the Garamantes and largely remained beyond permanent Roman control. However, the Romans had extensive contacts with the Garamantes. For instance, a mausoleum at their capital, Germa/Garama, shows extensive Roman influence. And on occasion, Roman expeditions did penetrate the area.

For instance, in 19, BC L. Cornelius Balbus campaigned in the Fezzan. And after the Garamantes attacked Roman coastal areas in the first century AD, Festus, a Roman governor, launched a punitive campaign. And an expedition south from Libya under Septimius Flaccus lasted some months and ended up in the middle of the "Aethiopians." Unless the expedition was far off course, this presumably refers to black people, and Flaccus may have reached as far south as the Tibesti Mountains, which are mainly located in northern Chad. An expedition under Julius Maternus did get as far as the land of Agisymba, a land where the expedition encountered rhinoceroses. This may well have been in the region of Lake Chad, and if so, their route could have taken them through Chad.

Cyrenaica saw bitter fighting during the reign of Trajan, when the Jewish community in the area rose in rebellion.

And under the African emperor of Rome, Septimius Severus, born in what is now Libya, Roman troops again advanced in the south, reaching as far as Germa/Garama.

Armed Italians would return to Libya in the Middle Ages. For instance, in 1146, the fleet of Roger II of Sicily captured Tripoli and it became part of his Kingdom of Africa for a while. And in 1335, Genoese pirate Filippo Doria again seized Tripoli before selling it.

In the period after the Middle Ages, pirates based in North African ports, including Tripoli, caused major problems for Europe, and both Italian fleets attacked them on a number of occasions. For instance, the Royal Sardinian Navy attacked Tripoli in 1825, and a Neapolitan naval force attacked the same target three years later.

However, it was the twentieth century that saw the most intense Italian military involvement with Libya since the Roman period.

Looking to expand its overseas territories, in 1911 the Italians set their sights on Libya. In October, the Italian Navy shelled shore forts and then landed men to seize Tripoli. Intense fighting followed, but eventually, as 1911 turned into 1912, Italy consolidated its control of the coastal area. In terms of the overall history of warfare, the war is now chiefly remembered for the first deployment of aircraft in combat. On November 1, 1911, Giulio Gavotti dropped the first bombs from a plane in combat. On May 2, 1912, Captain Marengo bombed by night for the first time.

Finally, in October 1912, the Ottomans ceded control of their territory to the Italians. In the period after World War I, the Italians would pick up extra chunks of border territory from neighboring French and British colonial authorities. The fighting was not, however, over for Italy. Libyan resistance followed, led especially by Omar Mukhtar. This rebel leader was finally captured by Italian armed forces and hanged in 1931.

With the arrival of World War II, Libya once again became a battlefield for Italian forces. In September 1940, Italian troops invaded Egypt from Libya. However, a British counteroffensive forced Italian troops back into Libya. After the arrival of the Afrika Korps, however, Axis troops proceeded to force British forces back. A period of fighting in Cyrenaica and around the Egyptian border ensued before the Axis forces were finally able to capture Tobruk, in eastern Libya, and once again push across the border into Egypt. The Axis offensive, however, ground to a halt with the British victory at El Alamein in late 1942. As Allied superiority in supplies began to have a decisive effect, the Axis forces were thrown into retreat, forced back in a series of actions across Libya and into Tunisia. Tripoli fell to the British on January 23, 1943.

During the 2011 NATO operation against Gadhafi's forces in Libya, Italian naval forces and aircraft played a significant role.

LIECHTENSTEIN

WHEN THE ROMANS ARRIVED IN THE AREA of what is now Liechtenstein, they found a people called the Raeti living there. Now, it is possible that the Raeti were the first invaders of Liechtenstein with Italian links, since Pliny describes them as being originally Etruscans driven into the area by Gallic pressure. Modern archaeology has suggested links between parts of Raetia and Etruria, though in the farther northern areas of Raetia, these may have been restricted more to trade links and cultural influence.

P. Silius Nerva defeated the Raeti in a battle in 16 BC. Then things got even worse for the Raeti on the independence front, when Drusus the Elder and Tiberius conquered and occupied the whole region, including the little bit that's now Liechtenstein. They eventually created a province they called, not very imaginatively, Raetia.

Roman rule did not bring total security to the area. For instance, the Marcomanni swept into Raetia, causing havoc in the second century AD; and in the third and fourth centuries, the Alamanni would repeatedly invade the area. The Romans would constantly clash with them and try to expel them, but in the end, the Alamanni would settle the entire area in the fifth century.

At various times after that, soldiers with Italian connections did enter Liechtenstein. Italian-speaking parts of Switzerland border Liechtenstein to the south. In 1499, at the Battle of Triesen, the forces of the Three Leagues, an entity including some Italian-Swiss regions, were among those that defeated the troops of the Hapsburgs and the Swabian League.

And, in the early nineteenth century, the forces of Napoleon Bonaparte, the French emperor with the Italian heritage, also occupied Liechtenstein. Their commander was one General Masséna, a man born near Nice in an area that had been frequently a subject of dispute between France and Italian powers. Masséna had joined the French army's Royal

Italian Regiment in 1775, then became an officer in the revolutionary government's Army of Italy.

The army of Liechtenstein was abolished in 1868. It's worth pointing out, however, that on some slightly bizarre level, Liechtenstein can claim to be the last extant bit of the Holy Roman Empire. The prince of Liechtenstein and his successors were made princes of the Holy Roman Empire, and while the empire is gone, they live on.

LITHUANIA

THE DISCOVERIES OF ROMAN COINS and other Roman artifacts in Lithuania are probably linked to the well-documented trade in amber that took that precious commodity from the Baltic region into the empire.

In the sixteenth century, Bona Sforza, from Milan's powerful Sforza family, as wife of Sigismund I the Old, played a powerful role in the Grand Duchy of Lithuania.

In 1812, as Napoleon hurled his Grande Armée across the Nieman River and into the Russian Empire, Eugène de Beauharnais, Viceroy of Italy, Prince of Venice, and commander of IV Corps, which included a substantial body of Italian troops, crossed the river at what is now Prienai in Lithuania on Napoleon's right flank. Napoleon, headed for the Lithuanian capital Vilnius, crossed the river at Kaunas and headed in the opposite direction. Six months later, a very petite Armée, all that was left of the Grande Armée, endured the horrific retreat from Moscow with the Russian Army and Cossacks in hot pursuit.

Meanwhile, another Italian military commander was having a rather more successful time of it in Lithuania. Paulucci (see Latvia), born in Modena but at that stage a commander in the Russian army of Tsar Alexander I, helped negotiate the Convention of Tauroggen with Prussian troops that had previously been fighting for Napoleon. The Convention was a turning point in Prussian history, and perhaps a turning point in European and even world history. The Convention would eventually lead to a Prussian revolt against Napoleon, which in turn played not only a major role in the downfall of Napoleon, but was a key point in the rise of Prussia as a European power in the nineteenth century world and beyond. Another member of the team involved in negotiating this historic agreement was one Prussian who also had been fighting for the Russians: Carl von Clausewitz, who would become much more famous in military history for a hugely influential book simply titled *On War*. After the negotiations at Tauroggen, Paulucci led forces to capture the major Lithuanian city, Memel/Klaipėda.

In 1919, another Italian military commander played an important role again over Tauroggen. General Marietti was the Italian member of the Allied Commission in the Baltic States that was trying, with some eventual success, to sort out the chaotic situation in the Baltic States after World War I and ensure German troops and Freikorps evacuated the area as peacefully as possible. At Tauroggen, for example, they intervened on one occasion to try to prevent any side using it as a military base; and tried to coordinate peaceful liaison between German, Latvian, and Lithuanian forces in the area. After the final German retreat, Italian troops were deployed to assess some of the damage they left behind.

Late in World War II, a number of small Italian units, including specialist "smoke cover" battalions still fighting alongside the Germans, found themselves in the Baltic region attempting to defend Baltic ports against advancing Russian forces.

And now, in the post-Soviet era, Italian forces are once again deployed to Lithuania. In January 2015, Italian Air Force planes took over NATO's Air Policing mission in the Baltic States, and Italian Eurofighter Typhoon fighter jets had already visited the air base at Šiauliai in Lithuania in preparation for that.

LUXEMBOURG

A SMALL COUNTRY, BUT ITALY HAS HAD A BIG IMPACT on it, starting largely with one of the most famous Italians of them all.

Julius Caesar turned up in the region on his way to Britain, and at first things went relatively smoothly with the local tribe, the Treveri. The Treveri, apparently renowned as warriors, even sent cavalry to fight alongside Caesar's forces. But then a power struggle within the Treveri caused a few problems for the Romans. One of the tribe's leaders, Cingetorix, was quite keen on Rome, but his rival for power (and father-in-law—must have been a happy family), Indutiomarus, not so much.

At first, Caesar managed to intimidate Indutiomarus and took hostages to ensure good behavior, and in the meanwhile promoted Cingetorix. But when Caesar dispersed his troops in winter quarters, Indutiomarus finally struck. Not to much effect in the end. Romans ambushed Indutiomarus while he was besieging one of their camps and killed him. Cingetorix was left in charge, and the scene was set for about five hundred years of Roman control of the area. It wasn't without hiccups. For instance, in 30 BC, the Treveri rebelled, and Marcus Nonius Gallus waded in to suppress the revolt. Some of the Treveri joined another revolt in AD 21; and in AD 70, many of them joined the Batavian rebellion. Things did eventually settle down. However, by the third century, as well as assorted civil wars in the area, the Treveri were also becoming vulnerable to major Germanic incursions from beyond the imperial frontier. That situation continued in the fourth century and on into the fifth, until Roman control of the area disappeared.

Over the centuries to come, assorted Italians had military links with Luxembourg. For instance, in 1543, an Italian military engineer arrived in Luxembourg along with a whole bunch of other Italians to restore Luxembourg's fortifications on behalf of Francis I of France. Later in the seventeenth century, the famous Italian general Alexander Farnese, Duke of Parma and Piacenza, controlled Luxembourg in the name of the Spanish king. In 1792, Filippo Brentano Cimaroli, a general in the Austrian Army, was in command of Austrian troops in Luxembourg. However, it would be the forces of Napoleon that would control Luxembourg for a period.

In addition, starting at the end of the nineteenth century, a wave of Italian immigration into Luxembourg played a crucial role in creating an industrial base in the tiny country.

Many Italian American soldiers are buried around their commander, General George S. Patton Jr., at the Luxembourg American Cemetery in Hamm, near Luxembourg City. Many of these fell in fighting during the Battle of the Bulge.

Also, along with Italy, Luxembourg is a fellow member of NATO.

MACEDONIA

THE ANCIENT KINGDOM OF PAEONIA occupied much of what is the modern nation of Macedonia (the former Yugoslav Republic of Macedonia). It was, however, faced with threats to its independence from the Dardani to the north and the Macedonians to the south.

In 217 BC, Philip V of Macedon advanced north into Paeonia and captured the key town of Bylazora. So when the Romans in 168 BC, after the Third Macedonian War, put an end to the united Kingdom of

Macedon and split it up into separate republics as Roman protectorates, Paeonia became part of that process. Eventually, after more fighting, Rome would take full control.

Northern parts of what is now Macedonia, still occupied by the Dardani, did not come under full Roman control until sometime in the late first century BC or early first century AD.

Soldiers from Italy invaded the area again in the Middle Ages. For instance, in the 1080s, the campaign by Bohemond of Taranto against the Byzantine forces in the area took him as far as Ohrid. And in 1464, Venetian forces with Albanian forces under Skanderbeg won a victory over Ottoman forces at the Battle of Ohrid.

While campaigning against the Turks in 1689, Italian Imperial General Piccolomini captured and then burned the city of Skopje before dying of the plague, which he had caught there.

Italian forces made it into the area in the twentieth century as well. During World War I, Italian troops were stationed in neighboring southern Albania. They advanced into territory inside Macedonia, including around Bitola and even eventually as far as Krusevo in the last weeks of the war. Italian troops also occupied parts of Macedonia during World War II.

During the Kosovo crisis in 1999, Italian forces were stationed in Macedonia. They were in Macedonia again during the political crisis there that started in 2001. Italian military personnel took part in successive multinational operations, such as Essential Harvest, Amber Fox, and Allied Harmony, between 2001 and 2003.

MADAGASCAR

MADAGASCAR'S A BIG, BIG ISLAND, but it's also far, far distant from the Mediterranean. It's a matter of some debate as to whether the Greek and Roman worlds knew anything about the island. A Roman coin of Constantine was found on the island, but on its own it doesn't prove a huge amount.

Nor does it necessarily prove a huge amount that an Italian named the island. Yep, Madagascar gets its name from a secondhand description of a wealthy island in the works of Marco Polo. In fact, it's uncertain whether Marco Polo was actually referring to the island of Madagascar, but Renaissance cartographers reckoned he was and the name remained.

The Portuguese, with Italian involvement, were the first Europeans to encounter Madagascar definitely, allowing those cartographers to put it on their maps. On their voyages to India, the Portuguese and Italians experimented with routes skirting both the west and east coasts of Madagascar, routes plenty of other Italian sailors were to take later.

But Madagascar would eventually become a French colonial territory. Among those who played a role in extending French rule across the island was Joseph-Simon Gallieni, a military officer and later a general, and son of Italian-born Lieutenant Gallieni. He forced Queen Ranavalona III into exile.

Italian submarines heading for a new base in Bordeaux after the fall of Italian East Africa in 1941 steered a course between Mozambique (the Portuguese were neutral) and Madagascar (then under the control of Vichy French authorities). When the British invaded the Vichy-held island in 1942, British planes attacked and sank two Italian ships there, the *Somalia* and the *Duca degli Abruzzi*.

In recent years, the Italian Navy has once again been sailing in the waters off Madagascar, this time as part of the international antipiracy effort in the Indian Ocean. For instance, in early 2014, the ITS (Italian ship, NATO designation) *Francesco Mimbelli* (named after a commander of torpedo boats during World War II) visited Antsiranana, liaising with Malagasy authorities. The same year, the Italian aircraft carrier *Cavour* and escort ships also visited Madagascar.

MALAWI

N OT A COUNTRY THAT'S HAD MUCH INVOLVEMENT with Italian soldiers on its own territory.

Some Italians did move to live there in the twentieth century, and some of these were interned during World War II. Troops from what was then British-controlled Nyasaland fought Italian troops in a number of locations, including Kenya and Somaliland.

MALAYSIA

F OR A START, TRADE ROUTES probably linked the Roman Empire to this area. The description of the region by the geographer Ptolemy suggests to some that he was aware of a route that Indian ships took in order to reach Borneo, an island now divided between the countries of Malaysia and Indonesia. And Rouletted Ware (a pottery produced in the period from about 500 BC to AD 200 and which seems to have originated in India) is found as far west as Berenike in Egypt and as far east as Bali in Indonesia, indicating some of the spectacular long-distance links in operation even at that early stage.

More definite Italian involvement followed. Marco Polo passed through Malaysian territory on his return journey, and the Venetian Niccolò de' Conti seems to have spent time in the region in the mid-fifteenth century.

Genoese trader Girolamo da Santo Stefano had already made it to what is southern Malaysia by 1497; and certainly when the Portuguese opened up a sea route from Europe to the East at the very end of the fifteenth and the beginning of the sixteenth century, Italians played a significant role. As early as 1510, for instance, Florentine merchant Girolamo Sernigi sent a fleet of four to Malacca in what is now Malaysia. The local Portuguese commander dragged them into an attack on Goa and then on Malacca (in Malaysia). Malacca was captured in 1511, and one of the Italians involved in the assault records how local heavy guns killed significant numbers of the attackers.

The great early-sixteenth-century Italian explorer Andrea Corsali also acquired knowledge of the area, describing, for instance, the Malacca peninsula.

And in the late nineteenth century, as Italy tried to catch up with its European competitors in the race to establish colonies around the world, Italians once again headed for what is now Malaysia. In 1870, an expedition on the Italian Navy corvette *Principessa Clotilde*, under the command of Carlo Racchia, headed for northern Borneo and territory controlled by the Sultan of Brunei in the area of Gaya Bay, with the aim of establishing a penal colony there. Opposition from the United States, the United Kingdom, and the Netherlands prevented the plan being put into operation.

Italian naval forces were in Malaysian waters again during World War II. In particular, Italian submarines based at Bordeaux operated a service transporting goods important for the Axis war effort. When the armistice was announced in September 1943, the *Cappellini*, the *Guiliani*, and *Torelli*, which were all in the region, were taken over by the German U-boat command. With the assistance of the Japanese occupiers at Penang, the command was based in what is now Malaysia. The *Reginaldo Guiliani*, which had a mixed German and Italian crew by then, was torpedoed and sunk by the British submarine *Tally-Ho* on February 14, 1944, in the Straits of Malacca, where Girolamo Sernigi's fleet had first arrived over four hundred years earlier.

MALDIVES

THE MALDIVES WERE NEVER PART OF THE ROMAN EMPIRE, and they don't seem to have been a major destination on Roman trade routes, but we do have some evidence that the Romans were at least aware of the Maldives.

At least one Roman coin has been found on the islands. A Republican denarius was excavated in 1958 in the reliquary of a Buddhist stupa in the north-central region of the Maldives archipelago. It was a coin of Caius Vibius Pansa minted in either 90 or 89 BC, heavily worn with long use, and pierced for use in jewelry. It is uncertain how and when it came to the islands, though it presumably must have been before the islands became Muslim. The *Periplus of the Erythraean Sea* does refer to islands off Limurike, its name for Malabar, that produced tortoiseshell, and this could be a reference to the Maldives. And the historian Ammianus Marcellinus does refer to the Roman emperor Julian receiving ambassadors from the Divi and the Serendivi in 362. It is assumed that the Serendivi is a reference to Sri Lanka, and some argue that the Divi are the Maldives.

Since then, Italian sailors and ships have called in on numerous occasions. And during World War II, on February 27, 1941, the Italian auxiliary cruiser and converted banana boat *Ramb I* encountered the New Zealand light cruiser HMNZS *Leander* near the Maldives. The *Ramb I* initially tried to bluff the British ship, but when this failed, it opened fire on the *Leander*, doing some damage with its first salvo. The British cruiser, however, returned fire with five salvoes, leaving the *Ramb I* severely damaged. After most of the Italian crew abandoned ship, it exploded. The

Italians were transported first to Addu Atoll, in the Maldives, and then to a prisoner of war camp in Sri Lanka.

In 1972, Italians played a key role in kick-starting the Maldives tourist industry.

MALI

NOBODY IS QUITE SURE whether the Romans ever made it to Mali.
Roman items have been found in southern Algeria, about 125 miles from what is now the Algerian border with Mali, on a caravan route that runs south into Mali. For instance, Roman jewelry and items from the third and fourth centuries were found at Abalessa in Algeria, and Roman coins have been found even farther south at Timmissao. And Roman troops did operate in the vicinity.

In 19 BC, Cornelius Balbus attacked the Garamantes in southern Libya and then pressed farther south until encountering a river called the Dasibari—which may have been the Niger River—somewhere near Gao. And in AD 41, C. Suetonius Paulinus, pursuing Moorish rebels, took troops across the Atlas Mountains into the Sahara beyond. Nobody is quite sure how far they got or in which direction, but eventually they had to retreat because his men were suffering from heatstroke and thirst.

In the nineteenth century, France became the colonial power in Mali, but it was the soldier son of an Italian who first established French rule there. Joseph-Simon Gallieni was the son of an Italian-born lieutenant, and he too became a soldier. On March 29, 1887, then Captain Gallieni turned up at Bafoulabé in southeastern Mali and signed a deal with local chiefs, establishing French control in the area.

In response to the chaos that hit Mali in 2012, the French and other nations sent troops to prevent the south from being captured by Islamist rebels from the north. The EU established EUTM, the French-led European Training Mission, to help the Malian Armed Forces. Italy has sent military personnel to Mali to assist.

MALTA

MALTA IS A GROUP OF ROCKY LIMESTONE ISLANDS lying at the approximate center of what the Romans called the Mare Nostrum (Our Sea). Over its long history, it has been a magnet for invasions from many nations, including its neighbor Italy.

The first humans who ever arrived on Malta, perhaps as many as 60,000 years ago, almost certainly came from Sicily, which lies just sixty miles due north.

The Phoenicians arrived from the Levant in about 800 BC. The Carthaginians invaded in 480 BC and pretty much dominated the island until its final conquest by the Romans during the Punic Wars in 218 BC. In AD 60, St. Paul visited the island. The Arabs conquered the island in 870, converting it to Islam.

Count Roger I of Sicily, an Italian-based Norman warrior, led an invasion of Malta in 1090. The island was restored to its Christian heritage, which endures to this day.

After a brief Spanish reign, the Knights of St. John, a Roman Catholic military order, arrived to assume control of the island in 1530. In 1565, the Ottomans launched the Great Siege of Malta. On September 7 of that year, twenty-eight ships and eight thousand soldiers led by García Álvarez de Toledo, the Viceroy of Sicily, arrived to break the siege. It was, therefore, an Italian intervention that turned the tide of the Great Siege of Malta in favor of the Knights of St. John.

In 1798, the long reign of the Knights was brought to an end by an invading general with a very Italian sounding name—Napoleone di Buonaparte. Napoleon was proud of his Italian heritage, insisting that "I am of the race that founds empires." He would later become King of Italy.

The Maltese soon rebelled against French rule and were aided by the British and the Kingdom of Naples. The British would retain Malta as a colonial possession until the Union Jack was finally lowered in 1979.

While Malta may have been politically British, she was also subject to deep historic ties to Sicily and to waves of immigration from Sicily and Italy. The Maltese Roman Catholic Church, for example, answered to the Archbishop of Palermo.

During the First World War, these divided loyalties presented no problem as British-held Malta was aligned with Italy.

On June 10, 1940, Il Duce joined Hitler's war on Britain and launched the second Siege of Malta. The next day, a relentless three-year bombing campaign was initiated against the island. After enduring over 3,000 bombing raids, Malta became then the most bombed place on the planet.

And Italy didn't just attack from the skies. The Italian Navy attacked Malta on the night of July 26, 1941, with motor torpedo boats. Searchlights illuminated the Grand Harbour and the E-boats were annihilated. Major Teseo Tesei of the Italian Navy was killed in action that night.

American readers are familiar with the incarceration of Japanese Americans during World War II. Some Maltese inhabitants of Italian extraction fell under similar suspicions during the war. Some forty-nine Italian-speaking Maltese were deported by British authorities to Uganda for the duration of the war.

Some Maltese were even involved in espionage for the Axis. One university student, Carmelo Borg Pisani, volunteered to spy on his native land. Commander Junio Borghese, known as the Black Prince, brought Pisani to Malta on an Italian submarine, dropping him off at the Dingli Cliffs. Pisani was soon caught and later hanged. Soon after, he was awarded the Gold Medal of Military Valor by King Victor Emmanuel III.

Although the Italians bombed Malta and attempted to strangle its supply line, they never tried to invade the island. Mussolini's failure to invade Malta at the onset of war, when the island was lightly defended, was a major strategic blunder. Certainly Royal Navy submarines and RAF aircraft punished Italian shipping convoys on their way to supply Axis forces in North Africa. The British presence in Malta crippled the logistical plan for the Axis in North Africa.

Today a ferry service runs between Sicily and the Republic of Malta, allowing for peaceful invasions between the neighboring islands.

MARSHALL ISLANDS

THE MARSHALL ISLANDS ARE IN THE PACIFIC on the opposite side of the globe from Italy. The Spanish were the first Europeans to arrive. These islands passed from German to Japanese control after World War I.

Italian Americans participated in the 1944 invasion of Eniwetok, which was an important Japanese base. US marine Anthony Damato, of Shenandoah, Pennsylvania, was awarded a posthumous Medal of Honor for his heroic service on Eniwetok.

Captain Frank "Delo" Delorenzo of Milwaukee, Wisconsin, flew air strikes on targets in the Marshall Islands. He was also one of the US Navy pilots that flew Admiral Chester Nimitz to Honolulu in his PB2Y Coronado on Christmas Day, 1941.

MAURITANIA

YOU'D THINK WITH A NAME LIKE THAT, this country ought to have been a major area of Roman activity. Actually, from the Roman point of view, the name's a bit deceptive.

What the Romans mostly referred to as Mauritania, or Mauretania, the land of the Mauri or the Moors, was mostly farther north in what is now Morocco and Algeria. Confusing, eh?

However, this doesn't necessarily mean that what is now the modern territory of Mauritania never saw Romans. Roman coins have been found in Mauritania, at Resseremt and Tamkartkart, and indicate at least links to Roman-held territory.

And in AD 41, a certain Suetonius Paulinus led a military force south into the Atlas Mountains. Having passed beyond the peaks, he entered a region that Pliny the Elder tells us was uninhabitable due to heat, even though it was winter. Nobody is entirely sure where Paulinus ended up; but according to Pliny, not far off were Aethiopians, presumably meaning black people rather than the people we call Ethiopians, unless Paulinus was by this stage far, far off track by about two thousand miles.

Paulinus is more commonly known to history as the man who massacred the Druids of Anglesey and defeated the rebellion by the flame-haired Queen Boudicca in Britain (see United Kingdom). Clearly he was not a man to be easily defeated by extreme changes of climate, or, indeed, by the thought of extreme violence. In the end, though, he was a man who was defeated by choosing the wrong side in the civil war that followed the death of Nero.

The Carthaginians and Phoenicians had explored the coast of Mauritania in the pre-Roman period, and it seems reasonable to assume that Roman ships visited it too.

However, it was not till well after the end of the Roman period that Italian sailors played a significant role in the area again. For instance, in the Middle Ages the Genoese took control of much trade with Morocco's Atlantic coast; and in 1455, Venetian Alvise Cadamosto cruised along the coast of Mauritania en route to explore the African coast farther south. And during World War II, Italian submarines were in action in the area. For instance, on January 5, 1941, the Italian submarine *Cappellini* took part in a gun battle with the British steamer *Shakespeare*. One Italian crew member was killed; the *Shakespeare* was sunk. Twenty members of the *Shakespeare*'s crew were killed, but the *Cappellini* rescued twenty-two more and took them to one of the islands of Cabo Verde.

MAURITIUS

THE SMALL, BEAUTIFUL ISLANDS OF MAURITIUS are far, far distant from Italy.

Having said that, the earliest definite historical evidence that Europeans had become aware of Mauritius is a 1502 map produced by the Italian cartographer Alberto Cantino. At that time, of course, Italians were playing a major role in Portuguese discoveries in the Indian Ocean, and Mauritius was on one of the Portuguese routes linking Portugal and India. It is possible, therefore, that Cantino may have received his information openly from other Italians. It's also possible, however, that something more surreptitious was going on. Cantino seems to have been sent to Spain by the Duke of Ferrara, ostensibly to conduct horse-trading, but perhaps with the secret intention of getting the latest and commercially sensitive news on the status of exploration by the Portuguese (and those Italians working for them). The duke apparently paid twelve gold ducats for the map, a significant amount, and suggestive of the importance attached to it.

Mauritius came under Dutch colonial control, and in 1692 Roelof Diodati became governor. He had Swiss-Italian ancestry and he came too late for the dodos, the last of whom had been wiped out under the previous governor.

And for a time, nearby Réunion had an Italian name. Well, sort of. It was called Île Bonaparte after Napoleon himself.

As part of the British Empire, Mauritius was enemy territory for Italian submarines until 1943. It was used by the British as a base for Operation Supply in March 1941, aimed at Italian submarines redeploying as Italian East Africa was occupied.

MEXICO

T HE MILITARY INVOLVEMENT BETWEEN ITALY AND MEXICO starts with
the arrival of the first Europeans in the country.

Italians played a vital role in the original European conquest and
occupation of Mexico.

Italian explorer Amerigo Vespucci entered the Gulf of Mexico in
1497 and may have reached Campeche Bay.

And among the troops of Hernán Cortes were Italian soldiers and
veterans of wars in Italy. Bernaz Díaz del Castillo, who was on the
expedition and wrote a first-hand account of it, mentions an Italian soldier
called Botello who had been in Rome, who was reputed to have a great
knowledge of astrology, and who acted as an adviser to Cortes. Botello was
killed in an attack by the locals.

Many other Italians followed him to Mexico, including Italian explorer
Lorenzo Boturini Benaduci, who played a vital role in collecting and preserving
documents from the local cultures, including the famous Boturini Codex.

And Italians kept on moving to Mexico. Italian immigrants from
the Italian diaspora founded the town of Nueva Italia in Mexico. Caesar
Cardini, the inventor of the Caesar salad, was born in Italy but operated a
restaurant in Mexico City.

Italian soldiers also came to fight in Mexico. For instance, Guiseppe
Avezzana, who was born in Chieri, Piedmont, in 1797 and had fought in
the Napoleonic Wars at a young age, found himself fighting the Spanish
on Mexican territory in 1827; and in 1832, he played a vital role in a
revolution that seized power in Mexico.

General Vicente Filisola, born in Ravello, was Santa Anna's second-
in-command at the Siege of the Alamo, which lasted from February 23 to
March 6, 1836. Mexican forces finally defeated the Texans and gave no
quarter. Filisola was also present at the Battle of San Jacinto on April 21,
1836, where he succeeded Santa Anna in command after the Mexican
general's capture by the Texan forces. Filisola led the withdrawal to Mexico
and abandonment of the Alamo that followed this battle.

Mexicans of Italian descent also made an impact. Manuel María
Lombardini, for instance, came from a family with Italian blood and had
an extensive career as a Mexican general, including fighting US troops in
the Battle of La Angostura in 1847, before eventually serving as president
of Mexico in 1853.

Perhaps Mexico's most profound impact on the history of Italian invasions, though, derives from a name. On July 29, 1883, in the village of Dovia di Predappio, a child who would one day order a number of Italian invasions was born. Mussolini's mother was a schoolteacher. His blacksmith father was a socialist who named him Benito. He gave him that name in honor of Benito Juárez, who had led the fight against the French-imposed emperor Maximilian in the 1860s. Meanwhile, some Italians also served Maximilian while in the French Foreign Legion. The unfortunate Maximilian was shot once by a Mexican firing squad and then shot in paint by Édouard Manet.

Giuseppe Garibaldi II, the Australian-born grandson of Garibaldi, served as an officer in the Mexican Revolution. He was second in command at the Battle of Casas Grandes on March 6, 1911. He fell out with Pancho Villa, but the Plaza Garibaldi in Mexico City is named after him.

Mexico declared war on Italy and the other Axis nations in May 1942, following the sinking of Mexican vessels by German submarines. Italian submarines, such as the *Leonardo da Vinci*, did operate in the Caribbean not far from the eastern coast of Mexico.

There are over one and a half million Italo-Mexicans living in Mexico today. Among many Italo-Mexican celebrities is Daniel Mastretta, the creator of the Mexican sports car, the Mastretta MXT, which was recently featured on Britain's *Top Gear*.

MICRONESIA

FERDINAND MAGELLAN, whose crew was more than 10 percent Italian, was the first European to reach Micronesia though he seems to have focused on Guam and the Marianas, neither of which are part of the Federated States of Micronesia. The diary of Antonio Pigafetta records the first contact between Europeans and natives in Micronesia, which was violent. After natives seized one of Magellan's skiffs, the captain sent a party "on shore with forty armed men, burning forty or fifty houses … and killed seven men of the island."

The Italian warship *Vettor Pisani* sailed in this area during its exploration of the Pacific in the nineteenth century.

During World War II, Italian Americans serving in the US armed forces participated in action against Japanese forces on some of the islands, including air and naval attacks on the Japanese base at Truk.

MOLDOVA

MOLDOVA WAS PRETTY MUCH ON THE EDGE of the Roman world, but it is likely that some Roman troops entered what is now the territory of Moldova at some stage.

It's not entirely clear what was going on in Moldova at the time of figures like Consul Plautius Silvanus Aelianus and Emperor Trajan.

However, Roman troops, including naval units, were stationed on the Black Sea coast at Tyras, just outside the mouth of the Dniester River, the river that marks the border between Ukraine and Moldova.

And a major Roman base at Noviodunum (in what is now Romania) lay to the south of the Danube, which in that area marks the border between Romania to the south and Moldova and Ukraine to the north. In 369, Emperor Valens took an army north across the Danube from Noviodunum and won a victory there.

Italians have operated in the vicinity since then. For instance, in the Middle Ages, the Genoese had a colony at Caladda on the Danube.

During the eighteenth century, the Marchese Victor Amadeus Solare di Govone gave up his career as a Piedmontese officer and headed for Moldavia to fight the Turks.

In 1807–1809, the Russian Army of Moldavia campaigned against the Turks in what is now Moldova and Romania. Among its officers was one Yegor Gavrilovich Zuccato, a Russian from an Italian family.

And during the invasion of the Soviet Union in July 1941, Italian troops did advance through Moldavia and Bessarabia en route to Ukraine. Italian units crossed into Ukraine from the northern Moldovan town of Soroki/Soroca.

In January 2014, Italy and Moldova signed a technical agreement to allow Moldovan troops to serve alongside Italian troops in Kosovo.

MONACO

MONACO IS A TINY PRINCIPALITY surrounded by French territory, but it's only a few miles along the coast from Italy and has seen so many Italian military men pass through its land and waters that, frankly, it's only possible to give a brief summary here.

What is now the territory of Monaco has long been an area of mixed influences. At an early stage it had Ligurian influence, Greek influence, and the influence of powerful Celtic tribes to the north. Roman influence in what is now southwestern France and along the Mediterranean coast had been expanding from quite an early date.

Julius Caesar himself visited Monaco after the Gallic Wars, although the expression "the die is cast" had nothing to do with his experiences at the gaming tables of Monaco's famous casino. Those came along much later.

And Roman power in the hills inland from Monaco was not firmly established until the reign of Augustus. Augustus campaigned against the tribes in the region between 16 BC and 7 BC. In 6 BC, the Tropaeum Alpium, much of which can still be seen at La Turbie near Monaco, was constructed.

The Roman poet Virgil mentioned Monaco in the *Aeneid*, writing about "the citadel of Monoecus."

In the period after the end of the Roman Empire, various invaders from various directions (including Italy) occupied the area. Then in 1191, Holy Roman Emperor Henry VI allotted the territory to Genoa; and in 1215, a Genoese detachment started building a castle there.

Francesco Grimaldi of Genoa seized the rock of Monaco in 1297. Descendants of Francesco on his cousin's side would later found the dynasty that rules Monaco to this day.

Napoleon controlled Monaco at one stage, but the Congress of Vienna then handed Monaco to the Kingdom of Sardinia as a protectorate. This was the situation until 1861, when Monaco left Sardinian control.

In World War II, Monaco sought to remain neutral. Instead, she suffered three separate invasions, including one by the Italians.

In November of 1942, after a few days of fighting, French forces in North Africa surrendered to the Allied forces that had landed in Operation Torch. Several French divisions based in North Africa simply switched sides. Hitler responded by invading Vichy France, which represented the southern portion of France that bordered the Mediterranean.

Mussolini saw this as an opportunity to carve up his portion of the spoils, and he promptly ordered a proper invasion of Monaco. A parachute battalion and the San Marco Marines were landed on the Riviera coast. It would be Mussolini's final conquest. Many of the principality's citizens were of Italian descent and actually welcomed the troops.

After the fall of Mussolini's government in September 1943, Monaco was invaded by the Germans, who were followed a year later by the

Americans. The beautiful actress Grace Kelly led another American "invasion" of Monaco in 1956 ... but that's another story.

MONGOLIA

MONGOLIA MAY SEEM A WORLD AWAY from Italy, but it was not always so. When a Mongol army invaded Italy's neighbor, Austria, in 1241 and laid siege to Vienna, Europe was deeply divided. The Italians of the Lombard League were, meanwhile, fighting against Austria's chief defender, Holy Roman Emperor Frederick II. In spite of having been excommunicated by Pope Gregory IX, Frederick II smashed the Lombard League at the Battle of Cortenuova. When the Holy Roman emperor turned his attentions to the Mongol threat, Italians in cities such as Viterbo revolted. Pope Innocent IV would eventually convene a council in Lyon to unite Christendom against the Mongol threat.

The Venetian trader Marco Polo did famously journey to Mongolia, visiting Karakorum, which Genghis Khan had established as his capital.

Mongolia hasn't exactly seen massive amounts of Italian military involvement. In fact, it's seen hardly any. Italian prisoners of war (who had been captured while serving in the Austro-Hungarian forces) traveled close to Mongolia on the Trans-Siberian Railway when fleeing Russia after the Russian Revolution; and Italian troops and the liberated Italian POWs who now served with them weren't far distant during the Allied Intervention in Siberia in 1918 and 1919.

In 1942, the extraordinary Rome-to-Tokyo journey, conducted by a single long-range Italian aircraft, certainly took the plane close to, and perhaps through, Mongolian airspace (see Russia, China, Japan).

MONTENEGRO

THIS IS A COUNTRY THAT AT LEAST in the English-speaking world tends to be known by an Italian name that means *black mountain*. But then, the country is situated just across the Adriatic from Italy, and it has had a lot of armed Italian involvement.

When the Romans first encountered the area now known as Montenegro, it was occupied by a people known as the Illyrians. The

Romans fought several wars against them. In the First Illyrian War, they fought Queen Teuta, who had her capital at Rhizion, which seems to have been somewhere near the Bay of Kotor in present-day Montenegro.

And in 167 BC, a Roman force advancing northward from what is now Albania captured much of the Illyrian royal family at Meteon or Medun—just inside Montenegro. Roman garrisons arrived, and eventually the area became part of the Roman province of Illyricum.

In the later Middle Ages, Venice began to exert authority over much of the Albanian coast and the area around the Bay of Kotor. And while it lost Albania to the advancing Ottoman Empire in the late fifteenth and early sixteenth centuries, it managed to hang on to the Bay of Kotor area much longer.

In fact, Kotor was Venetian from 1420 to 1797, except for a couple of short periods when the Ottomans managed to seize it temporarily. Fighting took place in the region between Venetian and Ottoman forces during the Morean War of 1684–1699. The area was returned to the Napoleonic Kingdom of Italy for a few years, but at the end of the Napoleonic Wars, it went to the Hapsburgs.

Kotor became a major Austro-Hungarian naval base, but at the end of World War I, Italy sent its navy in. Italian occupying forces occasionally clashed with forces of the new nation, Yugoslavia, which were attempting to assert Yugoslav sovereignty in the area. Eventually, the Yugoslavs triumphed.

In April 1941, however, Italian forces joined with the German Army in the invasion of Yugoslavia. At the time, the Queen of Italy was Elena of Montenegro, daughter of King Nicholas I of Montenegro, which gave something of a personal angle to the invasion.

Mussolini promptly annexed to Italy the area around the Bay of Kotor as the Province of Cattaro (Italian for Kotor), and Italian troops occupied the rest of what was then Montenegro. After the armistice with the Allies in the autumn of 1943, German forces invaded. Italian troops resisted the Germans in some places, and some Italians joined the Yugoslav partisans in Montenegro.

MOROCCO

MOROCCO IS ANOTHER ONE OF THOSE AREAS where Roman power came gradually at first.

When they first became a power in the region during the Punic Wars, the Romans encountered the Kingdom of Mauretania—a name like the country that today is called Mauritania, but, confusingly, in different locations. The ancient Kingdom of Mauretania had a Mediterranean coastline in what is now Algeria and Morocco, and a rather shorter Atlantic coastline in what is now Morocco.

As the Romans developed their power base in territory formerly controlled by Carthage, centered in what is now Tunisia, their initial focus was on the Kingdom of Numidia, which lay between their territories and Mauretania. The Mauretanians at times became involved in the power struggles in Numidia, but in the end, when Julius Caesar crushed Pompey's forces at Thapsus and his ally Sittius did the same to the forces of King Juba I of Numidia, King Bocchus of Mauretania—who had been wise enough to ally with Caesar—found himself rewarded with a chunk of Numidia.

Bocchus died in 33 BC, and the Romans moved in. However, in 25 BC, having raised him to be pro-Roman, they put Juba I's son, Juba II, on the throne of Mauretania. This Juba died in AD 23, and his son Ptolemy took over. Juba II and Ptolemy had major problems with a rebel leader called Tacfarinas (see Algeria); however, the situation looked hopeful for the royal house of Mauretania. That is, until AD 40, when Ptolemy went to Rome and was murdered on the orders of Caligula. With the king dead, the Romans took direct control again, but the locals rebelled. The Romans moved in to crush the rebellion, sending Gaius Suetonius Paulinus. He not only crushed the revolt but also led an expedition across the Atlas Mountains in one of the few major Roman military expeditions that penetrated far into Africa.

Roman control of territory in what is now Morocco focused keenly on the northern coastal strip to the east and west of the Straits of Gibraltar. Roman control of any inland territory significantly to the south of that was less stable and less long-term. For instance, the great city of Volubilis, which had been a key Roman defense point, was abandoned in the third century; and by the end of that century, the local tribe, the Baquates, were in power there, though they remained in alliance with Rome. The Germanic Vandals arrived from Spain in the fifth century, and eventually Morocco became part of the Muslim world.

In the Middle Ages, though, Italians once again played a major role in Morocco. The Genoese, for instance, became a major trading power in Morocco. As early as 1162, the Genoese had reached Salé on Morocco's Atlantic coast; and by 1253, they had made it as far south as Safi.

In the end, it was other European powers, particularly Portugal, Spain, and France, that would battle for influence over Morocco, but Italians did play a role in these battles. For instance, in 1578, a Portuguese and Moroccan army that was defeated by another Moroccan army at the Battle of Ksar El Kebir included hundreds of Italians.

In the period before the French occupation of Morocco in 1912, Italy did have some military links with the Moroccan government. An Italian Military Mission was sent, and Italians took control of the arms factory at Fez. However, the links never developed into anything more substantial.

Later, Italians would serve with the French Foreign Legion during the French occupation of Morocco.

Between the two world wars, Mussolini did make some effort to expand Italian influence in the then international city of Tangier. For instance, in 1927, he sent the Prince of Udine to the city with three warships; and the Revised Statute of Tangier did for a time give Italy enhanced status in the city and the running of it.

During the Spanish Civil War, Italian sailors in Tangier attacked and did major damage to the offices of a Republican newspaper in the Petit Socco there. And, in an event that would be central to the outcome of the war, aircraft of the Italian Air Force airlifted large numbers of Franco's troops from Tétouan, in then Spanish-controlled Morocco, to Spain.

Italian submarines operated in the waters off Morocco during World War II. And Italian naval vessels have, of course, been in Moroccan waters more recently. The 30th Naval Group called in on Casablanca on its long-distance cruise in 2014.

Italy has contributed military personnel to the United Nations Mission for the Referendum in Western Sahara (MINURSO).

MOZAMBIQUE

THE ROMANS MAY HAVE BEEN AWARE, at least from secondhand reports, of the coastline of Mozambique (see Tanzania), but clear Italian involvement with the area comes much later.

Mozambique used to be a Portuguese colony, which gives a good clue to initial Italian actions in the area. Italians played a role in early Portuguese penetration of the region. For instance, the Italian-financed *Anunciada* was one of six ships in the Second Portuguese Armada (1500) to make it to India, after a stop at Mozambique Island. And two Italians,

Thomaz de Carmona, or Cremona, and Giovanni Buonagrazia, captained ships in the Fourth Portuguese Armada (1502); and they spent time during it on the coast of Mozambique, including stops at Mozambique Island.

The Italian warship *Staffetta* called in on its long cruise around Africa in 1887–1888.

During the Boer War, elements of the Italian Scouts, which had been fighting alongside the Boers, retreated into Mozambique as Boer resistance finally collapsed. They had acted as a rearguard for the Boer forces as they retreated from the Tugela to Komatipoort on the border with (then Portuguese-controlled) Mozambique, blowing up rail bridges behind them as they went, in order to delay the British advance. And Camillo Ricchiardi himself, their commander, was briefly held prisoner in Mozambique, until he promised not to return across the border into the Transvaal.

Italian submarines heading for a new base in Bordeaux after the fall of Italian East Africa in 1941 steered a course between Mozambique (the Portuguese were neutral) and Madagascar (then under the control of Vichy French authorities). Italy also had an intelligence operation running from the Italian consulate in the capital of Mozambique (then Lourenço Marques, now Maputo), working with German intelligence to monitor shipping movements. In May 1943, British agents seized Alfredo Manna, head of the Italian operation, and smuggled him out of the country for interrogation.

In 1993, Italian troops deployed as part of the United Nations Operation in Mozambique (ONUMOZ) to help implement the Rome General Peace Accords, in order to end the conflict between the Mozambican National Resistance (RENAMO) and the government of Mozambique. The UN mission included monitoring the ceasefire, disarming fighters, and collecting weapons.

And in 2014, the Italian and Mozambique navies started cooperating on antipiracy measures.

NAMIBIA

N OT A COUNTRY THAT'S SEEN A LOT of armed Italians in its time.
Italians probably played a role in the original Portuguese exploration of the area. And a major part of Namibia is actually named after an Italian. A military man from an old Italian family, Georg Leo Graf von Caprivi de Caprera de Montecuccoli, was head of the German Navy

from 1884 to 1888 and German chancellor from 1890 to 1894, at the time when Germany was imposing colonial rule on the area that would become Namibia. The Caprivi Strip is named after him. He did a deal with Britain to extend German holdings in southwest Africa as far as the Zambezi River. Hence, the Caprivi Strip.

And Italian submarines may have been not too far distant at times during World War II.

However, for a few months in 1989 and 1990, the Italian Army was here. Not all of it, obviously. In fact, only a very small bit of it, but here, nonetheless.

The United Nations Transition Assistance Group (UNTAG) had been sent in to supervise a ceasefire and elections leading to Namibia's independence. Among other military personnel, Italy sent a helicopter squadron to help.

NAURU

IT'S A LONG WAY FROM ITALY, and frankly, Italy hasn't had that much involvement with military situations there, though obviously its waters have seen Italian ships.

In the decades before World War I, the island was a German colony. This was then captured by the Australians during the war.

After the war, even though Australia was supposed to share control with New Zealand and the United Kingdom, according to a League of Nations mandate, Australia pretty much retained its grip. Italian League of Nations Mandate Committee Chairman Marquis Alberto Theodoli made some efforts to rectify the situation but doesn't seem to have achieved too much, and de facto Australian control remained over Nauru.

In World War II, on June 5, 1940, with the possibility of Italy entering the war, the Italian liner *Romolo* escaped from Brisbane in Australia. The Australian-armed merchant cruiser HMAS *Manoora* was sent to track her, but when the situation was still uncertain, the tracking was called off. Italy entered the war on June 10, and the hunt was back on, in earnest. The *Manoora* caught up with the *Romolo* just southwest of Nauru; and rather than be captured by an enemy vessel, the crew of the *Romolo* scuttled her. *Manoora* rescued crew and passengers and returned to Australia with them.

NEPAL

THE FIRST UNIFORMED ITALIANS TO REACH NEPAL were likely the Jesuits, who visited in Nepal in 1662, followed by Capuchin friars in 1715.

Italians may have never, strictly speaking, invaded Nepal. The Nepalese, on the other hand, have definitely invaded Italy. The 43rd Gurkha Infantry Brigade participated in the Allied invasion of Sicily in July 1943. These hardy troops, accustomed to high altitudes, fought the Germans in the Italian Apennines. The Rimini Gurkha War Cemetery is the final resting place of many Nepalese soldiers.

In 1973, five men in a large expedition led by Guido Manzino managed to reach the summit of Mount Everest, becoming the first Italians to reach the "roof of the world."

THE NETHERLANDS

JULIUS CAESAR FIRST BROUGHT ROMAN POWER to what is now the Netherlands during his campaigns in the region between 57 and 53 BC. In 53 BC, after Ambiorix, leader of the Eburones, destroyed a Roman legion, Caesar retaliated by ruthlessly destroying the Eburones.

Assorted fighting in the region followed, and the Romans subsequently tried to push into what is now Germany, until the decisive defeat of Varus at the Battle of the *Teutoburger Wald* in AD 9. After that, the Roman frontier in the region was consolidated along the course of the Rhine, leaving what is now the southern part of the Netherlands under long-term Roman control.

Assorted fighting in the area would follow, in particular during the great Batavian Rebellion of AD 69; and increasingly in the third and fourth centuries, the area became vulnerable to incursions from the east.

However, Italians were involved in major fighting in the area again in the sixteenth and seventeenth centuries. Italians formed a major component of the Spanish armies that fought the Eighty Years War from 1568–1648, as the Netherlands fought to free themselves from Spanish control. And a number of key commanders on the Spanish side were, in fact, Italian. In the late sixteenth century, for instance, at a key point in the war, Alessandro Farnese, Duke of Parma, reconquered much of what is now Belgium and parts of what is now the Netherlands. And in the early seventeenth century, Genoese aristocrat Ambrosio Spinola, Marquis of the Balbases and Duke of Sesto, was another major commander on the Spanish side, achieving victories that included the Capture of Breda in 1625.

During the Napoleonic Wars, the French emperor with the Italian heritage controlled the Netherlands for a significant period. He eventually put his brother, Louis Napoleon, on the throne (briefly followed by the son of Louis) before annexing the Netherlands to France.

Many Italian Americans and Italian Canadians took part in the liberation of the Netherlands in World War II. Major General "Terrible Terry" de la Mesa Allen Sr. was the grandson of a Spanish veteran of the Garibaldi Guard in the US Civil War (see United States). Allen would command the 104th, or Timberwolves, division that liberated Zundert in October 1944.

The Netherlands is a founding member of NATO, along with Italy.

NEW ZEALAND

E VER HEARD OF THE ITALIAN INVASION of New Zealand?
No? Well, one Italian naval commander did lead a sort of invasion of New Zealand in the late eighteenth century.

By 1770, Antonio Ponto, a sailor from Venice serving on board Captain Cook's HMS *Endeavour*, had been the first Italian and one of the first Europeans to set foot on New Zealand soil.

Another Italian naval man wasn't far behind.

In February 1793, a Spanish naval expedition commanded by Alessandro Malaspina from Tuscany that was exploring parts of the Pacific arrived on the shores of New Zealand. It wasn't a lengthy stay. They explored Doubtful Sound on South Island and then left for Australia. However, still today a few place names remain as proof of Malaspina's landing. Bauza Island is named after the cartographer, and Febrero Point is named after the month in which Malaspina landed. Marcaciones Point (Observation Point) has an official plaque marking Malaspina's landing.

Italians began to immigrate to New Zealand in the nineteenth century. For instance, families from Stromboli helped start the fishing industry at Island Bay. And many more Italians arrived in the twentieth century.

Coin of Julius Caesar (100–44 BC). "Veni, Vidi, Vici." Aureus. (*Photo courtesy of Chris Kelly.*)

Caesar Augustus or Octavian (63 BC–14 AD), founder of the Roman Empire. Aureus. (*Photo courtesy of Chris Kelly.*)

Gaius Caesar, aka Caligula (12–41 AD). The emperor Tiberius predicted that Caligula would be "a viper in Rome's bosom." Aureus. (*Photo courtesy of Chris Kelly.*)

Claudius (10 BC–54 AD). Emperor who initiated the conquest of Britain. Aureus. (*Photo courtesy of Chris Kelly.*)

Nero (37–68 AD). Shakespeare called him "an angler in the lake of darkness." Aureus. (*Photo courtesy of Chris Kelly.*)

Vespasian (9–79 AD). Roman general who took part in the invasion of Britain and became emperor in 69—the bloody year of four emperors. Aureus. (*Photo courtesy of Chris Kelly.*)

Head of Julius Caesar. "All Gaul is divided into three parts." Found in the Rhone River, 2007. Musée de l'Arles et de la Provence Antique, Arles, France.

Statue of Caesar Augustus (63 BC–14 AD). After the defeat at *Teutoburger Wald*, he said, "Quinctilius Varus, return my legions to me." Musée de l'Arles et de la Provence Antique, Arles, France.

Head of Mithridates the Great (134–63 BC). Also known as Mithridates VI or Mithridates of Pontus. An enemy of the Roman Republic from Asia Minor. Louvre Museum, Paris, France.

Head of Marcus Aurelius (121–80 AD). Philosopher-emperor who wrote that "life is warfare, and a visit in a strange land." National Archaeological Museum, Athens, Greece.

Roman Forum, Rome, Italy

Arch of Titus. Commemorates the capture of Jerusalem in 70 AD. Via Sacra, Rome, Italy.

Roman chariot replica, Roman Army Museum, Vindolanda Charitable Trust, Carvoran, United Kingdom

Trajan's Column. Completed 113 AD, commemorates Trajan's victory over the Dacians. Rome, Italy.

Bust of Hadrian (76–138 AD). Emperor of Rome, born in Spain, ordered the construction of a defensive wall in Britain. Uffizi Gallery, Florence, Italy.

Hadrian's Wall was mainly built by three Roman legions over at least six years. United Kingdom.

Hadrian's Wall runs 73 miles from Bowness-on-Solway to Wallsend across northern Britain, United Kingdom.

Statue of Christopher Columbus (circa 1450–1506) with Queen Isabella of Spain. Genoese explorer and navigator who "discovered" the New World and transformed our world. Capitol Building, Sacramento, California. (*Photo courtesy of Kate Paloy.*)

Statue of Amerigo Vespucci (1454–1512). Italian explorer and navigator after whom North and South America are named. Outside Uffizi Gallery, Florence, Italy.

Statue of Christopher Columbus. Sculptor: Vittorio di Colbertaldo. Erected 1957, Pioneer Park, San Francisco, California.

Model of La Niña, a Spanish caravel used by Columbus on his voyage of discovery in 1492. (*Collection Nina Van Rensselaer.*)

Equestrian statue of Cosimo I (1519–1574). Became head of Florentine state at age seventeen, besieged Siena, named Grand Duke of Tuscany. Florence, Italy.

Francesco Petrarch (1304–1374). Italian humanist and poet of the Renaissance. Outside Uffizi Gallery, Florence, Italy.

Exterior of Basilica of Santa Maria Novella, Florence, Italy

Statue of Niccolò Machiavelli (1469–1527). Florentine historian, the "Philosopher of Invasions." Outside the Uffizi Gallery, Florence, Italy.

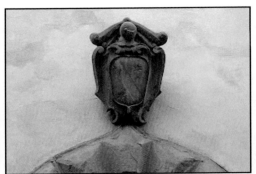

Buonaparte family crest, San Miniato, Italy

Bust of Napoleon. Napoleon said,
"I am of the race that founds empires."
Grand Curtius Museum, Liège, Belgium.

Napoleon Crossing the Alps, Peter Saul, 1976 (*Author's collection*)

Bust of Napoleon (1769–1821).
King of Italy from 1805–1814.
Museo Napoleonico, Rome, Italy.

Statue of Giuseppe Garibaldi (1807–1882).
Italian general during the Risorgimento,
captured Sicily with the Thousand. Milan, Italy.
(*Photo courtesy of Siobhan O'Connor.*)

Luigi Palma di Cesnola
(1832–1904). Colonel
Union Army in US Civil
war, US Consul to
Cyprus, first director
of the Metropolitan
Museum of Art. Kensico
Cemetery, Valhalla, New
York. (*Source: Wikiwand*)

Monument to the New York 39th Volunteers known as the
Garibaldi Guard. Hancock Avenue, Gettysburg, Pennsylvania.

Marker Lieutenant Colonel George A. Custer, 7th US Cavalry, Little Bighorn Battlefield National Monument, Montana

Custer's last letter. "Bring packs." West Point Museum, United States Military Academy, West Point, New York.

Giovanni Martini, aka John Martin (1852–1922). Custer's trumpeter at Little Bighorn; carried Custer's last message. (*Photo used under license with the Denver Public Library.*)

French Foreign Legion parade ground, Aubagne, France

"The Legion is our home." Latin motto of the French Foreign Legion on drum. French Foreign Legion Museum, Aubagne, France.

Virginia Oldoini, Countess of Castiglione (1837–1899). Cavour's cousin and mistress to Napoleon III. Countess di Castiglione, painted in Paris in 1862 by Michele Gordigiani.

Napoleon III (1808–1873), Emperor of the French. Defeated the Austrians at Magenta and Solferino in support of Italian unification. French Foreign Legion Museum, Aubagne, France.

Claxton Gun (circa 1868). "The Pope's Machine Gun." Invented by American F. S. Claxton with six 25mm cannons. This type of gun was used by the papal forces at the siege of Rome in 1870. Grand Curtius Museum, Liège, Belgium.

Thomas Tileston Wells (1865–1946), author of *An Adventure in 1914*. New York City lawyer and American consul general to Romania.

Caproni Ca.20 (1914), world's first fighter plane. Used by Regia Aeronautica in World War I. Museum of Flight, Seattle, Washington.

Memorial to the fallen sons of Monterosso from WWI and WWII, Monterosso, Italy

"Pilot Giovanni Ruazzi was killed while flying in the Regia Aeronautica over Ethiopia in 1938." San Cassiano, Italy.

Macchi MC.200 Saetta monoplane used by the Regia Aeronautica in World War II. National Museum of the United States Air Force, Dayton, Ohio. (*Photo courtesy of the US Air Force.*)

Fiat CR.42 Falco. Single-seat biplane flown by the Regia Aeronautica before and during World War II. (*Photo courtesy of the Royal Air Force Museum, London, United Kingdom.*)

Benito Mussolini (1883–1945) aka Il Duce. Led Kingdom of Italy from 1922 until his deposition in 1943. Led the Italian Social Republic from 1943 until his execution in 1945. (*Source: EUR SpA, Rome Italy.*)

Tobruk road sign from Italian Libya, The Tank Museum, Bovington, United Kingdom

Garibaldi and Mussolini toy soldiers, Florence, Italy

Statue of John Basilone (1916–1945). US Marine, winner of the Medal of Honor and Navy Cross, killed on Iwo Jima. Raritan, New Jersey.

Pentagon, Washington DC. Based on Italian star fortification plans used during the Renaissance. (*Photo used under license with Corbis Images.*)

Joe DiMaggio (1914–1999). Display case. The "Yankee Clipper" joined the US Army Air Corps in 1943. National Baseball Hall of Fame and Museum, Cooperstown, New York.

PB2Y Coronado, the type of plane flown by US Navy pilot Captain Frank "Delo" DeLorenzo, that flew Admiral Chester Nimitz to Honolulu on Christmas Day, 1941. National Naval Aviation Museum, Pensacola, Florida.

Dominic Paul DiMaggio (1917–2009). Boston Red Sox and US Navy veteran. Fisherman's Wharf, San Francisco, California.

Italian training ship *Amerigo Vespucci* (launched 1931). Used to train the officers of the Marina Militare. Venice, Italy.

A Centauro wheeled tank destroyer of the Italian army operating with IFOR (Implementation Force) in Bosnia in early 1996, a few months after the end of the Bosnian War. It was part of a multinational effort to implement the Dayton Peace Accords. (*Photo courtesy of Stuart Laycock.*)

Surface vessels of the Marina Militare, La Spezia, Italy

Toy soldiers of UN Blue Helmets and Marines from the San Marco Regiment, Florence, Italy

Piazza Santa Croce. Pageantry preceding Calcio Storico (Historic Soccer). Florence, Italy. (*Photo courtesy of Matteo Pierattini.*)

Calcio Storico is soccer without limits. Florence, Italy.

The Italian Navy dropped in occasionally in the nineteenth century. For example, the corvette *Vettor Pisani* called in at Auckland in the spring of 1873 during its Pacific voyage of exploration.

More recent links include using New Zealand as a stop on the route to the Italian Mario Zucchelli station in the Antarctic.

NICARAGUA

CHRISTOPHER COLUMBUS WAS THE FIRST EUROPEAN to explore the Nicaraguan coast when he sailed along it in 1502 during his fourth voyage.

Italians also played a major role in the Spanish colonial occupation of Nicaragua. For instance, the *Santiago*, a Spanish ship built in Nicaragua, is recorded as setting sail on its first voyage in 1550, headed for Peru. Five Italians were among the crew, and the pilot was Italian as well. The voyage wasn't a great success. In fact, it wasn't a success at all. The pilot didn't know the port that was the *Santiago*'s first destination; and when it got there, it went aground and had to be abandoned.

Nicaragua saw a significant number of Italians move there in the nineteenth century.

One person of Italian descent who played a huge role in the wars and politics of Central America in the early nineteenth century was Francisco Morazán, whose grandfather was Corsican. Morazán traveled to Nicaragua to find arms and troops prior to his invasion of Honduras, which produced victory at the Battle of La Trinidad in November 1827. Nicaraguans were again in his army when he invaded El Salvador in 1828. However, Nicaraguans also fought against him, including those he defeated at the Battle of San Pedro Perulapán in 1839. From 1830–1839, Morazán was president of the Federal Republic of Central America. Puerto Morazán in Nicaragua was founded in 1945.

Italians were in action in Nicaragua again later in the nineteenth century. They were among those involved in the fighting as US adventurer William Walker was elected president of Nicaragua in 1856.

Nicaraguan dictator Somoza had some links with Mussolini, and a tank near the statue of Sandino in Managua is said to have been given to Somoza by Mussolini. At one stage, Somoza even had a photo of Mussolini in his study. Nevertheless, Mussolini's photo was replaced by Roosevelt's, and in December 1941, Nicaragua declared war on Italy.

NIGER

I T'S NOT CLEAR WHETHER ANY ROMANS ever marched into Niger. Roman artifacts have been found north of the Algerian border with Niger. For instance, Roman ceramics and fourth-century Roman coins have been found in the Tassili N'Ajjer area, and fourth-century Roman glass and ceramics have been found in tombs at Tin Alkoum. A caravan route leads south from Algeria into Niger. Metal debris and ingots from Marandet in Niger show some links with metal from Kissi in Burkina Faso, an area that metallurgical evidence suggests may have had links with the Roman Empire.

And assorted Roman expeditions in this region did penetrate far to the south of the territory they permanently controlled in the north. An expedition under Julius Maternus did get as far as the land of Agisymba, where the expedition encountered rhinoceroses. This could have been the region of Lake Chad, and if so, their route may have taken them through Niger.

Italy did try to get control of a big chunk of Niger during the Mussolini period. The 1935 Franco-Italian Agreement would have pushed the border of Italian-controlled Libya a lot farther south, into what is now Niger. The agreement was never fully implemented in this respect, but it later formed the basis of attempts by Colonel Gadhafi of Libya to claim tens of thousands of square miles of Niger.

In recent years, Italy has contributed a small number of personnel to the European Union's Capacity Building (EUCAP) Sahel Niger mission, which aims to develop the abilities of Niger's security forces.

NIGERIA

I T SEEMS UNLIKELY THAT MANY ROMANS made it as far as Nigeria.
It has been proposed that a reference in the story of the Carthaginian explorer Hanno of his seeing a mountain with flames coming from the top is a reference to Mount Cameroon. If so, Hanno would have sailed past Nigeria to reach it, but a number of other explanations have been suggested for Hanno's fiery mountain, that it was in areas far to the west and much closer to known areas of Carthaginian exploration.

Roman coins have allegedly been found in Nigeria, and it could be that Maternus, a Roman explorer who journeyed south from Libya, reached the Lake Chad region. Part of the shoreline of Lake Chad lies in Nigeria.

Italians did, however, definitely start getting involved in the area in the fifteenth century. They played a major role in the early Portuguese exploration and exploitation of this area. At one stage, from 1486–1495, Florentine banker Bartolomeo Marchionni had a sort of lease on the Niger delta for trading purposes.

The Portuguese approached from basically the direction Hanno would have come, if he did come. And in the nineteenth century, an Italian did come to Nigeria from sort of the direction that Maternus would have come, if he did come. OK, Italian explorer Pellegrino Matteucci didn't set off from Libya, he set off from farther east, but he did reach Lake Chad and then headed down to the Niger delta.

Italians got involved in actual fighting in Nigeria during the Biafran War (1967–1970). Former Italian marine commando Giorgio Norbato died fighting there.

In 2014, the Italian aircraft carrier *Cavour* and escort ships also visited Nigeria.

NORTH KOREA

I N 1866, THE ITALIAN NAVY'S SHIP *VETTOR PISANI* arrived at Wonsan in what is now North Korea, looking to establish links with the local rulers.

The Italian concession at Tientsin in China (1901–1947) is near North Korea, so Italian naval ships must have passed often through Korean waters.

Many Italian Americans served bravely with the US forces during the Korean War. Reginald Desiderio, for instance, was posthumously awarded the Medal of Honor for heroism in helping hold off an enemy attack near Ipsok on November 27, 1950.

Italians may not have entirely forgiven North Korea for beating them 1 to 0 in the 1966 World Cup, but they have not really invaded North Korea. In 2000, Italy became the first Group of Seven nation to recognize North Korea.

NORWAY

A VARIETY OF ROMAN COINS AND ARTIFACTS have been found in Norway, but the questions of how much influence Rome had on the area, to what extent Roman traders ever visited it, and if people from the area visited the empire are still a matter of some dispute.

One Italian who did make an early visit to Norway, northern Norway at that, even if unintentionally, was Venetian Pietro Querini. In 1431, he set off from Crete with three ships, taking wine and spices to Bruges in what is now Belgium. Well, that was the plan. Instead, the ships got caught in a massive Atlantic storm that drove them far out into the ocean, probably somewhere west of Ireland and Scotland. Some of the crew managed to live through the experience by taking to lifeboats. After drifting for a long time, those who were left, just eleven out of sixty-eight, ended up near Røst, in Lofoten. The locals took them in and cared for them until they could set off to return home. The Italians were hugely impressed by the physical beauty of the locals—and by the fact that they didn't lock up anything, the fact that they allowed their women lots of freedom, and the fact that at the end of the day they all undressed and went naked to bed without too much effort at concealment. When Querini returned to Venice, he took the Norwegian approach to stockfish (*stoccafisso* or *baccala* to Italians, salted cod to English speakers) with him, and some suggest it is he who made it popular in Veneto.

On at least one occasion, Italian soldiers do seem to have seen action in Norway. Assorted French and Italian deserters and prisoners of war left behind by the retreat of Napoleon's army from Eastern Europe were recruited into the Swedish Army. They saw action in Norway during the Swedish-Norwegian War of 1814. Norway lost, and the king of Sweden became king of Norway too.

Norway and Italy have, of course, now long been fellow members of NATO, which has led to a wide variety of shared military activity. For instance, members of the Italian Air Force recently took part in the Unified Vision 2014 Trial in Norway.

OMAN

THE ROMANS KNEW ABOUT THE AREA OF OMAN, the trade routes that ran through it, and its fame for pearls. A large number of gold coins of Tiberius were reported to have been found at Sohar in Oman in 1601.

The Venetians maintained a connection with the Persian Gulf and its trade routes during the Middle Ages. But in the early sixteenth century, the Portuguese arrived as they explored the sea route to the east around the Cape of Good Hope.

When Italy declared war on Britain on June 10, 1940, the Italian submarines based in Massawa, Eritrea, immediately went on the offensive. One of the submarines, the *Galvani,* was sent to intercept tankers in the Gulf of Oman. Instead, however, the *Galvani* was intercepted by HMS *Falmouth* and HMS *Kimberley* and sunk with a mixture of gunfire and depth charges. Twenty-six of its crew died; thirty-one were rescued and taken prisoner.

In recent years, the Italian armed forces have used facilities in Oman during a number of operations. For instance, the Italian destroyer ITS (Italian ship, NATO designation) *Mimbelli* recently called in on Oman during NATO's antipiracy Operation Ocean Shield.

PAKISTAN

IT'S CONCEIVABLE THAT ITALIANS entered what is now Pakistan with the forces of Alexander the Great (see Iran). And certainly Roman traders were well aware of the Pakistani coastline. The *Periplus of the Erythraean Sea* goes into some detail about a port city in the vicinity of what is now Karachi, and the goods that were imported and exported through it.

In the nineteenth century, a number of Italian soldiers had major involvement in what is now Pakistan.

In particular, Paolo Di Avitabile, born in Agerola in 1791, and Jean-Baptiste Ventura (Giovanni Battista Ventura), born in Modena in 1794, both played a major role in leading troops of the Sikh Army in the Punjab and helping modernize the army.

Avitabile, after fighting in the Napoleonic Wars and serving in Persia, was given a position of command in the artillery in the Punjab. He became governor of Wazirabad and then was a ruthless governor of Peshawar. Ventura was a veteran of the Napoleonic Wars as well; and he served in Persia and was part of the campaign that captured Peshawar. Eventually, he became governor of Lahore.

In the period leading up to and during World War II, Mussolini's government encouraged and aided anti-British activists from what is now Pakistan, including Mohammad Iqbal Shedai, who was born in Sialkot.

And Italian soldiers returned to the area in the period after World War II as part of the United Nations Military Observer Group (UNMOGIP) based along the ceasefire line between India and Pakistan, in the state of Jammu and Kashmir in northern India.

The Italian military has been involved in humanitarian activity in Pakistan as well. For example, after a devastating earthquake struck in 2005, two Italian C-130Js were rushed in as part of a NATO Reaction Force. The Italian military subsequently flew in troops to the devastated city of Bagh, about sixty miles northeast of Islamabad, to help with relief and reconstruction there.

PALAU

IT HAS BEEN SUGGESTED THAT PART OF THE MAGELLAN EXPEDITION, an expedition that included a number of Italians, had the first European contact with the islands of Palau.

The Italian warship *Vettor Pisani* sailed in this area during its exploration of the Pacific in the nineteenth century.

In 1885, Italian Pope Leo XIII, born Vincenzo Pecci near Rome, was given the job of deciding between a number of different European countries claiming control of the islands. He gave them to Spain but allowed the others economic concessions.

During World War II, Peleliu, one of the islands that make up the nation of Palau, was the site of bitter fighting between American and Japanese forces. In September of 1944, American forces arrived on the island. They included Italian Americans such as Marine Patrick Finelli, an underwater demolitions expert who cleared mines on the beach. The First Marine Division to which he belonged won a Presidential Unit Citation for its efforts in that bloody battle.

PANAMA

Yes, yet another country that had an early visit from Christopher Columbus, although in this instance, Columbus probably wasn't the first European to encounter the country. That seems to have been Rodrigo de Bastidas in 1501. But Columbus wasn't far behind. He turned up in 1502 and went places Bastidas hadn't.

And Italians played a major role as the Spanish imposed colonial control on the area. For instance, Giovanni Battista Pastene, from Genoa, explored the coast of Panama. Noted Italian military engineer Battista Antonelli also carried out planning work there in the early period of the occupation.

More Italians arrived in Panama in the nineteenth century, and Italian engineers worked on the construction of the Panama Canal itself. During its cruise in the area, the Italian Navy corvette *Vettor Pisani* called in to observe the construction of the canal and prepare a report. It then popped over to the Panamanian Las Perlas archipelago and Taboga Island, where the crew took part in the 1884 Carnival.

In December 1941, Panama joined many other nations in the area in declaring war on Italy and the other Axis powers.

At sea, Italian submarines did sink ships registered in Panama. For instance, on June 15, 1942, the Italian submarine *Archimede*, under the command of Gazzana-Priaroggia, fired two torpedoes into the Panamanian-flagged freighter *Cardina* off the Brazilian coast. The *Archimede* then surfaced and fired its deck gun at the *Cardina*, sinking it. All crew were eventually rescued alive. The *Archimede* itself was located by an Allied aircraft on April 15, 1943, in the South Atlantic. Unable to submerge, the submarine was bombed by two aircraft and broken in two. Some crew members lived through the bombing, and the plane dropped life rafts. Brazilian fishermen found one of the rafts twenty-seven days later with only one man alive, the last man alive from the whole crew of the *Archimede*.

Italian-Americans took part in the US invasion of Panama in 1989.

PAPUA NEW GUINEA

I N 1515, ANDREA CORSALI, an Italian working for the Medici family, wrote a letter to Guiliano de' Medici mentioning an island to the east of the Moluccas, which he called Piccinnacoli but which is generally reckoned to be the island of New Guinea.

In 1876, Genoese naturalist and explorer Luigi Maria D'Albertis "invaded" Papua New Guinea. He charted the Fly River for the first time, traveling hundreds of miles up it in a launch called the *Neva*, while collecting specimens and occasionally firing off exploding rockets to deter any locals who seemed hostile.

And in 1880, Italians were at the heart of an attempt by the French marquis de Rays to create a settlement in what he called Nouvelle France. That is now on the island called New Ireland in what is now Papua New Guinea. A lot of *new* here, particularly when you add New Italy at the end.

De Rays's expedition was a disaster. It had been advertised as a journey to an already well-established settlement where the members of the latest expedition would have the opportunity of great new lives. On this basis, hundreds of Italians were persuaded to join the expedition, some of them paying substantial amounts for the "privilege." Instead, when the Italians arrived at Port Breton, they found they had to start the settlement from scratch. Many died of disease, and the task proved impossible. In the end, the remaining settlers managed to escape to French New Caledonia, and eventually they were allowed to immigrate into Australia. There, some of them eventually did create, not New France, but New Italy.

Papua New Guinea saw bitter fighting during World War II, and Italian Americans played a vital role in it. Among them was Ralph Cheli. Born in San Francisco, he became a major in the USAAF (US Army Air Forces). On August 18, 1943, near Wewak in New Guinea, Cheli was leading his squadron in an attack on a Japanese airfield. His plane was hit two miles from the airfield, but instead of concentrating on saving himself, he concentrated on continuing to lead the squadron and ensuring the attack's success. His plane later crashed in the sea. For his vital role in the attack, Cheli was awarded the Congressional Medal of Honor.

PARAGUAY

ITALIANS HAVE BEEN PART OF THE SPANISH OCCUPATION of Paraguay from the start.

Exploration by Anglo-Venetian explorer Sebastian Cabot along the Paraná River and the Rio de la Plata opened up the path that would eventually lead the Spanish to what is now Paraguay.

In 1542, the inhabitants of Buenos Aires decided to abandon their existing colony because of attacks from the locals and establish a new colony inland, which would become today's Paraguayan capital, Asunción. Among the settlers heading inland to occupy new ground were the crew of a Genoese ship that had been wrecked close to Buenos Aires. That crew included three men: Antonio de Aquino, Thomasso Rizo, and Giovanni Baptista Trochi.

In the early nineteenth century, Italian Argentine General Belgrano (his father was Italian) led an invasion of Paraguay but was defeated at the battles of Campichuelo and Paraguari.

Italian immigrants continued to contribute much to Paraguay in the nineteenth century. For instance, a thriving Italian community developed in Aunsción, and the National Pantheon of the Heroes and the Municipal Theatre in the heart of Asunción were both designed by Italian architect Alejandro Ravizza.

In 1865, Italy's South American Naval Division established a base at Montevideo in Uruguay, with one of its missions being to protect freedom of movement along the Paraguay and Paraná Rivers. And on one occasion, the Italian Corvette *Ardita* was rushed to Asunción to sort out a dispute over the seizure of an Italian boat. Commander Ansaldo of the *Ardita* addressed the problem by seizing a Paraguayan government boat.

An Italian Paraguayan invaded the capital in 1869. Cirilo Antonio Rivarola led a rebellion that eventually brought him to power in Asunción. He became Paraguay's fourth president and presided over the end of the hugely destructive War of the Triple Alliance. He didn't last long in power, though. He was forced to resign in December 1871, and in 1878 he was assassinated.

An old Italian gunboat, the *Constance*, became the Paraguayan Navy's *Pirapo*. This was at one stage, in fact, the Paraguayan Navy's only vessel. It soon saw action. In 1888, a Paraguayan naval detachment forced the Bolivians out of Bahia Negra.

Paraguayan aviation pioneer Silvio Pettirossi was another famous Italian Paraguayan. He was killed in an aviation accident in 1916, but today a Paraguayan Air Force base and the Paraguayan Air Force's Airborne Brigade are named after him, as is Asunción's Silvio Pettirossi International Airport.

And again in the 1930s, Italy and Italian Paraguayans played a vital part in helping Paraguay win a much more serious war against Bolivia, or at least mostly win it.

In 1932, the twentieth century's bloodiest conflict in South America erupted as Bolivia and Paraguay clashed over the disputed Chaco region. An Italian Military Mission was sent to Paraguay in 1933 to help the hard-pressed Paraguayan forces. Soon the Paraguayans had also acquired Fiat CR.20 biplane fighters and Caproni Ca.101 bomber and transport planes. They received a few Ansaldo CV 33 tankettes as well. In the end, Paraguay won most of the battles and most of the land.

Among the Italian Paraguayans who played a vital role in the Chaco victory, José Bozzano was particularly important. Descended from a Genoese family, he joined the Paraguayan Navy in 1917 and trained as an engineer and naval architect. In 1927, he was put in charge of ordering two new gunboats for the Paraguayan Navy, and he traveled to Italy to organize the construction of *Paraguay* and *Humaitá*. During the Chaco War, these were vital armed transport ships, and Bozzano himself played a hugely influential role in munitions production and, ultimately, in the outcome of the war.

Bozzano died in 1969, but his Italian gunboats continued to play a major role in Paraguayan conflicts long after the Chaco War. During the Paraguayan Civil War of 1947, rebels took over the ships and sailed them up the Parana River. Bombed and shelled, the ships were eventually forced to retreat into Argentine territory, where they were interned. And as recently as 1989, the *Humaitá* played a key role in the coup that toppled President Alfredo Stroesser, shelling government troops and facilities.

PERU

YOU MIGHT THINK THAT PERU is so far from Italy that Italians couldn't possibly have invaded it, but actually, Italians have had some major involvement in the history of this country.

For a start, sixteenth-century Genoese explorer Giovanni Battista Pastene, while working for the Spanish, played a significant role in early European exploration of the Peruvian coast. And he was far from the only Italian helping establish the Spanish colonial presence in the region. Italians from Genoa, Florence, Venice, Pisa, Milan, Sicily, Naples, and a variety of other places are recorded among the early European inhabitants of Peru in this period. Those who had a direct role in the military aspects of the occupation include three conquistadors: Pedro from Milan, and Esteban and Simon from Genoa.

Italians continued to be instrumental in the colonial occupation. From 1716 to 1720, for instance, Peru was even ruled by an Italian, Carmine Nicolao Caracciolo, 5th Prince of Santo Buono, Viceroy of Peru.

In the early nineteenth century, Italian Argentine General Belgrano conducted a campaign in Peru.

Many more Italians arrived in the nineteenth century. Most settled in the coastal cities or in Lima, but an Italian colony was also founded in the mountains of Chanchamayo. It still exists there, retaining its Italian culture.

A son of an Italian immigrant became one of Peru's most famous soldiers. Francisco Bolognesi played a major role in building up the Peruvian Army. He was killed in 1880, during the War of the Pacific, heroically defending the then Peruvian port of Arica against attacking Chilean forces. Arica eventually fell to Chile.

Meanwhile, the Italian Navy was also getting involved in the region. In 1865, the Italian Navy's South American division had established a base at Montevideo in Uruguay. During the War of the Pacific between Chile, Bolivia, and Peru, another division was established at Callao in Peru with the three warships, *Vettor Pisani*, *Carraciolo*, and *Archimede*. Their aim was not only to defend the Italian community but also to bring some kind of order amid all the chaos of the war.

Peru in the 1930s did have some fascist sympathizers and admirers of Mussolini, and Italy had military links with Peru at this time. For instance, an Italian Military Mission (active from 1937–1940) had trained a Peruvian paratroop unit, a first for the region; and when war with Ecuador broke out in 1941, Peru entered it with a bomber squadron of Caproni Ca.310 aircraft, among other aircraft. Both the bombers and the paratroopers played a key role in Peru's rapid victory. On July 27, 1941, Peru's Italian-trained paratroopers landed in the port city of Puerto Bolivar, captured it, and held it until Peruvian ground forces reached them.

In 2010, Italy and Peru signed a Memorandum of Understanding on Cooperation on the Defense and Security issues, which allows Italy to offer Peru extensive assistance with military training.

PHILIPPINES

So HAVE ITALIANS EVER FOUGHT IN THE PHILIPPINES? Well, it turns out that they have.

Ferdinand Magellan, the Portuguese explorer, reached the Philippines in 1521. When his armada had put to sea from Spain, over 10 percent of the crew (30 out of around 280) were Italian. Antonio Pigafetta of Vicenza served as an officer and kept a diary of the voyage. Magellan was killed fighting in the Philippines on the island of Mactan, and Pigafetta was also wounded in the skirmish. An Italian Navy destroyer was named after Pigafetta during the fascist era.

The Italian corvette *Vettor Pisani* called in on the Philippines during its voyages in the 1870s and 1880s.

The Philippines became an imperial Spanish outpost in Asia. The Spanish-American War ended Spanish rule and marked the arrival of the Americans after Dewey's decisive victory at the Battle of Manila Bay in 1898.

In the late nineteenth century, Italian soldier Camillo Ricchiardi fought alongside General Emilio Aguinaldo in some of his campaigns.

Prior to World War II, John Basilone, an Italian American soldier from Raritan, New Jersey, served in the US Army based in the Philippines; he was even nicknamed Manila John. He would later, as a marine, win the Medal of Honor at Guadalcanal (see Solomon Islands) and was killed on Iwo Jima.

Another Italian American Medal of Honor recipient, Willibald Bianchi, was captured by the Japanese after their 1942 invasion of the Philippines and forced the endure the Bataan Death March. He survived but was later killed in 1945 when his Japanese transport ship was hit by an American air attack.

General Douglas MacArthur, who led the return to the Philippines, was not, of course, Italian, but he was awarded several Italian medals for his service in the Philippines, including the Knight Grand Cross of the Military Order of Italy.

The Italian military sent emergency assistance to the Philippines after typhoon Haiyan hit in 2013.

POLAND

NOBODY'S QUITE SURE HOW MANY ROMANS ever made it into what is now Poland.

Some did. Recent archaeological work has been exploring possible Roman marching camps in the far east of the Czech Republic, not far from the border with Poland. Pomponius Mela, Pliny, and Ptolemy include details of geography, admittedly confusing at times, that reach as far east as the Vistula River deep inside Poland. And Pliny also records that under Nero, a Roman equestrian was sent on a mission to acquire amber. He traveled north from Carnuntum in Pannonia (a site near the Slovakian capital Bratislava) to the coast, presumably the Baltic coast, which he then explored. And Roman goods and Roman coins have been found in significant quantities in Poland.

However, it has to be said that during the Roman period, invaders were more likely to be moving from what is now Polish territory into the Roman Empire than the other way around.

Some Italian knights, however, probably did operate in Poland during the Middle Ages.

As the Renaissance developed, Italians played an increasing role in Poland. Bona Sforza, of Milan's powerful Sforza family, became Queen of Poland when she married Sigismund I the Old. Italian thinkers and merchants and artists expanded their activities in Poland. So did Italian soldiers. Lucrezio Gravisi was one; he traveled to Poland and was knighted by the Polish king for his military services.

More Italians were to fight in Poland in the seventeenth and eighteenth centuries. For instance, Raimondo Montecuccoli, a general in the service of the Hapsburgs, led an invasion of Poland in 1657, capturing both Krakow and Poznan.

And during the Napoleonic Wars, Italian troops invaded Poland again. As Napoleon fought his way into Poland in 1806, Italian forces played a key role. Milan-born General Pietro Teulié of the Italian Division won victories at Stargard and Neugarten before surrounding and besieging the Prussian defenders of Kolberg (now Kołobrzeg in Poland). However, on June 12, 1807, he was wounded in fighting on the front line and died six days later. Napoleon took a Polish countess, Marie Walewska, as his mistress; she and their son, Alexandre Joseph, joined Napoleon for his brief exile on the Italian island of Elba.

And there was more fighting to come in the nineteenth century. After Polish volunteers had fought for Italy, Italian volunteers returned the favor by fighting for Polish freedom. Menotti Garibaldi, son of Giuseppe, helped organize the Garibaldi Legion, a small detachment of Italian volunteers that went into action against Russian forces in Poland in 1863. After victory against the Russians at Podłęże, the unit got badly mauled in the Battle of Krzykawka. The Poles and Italians had success initially, but then the Russians counterattacked with reinforcements. The Italian commander, General Francesco Nullo from Bergamo, was killed by a bullet while trying to charge. Of the volunteers who survived, some were taken prisoner and deported to Siberia, while others managed to escape the battlefield and eventually returned to Italy.

Italian military personnel served in what is now Poland in both world wars. During World War I, for instance, the Austro-Hungarian Army conscripted tens of thousands of Italians from parts of Italy then under their control. For obvious reasons, these soldiers were not employed in the fighting against other Italians in Italy but were sent to the eastern front to fight the Russians. After the First World War, a large Italian military contingent was sent to what is now Poland to help control the Silesia plebiscite. Italian troops were based in places like Strzelce Opolskie and Głubczyce. It was not an easy mission. A number of Italian soldiers were killed in clashes with Polish insurgents, including sixteen in a battle at Czerwionka in May 1921, after the Italian troops ran out of ammunition.

During World War II, Italian submarine crews were sent to train at a German submarine base on the Baltic coast at what was then Gotenhafen and is now Gdynia in Poland. Late in the war, the Battaglione IX Settembre, still fighting on the side of the Germans, took part in the defense of what was then Angerburg in East Prussia and is now Węgorzewo in Poland, against the Soviet Army. And in the same war, Polish forces fought alongside other Allied forces as they advanced through Italy.

The Italian military cemetery at Bielany, Warsaw, first set up in 1926, holds the bodies of more than eight hundred Italians who died during the First World War and even more Italians who died in World War II.

The most significant Polish "invasion" of Italy came with the papacy of John Paul II. The Polish pope is widely credited with having expedited the fall of Communism. His death in 2005 was marked with calls for "Santo subito!" ("Immediate sainthood!") in St. Peter's Square.

In recent years, Poland and Italy have both been members of NATO and have shared assorted military links in that context.

PORTUGAL

T HE ROMAN INVASION OF WHAT IS NOW PORTUGAL took place over a long time and involved a number of campaigns and numerous clashes.

The Iberian Peninsula was one of the major sites of fighting between Rome and Carthage in the Second Punic War. That ended with Carthage's defeat in 201 BC, and soon afterward the Romans were attempting further campaigns in the region.

A war between Rome and the Lusitanians, a people who at that stage inhabited not only much of what is now Portugal but also large parts of what is now Spain, started in 193 BC. In 179 BC, Lucius Postumius Albinus celebrated a triumph over the Lusitanians; a peace deal was reached, but it didn't last. War broke out again in 155 BC. A massacre by Roman troops ended that war in 150 BC; but again in 146 BC, war erupted as a man who would become legendary, Viriathus, led the Lusitanians against the Romans. This bitter war, fought both on territory that is now Portuguese and on territory that is now Spanish, dragged on until 139 BC, when Viriathus was assassinated by three of his own men. Then between 138 BC and 136 BC, Roman forces under Decimus Junius Brutus Callaicus advanced and captured much of what is now Portugal.

It was, not, however, the end of fighting in the region. Much more followed. For instance, Julius Caesar crushed a revolt in 60 BC when extensive fighting during assorted Roman civil wars took place in the area.

And in the Middle Ages, Italians again played a major role in Portuguese military matters. In 1322, Genoese Manuel Pessanha was made admiral of Portugal; and Italians were key to Portuguese naval success in the next centuries. The Italian community in Portugal became important and influential.

And Italians were fighting in Portugal again in the period after the Middle Ages. For example, during the Napoleonic Wars, Italian troops are recorded serving with the French forces fighting in Portugal.

Italian volunteers also played a significant role during the Portuguese Civil War of 1832–34.

Italian submarines operated in the seas off Portugal during World War II.

Portugal is a founding member of NATO.

QATAR

I TALIANS HAVEN'T HAD A LOT OF MILITARY INVOLVEMENT with Qatar.
The Romans never reached here; and even though, in the Middle Ages, the Venetians were well aware of the trade routes that ran through the Persian Gulf, direct contact with the area was limited.

In recent years, Italy has had a few military links with Qatar. For instance, Italy and Qatar both fought against Saddam's forces during the Gulf War and against Gadhafi's forces in Libya in 2011. In 2007, during the first visit of an Italian submarine to the region since World War II, an Italian Naval Task Group consisting of the submarine *Salvatore Pelosi* and the offshore patrol vessel *Comandante Bettica* visited Doha, the capital of Qatar, and conducted training with local naval personnel.

REPUBLIC OF THE CONGO

T WO NATIONS HAVE CONGO IN THEIR NAMES, which can get confusing.
This is the country that used to be a French colony, not the one that used to be a Belgian colony.

And that statement in itself indicates that this country has had far more historic and military links with France than with Italy. Having said that, at least one Italian had a huge influence on this country. Its capital, Brazzaville, is even named after him; and the country itself has sometimes been referred to as Congo-Brazzaville, to distinguish it from the other Congo nation.

Pietro Paolo Savorgnan di Brazzà, the son of a count from Udine, was born in 1852 at Castel Gandolfo outside Rome. He was the seventh child of a family of thirteen, including his brother Antonion, who went on to become Grand Master of the Malta Order. Pietro, however, went to a French naval college; and in 1871, he was aboard a French naval ship ferrying French reinforcements to Algeria to crush a rebellion by the locals.

It was in the service of France that he set off to explore new parts of Africa, including the area that would later become a French colony and, eventually, the Republic of the Congo. Generally, Brazzà acquired a reputation among Westerners for taking a more cautious approach to infiltrating new African territories and for being more considerate of

Africans than others, but it was still a process that could lead to violence. On one occasion, an encounter with the Apfouru people led to his expedition being attacked by tribesmen in thirty canoes.

Eventually, he would persuade King Makoko to put his kingdom under France's protection. He left behind a small number of soldiers, Senegalese Laptots, guarding French claims to the territory. In 1884, Brazzaville was founded; and the same year, the Berlin Conference gave official international recognition to French control of the area. Brazzà was made high commissioner in the region.

He died in 1905, and he was originally buried in Paris and then in Algiers. However, in 2006, in a lavish and controversial ceremony, his remains were disinterred in Algiers and reburied in a gleaming mausoleum (incorporating Italian marble) in Brazzaville, the city named after him.

In 2014, the Italian aircraft carrier *Cavour* and accompanying ships visited Pointe Noire in the Republic of the Congo.

ROMANIA

THERE'S A BIT OF ROMANIA THAT WAS ROMAN for a very long time and a bit of Romania that was only Roman for a much shorter time.

These days, the Danube River, along much of its final course to the Black Sea, marks the border between Romania to the north and Bulgaria to the south. It's a natural boundary. It was a natural boundary in Roman times.

Not surprisingly, it was mainly the bit south of the Danube that the Romans held most securely and for the longest, which is somewhat ironic since it's now the territory mainly north of the Danube that has *Roman* in its name (Romania) and has a language ultimately derived from Latin, unlike the Slavonic Bulgarian to the south.

However, during the first century BC, the Romans began to exercise increasing influence over territory deep inside what is now Romania. It's still actually south of the Danube, but the Danube veers northward close to the Black Sea, leaving the current Bulgarian-Romanian border behind. So the Romans came to occupy a coastal strip, and Roman cities such as Tomis developed. Mind you, it was still very much the edge of the Roman world at that stage. Shortly afterward, the poet Ovid was sent from Rome into exile to Tomis, probably on account of some saucy poetry and an association with the somewhat wayward daughter of Augustus, Julia. He did not suffer quietly but wrote about it, lamenting his fate as if he'd been sent to the Arctic rather than an attractive stretch of shore on the often sunny Black Sea.

The Romans, however, had eyes on the land to the north, the territory of the Dacians. They'd already had problems with the Dacians in the first century BC, when the Dacian king Burebista had taken an unwelcome (to Caesar) interest in Roman civil wars. Caesar apparently had plans to attack Burebista, but Caesar's assassins saved Burebista for a while. Until (different) assassins dispatched him as well.

The relationship between Rome and the Dacians wasn't always a smooth one in the first century AD either. For example, during the reign of Roman Emperor Domitian, a Dacian army rampaged south into Roman territory. The governor of Moesia, Oppius Sabinus, was killed. The Roman forces pushed the Dacians back, but then they suffered a defeat by the Dacians at Tapae inside what is now Romania. A subsequent Roman victory did not crush the Dacians; and eventually, Domitian, facing a variety of crises elsewhere in the empire, pulled out after agreeing to a humiliating (to the Romans) peace treaty with the Dacian king, Decebalus.

However, Decebalus was not to enjoy his victory for long. In 101, the emperor Trajan led his army north into Dacia. After another clash at Tapae and one at Adamclisi, the Dacians accepted defeat and agreed to peace terms. But Trajan had not seen the last of Decebalus and his Dacians. In 105, Decebalus attacked. Trajan struck back and captured the Dacian capital of Sarmizegetusa after vicious fighting. Decebalus killed himself rather than be captured, and Dacia became a Roman province.

But it would not stay Roman until the end of the empire. The area remained vulnerable to attack from outside the empire; for instance, during the Marcomannic invasions of the second century. And increasingly in the third century, the Goths threatened the area. However, in the 270s, Emperor Aurelian finally decided that crises elsewhere in the empire meant he could no longer hold onto Dacia, and he withdrew from most of the territory that had been taken by Trajan.

It was not, however, completely the end of Roman presence north of the Danube. Some troops remained there, particularly at Sucidava, and other Roman emperors would lead temporary invasions. For instance, Constantine the Great campaigned north of the Danube, and so did Emperor Valens prior to his crushing defeat at Adrianople.

Armed Italians would be on missions in Romania again in the Middle Ages. For instance, the Genoese established a colony at Constanța, and the Genoese lighthouse is still a tourist attraction today. The Crusade of Nicopolis, which had some Italian involvement, mainly focused on Bulgaria but also involved parts of Romania.

Italian military involvement continued after the Middle Ages. For instance, in 1564, Venetian Giovanni Andrea Gromo was present in Transylvania, training local troops in cavalry tactics. And shortly after that, another Italian, Morgante Monfrone, was to be found training royal household troops in Transylvania. One Italian even became the ruler of Transylvania. Giorgio Basta, born at La Rocca, became an Imperial general and led Imperial troops into Transylvania, taking power there after his victory at the Battle of Guruslău in what is now Romania, in 1601.

Italian troops in the Austro-Hungarian Army fought in the area during the First World War. And the Italian expeditionary force that invaded Russia in 1941 assembled in Romania prior to its advance.

Romania joined NATO in 2004.

RUSSIA

D ID THE ROMANS EVER INVADE RUSSIA, or at least what is now Russia? Russia's Black Sea coast was on the very edge of the Roman world. Rome had long-term control of a part of Georgia to the south of it, and at one stage it had troops stationed in Crimea to the west of it. And Greek colonies did exist on what is now the Russian Black Sea coast, at places like Gorgippa and Hermonassa.

Part of what is now Russia's Black Sea coast, the Taman Peninsula, was part of the Kingdom of the Cimmerian Bosporus. This was basically a Roman client kingdom rather than directly controlled by Rome. However, Roman troops were present at times in parts of the kingdom; and in AD 63, Nero seems to have actually deposed the then king, Tiberius Julius Cotys I, and taken direct control. This seems to have lasted only briefly; and in 69, Nero's successor, Galba, restored a local king, Tiberius Julius Rhescuporis I, to the throne.

In the mid-fourth century, the kingdom seems to have ceased to exist, possibly due to the arrival of the Huns.

In the Middle Ages, major Italian influence returned to the area with the development of Genoese colonies along the coast; for example, at Anapa and Matrega on the Taman Peninsula. Rulers emerged in the area with both an Italian and a local heritage. Prince Zakkaria Gizolfi, for example, was the son of Vincenzo di Gizolfi and a local princess.

Eventually, though, Russian influence spread in the region, and it became part of the Russian Empire. A number of Italians served with distinction in the Russian Imperial forces in the eighteenth and nineteenth centuries, but the next mass Italian invasion of Russia came, of course, in 1812.

Napoleon came from a family with minor Italian noble connections. When he invaded Russia, he took substantial numbers of Italian troops with him, particularly those in IV Corps commanded by his stepson Prince Eugène de Beauharnais, Viceroy of Italy and Prince of Venice; but also some Neapolitan troops led by Joachim Murat, King of Naples. Italian commanders such as General Lecchi, Italian Guard commander, played a major role in the campaign on Napoleon's side. For instance, at the Battle of Maloyaroslavets in October 1812, massively outnumbered Italian and French troops managed to hold out against repeated Russian attacks.

And Italians weren't just fighting for Napoleon during his 1812 campaign. Some were fighting against him. One of them, Colonel Geronimo Savoini from Florence, was in command of a Russian brigade at the Battle of Borodino and was severely wounded.

In 1833, in the Port of Taganrog on the Sea of Azov, just to the north of the Taman Peninsula, a young Garibaldi, who had arrived there while captaining a merchant ship, encountered fellow Italian patriots and swore an oath to liberate Italy.

Taganrog later came under attack from British and French forces during the Crimean War (1853–1856). Cavour sent over 15,000 Piedmontese troops to fight in the war against Russia. They distinguished themselves at the Battle of Chernaya in 1855.

Significant numbers of Italian soldiers who had been fighting with the Austro-Hungarian forces during World War I arrived in Russia as prisoners of war. After the Russian Revolution, though, when Russia left the war, the Italians were released and found themselves in a Russia in turmoil, soon engulfed by civil war and international intervention.

Some of the prisoners formed fighting units such as the Legione Redenta, which teamed up with Italian troops in China that advanced into Russia along the Trans-Siberian rail route from the east. As an example of the often confused and confusing state of the war, a British officer records arriving in Krasnoyarsk, deep inside Siberia, to find it garrisoned by a company of the British 25th Middlesex Regiment, an Italian battalion raised from Italian former prisoners of war who had been armed by the British, and a company of Czechs. The town also housed Serbs who had been armed to protect the civilians. And Bolsheviks had managed to seize the higher part of the town.

Italian troops also landed in northern Russia at Archangel, along with other international forces. In the end, the Bolsheviks would prove more effective than their Russian adversaries, and international forces eventually withdrew.

During World War II, though, Italian troops once again invaded Russia.

Germany invaded the Soviet Union on June 22, 1941, in the Italian-named Operation *Barbarossa*—the largest invasion in military history. In July 1941, the Italian Expeditionary Corps was sent to assist the invasion. Its initial fighting took place in Ukraine, but by the summer of 1942, the Italian force had expanded to become the Italian 8th Army, the Italian Army in Russia, and was in position on the Don River, northwest of Stalingrad. It took part in the Battle of Serafimovitch to destroy a Soviet bridgehead, and then engaged in bitter fighting against a Soviet counteroffensive in August, in which the attackers were eventually forced to abandon their advance and withdraw.

But in November 1942, the Soviets started the operations that would eventually lead to the encirclement of the German 6th Army at Stalingrad. The Italian forces were badly mauled in these attacks, and the Italian Alpine Army Corps took responsibility for leading a column that attempted to fight a path through the encircling Soviet lines and escape. After a desperate journey through bitter weather and bitter fighting, the column eventually defeated Soviet defenses at Nikolayevka on January 26, 1943, and reached the Axis lines on January 30. They were some of the very few troops to fight a path out of the Soviet trap. The last German troops in Stalingrad surrendered on February 2. In March and April, what was left of the Italian army in Russia returned to Italy.

In addition to the main body of Italian ground troops, Italian Air Force units also operated in Russia; and Italian naval units operated against Russian targets, both in the Black Sea and on Lake Ladoga in the north.

RWANDA

A MILITARY MAN FROM AN OLD ITALIAN FAMILY, Georg Leo Graf von Caprivi de Caprera de Montecuccoli, was German chancellor in 1893–4 when Count Gustav Adolf von Götzen first marched into the territory that would become Rwanda, with the intention of claiming it for Germany.

A number of Italians played a brave role during the massacres in Rwanda in 1994, including diplomat Pierantonio Costa, Italian consul in Kigali, who used his own money to rescue thousands from Rwanda. Antonia Locatelli, an Italian volunteer in Rwanda, was murdered after trying to save people by telling the world about the massacres. And in March 1994, Italian paratroopers took part in helping secure the area around Kigali International Airport as part of a limited international effort to try to rescue civilians.

SAMOA

I TALIAN WARSHIPS HAVE VISITED SAMOA. For instance, in 1904 the Italian cruiser *Liguria* visited Apia, Samoa's capital, with the Duke of Abruzzi, then a captain in the Italian Navy, on board.

And in December 1941, when it left Kobe in Japan, the Italian blockade runner *Pietro Orseolo* planned to pass by Samoa en route for Cape Horn and an Atlantic crossing to take it home to Bordeaux.

The *Orseolo* became one of the most successful blockade runners on the route before being finally sunk on December 18, 1943, by torpedoes from coastal command aircraft.

SAN MARINO

T HE ORIGINS OF THE TINY REPUBLIC OF SAN MARINO are traditionally said to be linked to the arrival, in the late Roman period, of Saint Marinus from the island of Rab in modern Croatia. Situated in the Apennine Mountains near Rimini, San Marino is now entirely surrounded by the Italian state. It has had its own written constitution since the sixteenth century, and it has had a long history of neutrality. Its castles are defended, to this day, by a corps of crossbowmen. You might be tempted to ask, "Why hasn't it been invaded and conquered by Italy?"

But, of course, it actually has been invaded by Italians. Traces of Etruscan and Roman civilization that predate the arrival of Saint Marinus have been discovered in San Marino. And although invading

San Marino may be taboo, Cesare Borgia, no great respecter of taboos, did occupy San Marino with his papal forces in 1503. In the eighteenth century, Cardinal Giulio Alberoni earned fame as a soldier and a gourmet—he loved truffles and inspired the name of a pork *salume*, Coppa del Cardinale. In October of 1739, Alberoni led papal forces that invaded and occupied San Marino. Pope Clement XII quickly ordered a withdrawal and restored San Marino's independence. And Napoleon recognized San Marino's independent status in the Treaty of Tolentino, signed in 1797.

San Marino's unique position inside Italy has allowed it to become a haven for political refugees. Garibaldi himself sought and found refuge from Austrian forces in 1849 during the Risorgimento, when he retreated into Sammarinese territory. After Italian unification in 1861, he gratefully provided important support for San Marino's continued independence.

During World War II, San Marino provided a safe haven for many political refugees, with its population swelling from 10,000 to 100,000 during those years. Many Jews were thereby saved from the Holocaust. During the later stages of that war, San Marino was invaded by German and Allied forces.

Today, Italian defense forces act on behalf of the Republic of San Marino. And if would-be attackers got past the Italians, they'd have those crossbowmen to worry about!

On May 8, 2010, Italian Army vehicles mistakenly invaded the Republic of San Marino, which immediately protested to the Italian Embassy.

SÃO TOMÉ AND PRÍNCIPE

THE PORTUGUESE WERE THE FIRST EUROPEANS to discover São Tomé and Príncipe, and Italians may well have played some role in that. Otherwise, it's not a country that has seen much of Italians invading.

SAUDI ARABIA

WHEN THE ROMANS FIRST ARRIVED IN THE AREA, they found much of what is now Jordan and northwest Saudi Arabia occupied by the

Nabataean Kingdom. After some initial fighting, the Nabataeans entered a long period as a client kingdom of Rome.

Even during this time, however, Rome imposed an official presence, instituting a tax and customs post at a port called Leuke Kome, situated on the coast of what is now Saudi Arabia.

When Rabbel II, king of Nabataea, died in AD 106, Trajan decided to send in the legions. The invasion does not seem to have taken much time or effort, and thus Roman rule was established in part of what is now the mainland of Saudi Arabia.

And not just the mainland. At some stage, perhaps at about the same time, the Romans established a military presence on the Farasan Islands, now part of Saudi Arabia.

At the time, it was one of the most remote outposts of the empire, hundreds of miles south of the empire's borders. An inscription from AD 120 records the presence of troops from Legio VI Ferrata; and another from AD 143–144 records the presence of Roman commander Castricius Aprinus and troops of Legio II Traiana Fortis. The post seems to represent an army and naval presence in the Red Sea with aspirations to control much of it as far south as the point where it meets the Indian Ocean.

And the Italian Navy was in action again in the area at the beginning of the twentieth century. During the Italo-Turkish War, on January 7, 1912, the Italian protected cruiser *Piemonte* and two Italian destroyers, the *Garibaldino* and the *Artigliere*, encountered twelve Ottoman ships, and in the Battle of Kunfuda Bay largely destroyed the Ottoman force.

The Italian Navy operated in the Red Sea during World War II. In April 1941, an attempt by Italian destroyers to attack British facilities at Port Sudan came under heavy attack from British naval forces, and two of the damaged Italian destroyers were scuttled on the Saudi Arabian coast.

And on October 10, 1940, Italian SM.82 bombers took off from an Italian air base on the Mediterranean island of Rhodes. They flew over Vichy-French-controlled Syria, where one plane detached from the formation near Damascus, which then continued on to Kuwait and eventually reached Bahrain. Their target was the oil facilities there, which the planes still in formation bombed. The lone detached bomber hit Dahran, thirty miles to the west in Saudi Arabia. Then the detachment successfully flew across Saudi Arabia and the Red Sea to land at an Italian air base at Massawa, Eritrea. It was the longest bombing mission ever at that point in history.

As we noted in our earlier book *America Invades*, this Italian attack had an enormous impact on world history, as the Kingdom of Saudi Arabia turned to the United States for protection, with FDR meeting the Saudi king on board the USS *Quincy* in the Suez Canal in 1945.

SENEGAL

R OMAN MATERIAL HAS BEEN FOUND IN MAURITANIA, to the north of Senegal, and it is at least possible that ships from the Mediterranean did visit the waters off Senegal during the Roman period.

Certainly, when the Portuguese probably became the first Europeans to explore much of the area in the second half of the fifteenth century, Italians played a major role.

For instance, in 1455, Venetian Alvise da Ca' da Mosto and Genoese Antoniotto Usodimare explored the coast of Senegal, with Ca' da Mosto even referring to the Senegal River as Rio de Senega, the first recorded instance of this. It was also in Senegal that Ca' da Mosto bought slaves, exchanging them at a price of one horse to ten or fifteen slaves.

And in 1501, Florentine explorer Amerigo Vespucci was in the Bay of Dakar. He was en route with an expedition to Brazil and met up in Senegalese waters with Portuguese ships returning from India. It has been suggested that the information about eastern lands supplied by the fleet returning from India prompted Amerigo Vespucci to think that what Italian, Portuguese, and Spanish explorers were investigating on the other side of the Atlantic was not, in fact, part of Asia, but was a complete New World.

France was eventually to become the dominant European colonial power in Senegal, meaning that, yes, Napoleon did rule parts of it (with the English occasionally seizing those parts during their wars with Napoleon).

Among those who would play a role in extending French rule across what is now Senegal was military officer and later General Joseph-Simon Gallieni, son of Italian-born Lieutenant Gallieni.

In 1938, Mussolini's son Bruno descended on Dakar with a squadron of three Savoia-Marchetti SM.79 planes from Rome, before making an experimental long-distance flight to Rio de Janeiro.

Italians serving in the French Foreign Legion were among the troops assigned to the unsuccessful Allied Operation Menace in 1940, which was aimed at capturing Dakar. Italian submarines operated in the seas off Senegal during World War II.

In recent years, Italy has had assorted military training links with Senegal, including West African Training Cruise 2005. The naval Hera

Contingent was sent to Senegal to help control the flow of migrants toward the European Union. Italian military personnel were deployed on the sea and in the air off Senegal in 2006 as part of a European operation to prevent migrants from reaching the Spanish Canary Islands.

SERBIA

ROMANS INVADED WHAT IS NOW SERBIA over a long period. They first penetrated parts of western Serbia during the Illyrian wars of the second century BC. And in 75 BC, they clashed with the Dardanians, leading to further invasions of the region. More territory was occupied later in the century, but then the Illyrian Revolt of AD 6—which saw bitter fighting across the region, including on land now part of Serbia—threw Roman control into question until the rebellion was crushed. The period of Emperor Trajan saw even further advances.

Roman civil wars also resulted in assorted fighting in the region.

Italians fought in the area again during the Middle Ages. For example, Pipo of Ozora, Italian mercenary commander, conducted his last campaign in Serbia before dying in 1426. And soldier saint John of Capistrano led troops into battle against the Ottomans at the Siege of Belgrade in 1456, helping Hungarian John Hunyadi win a major victory.

Italians would campaign in Serbia in the period after the Middle Ages as well. For instance, Italian Imperial General Piccolomini campaigned in southern Serbia and elsewhere in 1689. Another Italian Imperial general, Antoniotto Botta Adorno, played a major role in the capture of Belgrade from Ottoman forces in 1717.

During World War I, Italian forces were key in evacuating the retreating Serbian Army from Albania to safety on Corfu.

During World War II, Italian forces occupied small parts of Serbia, such as the area around Duga Poljana.

And during the Kosovo War, the Italian Air Force took part in the air campaign against Serbia.

SEYCHELLES

THE FIRST EUROPEAN TO SIGHT ISLANDS in the Seychelles group seems to have been Vasco da Gama on his second voyage. This was an expedition that included a number of Italian participants.

Eventually, however, first France and then Britain became the colonial powers in the Seychelles.

During planning prior to World War II, consideration was given to a recommendation that the Italian Navy should seize the Seychelles as a forward base, perhaps after establishing a secret base on Silhouette Island.

In recent years the Italian Navy (Marina Militare) has collaborated in antipiracy operations in the seas off the Seychelles; and in 2013, the Italian frigate *Zeffiro* conducted a joint exercise with the Seychelles Coast Guard.

SIERRA LEONE

OK, NOT A COUNTRY THAT ITALIANS HAVE had that much to do with militarily, but a few points can be made.

For a start, an Italian seems to have sort of given the country its name.

Ca' da Mosto's description of the region was the first to be published, and he included the name in a mixture of Portuguese and Italian that was subsequently maintained by influential Italian mapmakers. And Italians were involved in the early Portuguese exploitation of the area.

Italian explorer Giacomo Bove stopped in in the late nineteenth century, as did the Italian naval ship *Staffeta* on its cruise along the African coast in 1887–1888. And the Italian Navy was in action off Sierre Leone during World War II.

For instance, on June 2, 1942, the Italian submarine *Leonardo da Vinci*, under Longanesi-Cattani, sank the Panamanian ship *Reine Marie Stewart* with torpedo and gunfire just off the coast of Sierra Leone, which as part of the British Empire was enemy territory.

The *Da Vinci* itself was sunk with all hands in May 1943.

SINGAPORE

SINGAPORE WAS A BRITISH COLONY since its foundation until independence, so Italian involvement has been somewhat limited.

In 1869, Singapore was where Emilio Cerruti was going to assemble his force to occupy the Kei, An, and Batchiane Islands in the name of Italy (see Indonesia) before opposition from other Western powers brought it all to a halt.

In 1930, Mussolini's eldest daughter, Edda, and her husband, Count Ciano, called in on Singapore en route for Shanghai. She attended a gala dinner attended by members of the Italian community in Singapore, where she expressed the view that, in a fascist state, a woman's role was to have children and not interfere in politics.

Elements of the Italian Navy did spend time in Singapore as allies of the occupying power during at least one war. In 1942, Singapore fell to the invading Japanese. It had been a major port for Britain, and now it became a major port for the Japanese. As such, Singapore was one of the prime destinations for Italian submarines making the long and dangerous journey from Bordeaux, transporting materials vital for the Axis war effort between Japanese-controlled territory and German-controlled territory.

In September 1943, when the armistice between Italy and the Allies was signed, two Italian submarines, the *Guiliani* and the *Torelli*, were already fully loaded in Singapore and waiting to make the return journey; and another, the *Capellini* was subsequently escorted to Singapore. The boats were put under German control. The *Guiliani* was sunk by a British submarine in February 1944, but after the German surrender in May 1945, the *Capellini* and *Torelli* came under Japanese control.

The Italian Air Force and the Republic of Singapore Air Force today have training links.

SLOVAKIA

WELL, THE ROMANS DID MAKE IT into what is now Slovakia, and they even securely held a little chunk of it behind the established *limes* (Lat.) or border defences. The Roman fort at Gerulata near the Slovakian capital Bratislava, for instance, shows a stable presence.

Moving deeper into Slovakia, though, it's a messier situation. There was clearly plenty of Roman influence, judging by finds of Roman artifacts as well as Roman influence on the local culture and the local tribe, the Marcomanni. They may have had some kind of client status, but actual Roman control was much more intermittent.

The most well-known Roman invasion of the interior of Slovakia took place in the second half of the second century AD, under Marcus Aurelius. After invading Marcomanni had crossed the Danube in 169 and rampaged as far south as Aquileia in Italy, the forces of Marcus Aurelius struck north, in 172, into the lands of the Marcomanni. Then in 173, they hit another tribe, the Qadi. At that stage the philosopher-emperor was distracted by a rebellion in the east; and in 177, the tribes rebelled. No wonder he wrote that "life is warfare" in his *Meditations*! In 178, Marcus Aurelius began another campaign against the enemy. An inscription carved by troops from that campaign still exists, carved in rock below Trenčín castle in northwest Slovakia, about eighty miles north of the Danube. The Romans were victorious and plans were afoot to create a new province, but by 180 Marcus Aurelius was dead—though it is unlikely that he was killed by his own son as in the film *Gladiator*. His successor, Commodus, having little interest in philosophy or the campaign, made peace and gave up the newly conquered territories.

However, another major Roman invasion was to take place in the fourth century. This time, it was Emperor Valentinian I campaigning against the Qadi after a dispute over the construction of a Roman fort in their territory. In 374, Valentinian invaded, but after achieving some success, he too died on the frontier in 375. It seems to have been a bad area for Roman emperors.

And plenty more Italian soldiers were to serve in what is now Slovakia. The famous Italian general of Hapsburg troops, Raimondo Montecuccoli, for instance, was sent to Bratislava in April 1645 during the Thirty Years War, to organize its defenses and defenders.

The Italian architect Petro Ferrabosco redesigned Bratislava castle in the sixteenth century; during the Napoleonic Wars, in 1811, Italian soldiers helped accidentally devastate it with fire.

In 1809, in another example, Vincenzo Federico Barone Bianchi, Duca di Casalanza and a general in the Austrian Army, fought ferociously to defend Bratislava against attacking French troops. Meanwhile, other distinguished Italian officers, including Carlo Zucchi and Filippo Severoli, fought for Napoleon at Bratislava.

During World War I, the Italians formed a Czechoslovak Legion from volunteers. General Andrea Graziani first took control and then General Luigi Piccione. After the war, the legion was sent to the newly formed Czechoslovakia.

And troops were again sent on a mission in what is now Slovakia as new nations emerged from the ruins of the Austro-Hungarian Empire. Bratislava was disputed between Hungary and Czechoslovakia. On January 1, 1919, the Italian commander in the area, General Piccione, himself assisted Czechoslovak troops to take control of the city, and Italian Colonel Riccardo Barreca was appointed military commander of the city. It was not an easy mission. Hungarian demonstrators clashed with Czechoslovak soldiers on February 12. In the chaos, nine people died and Barreca was knocked down and injured. The city went on to become one of Czechoslovakia's major cities and is now the Slovak capital.

Slovakia joined NATO in 2004.

SLOVENIA

SLOVENIA HAS A LAND BORDER WITH ITALY, so, not surprisingly, what is now Slovenian territory has seen so much Italian military involvement over the centuries, this chapter can include only a few of the main events.

The Romans took control of what is now Slovenia in a number of different steps. Initially, in the last two centuries BC, they increasingly exerted control over the coastal area, then occupied by a tribe called the Veneti, who, naturally, also occupied territory within the borders of modern Italy, in places such as the Venice area.

Much of inland Slovenia, however, consisted of a region called Noricum, inhabited by a group of tribes collectively known as Norici. A Norican king, Voccio, helped Caesar in the civil war, but in 16 BC, the Romans invaded Noricum. No tribes except the Ambisontes resisted the invasion, and Noricum soon became firmly Roman-controlled territory.

Other, smaller parts of what is now Slovenia were incorporated into Roman territory at other times.

As a key point on the land route between the western Roman empire and the eastern Roman empire, and also as an area close to both the empire's frontier and to Rome itself, this territory had extensive involvement in Roman civil wars. Vespasian was, for instance, acclaimed emperor by the Danubian legions at what is now Ptuj in eastern Slavonia in AD 69 (the bloody year of the four emperors); and in the fourth century, the area became crucial during the attempts by both Magnentius and Magnus Maximus to seize and consolidate power.

It also saw fighting against external enemies, such as during the Marcomannic Wars of the second century.

The period after the end of Roman control saw assorted peoples move through the area, and, eventually, Slavic settlement. The land became something of a border region as different powers struggled to exert their authority. For instance, the north of Slovenia eventually became part of the Holy Roman Empire, but the important Slovenian coastal town of Koper, after first allying with the empire, came under the control of the Patriarchate of Aquileia, and then became a long-term part of Venetian territory.

The country's key strategic location inevitably meant entanglement with a number of conflicts, many of them involving Italians. Parts of Slovenia, for instance, saw fighting with Hungarians, with Turks, and during the Napoleonic Wars.

During World War I, the Italians fought a series of bitter battles called collectively the Battles of the Isonzo, with much of the fighting taking place on Slovenian soil as Italy tried to push forward against determined defenders from the Austro-Hungarian Army. In 1917, the Italian Army suffered a catastrophic defeat at Caporetto, now Kobarid, in Slovenia.

However, at the end of the war, Koper, which had been Venetian until 1797, once again became Italian, along with much of western Slovenia.

In 1941, Italian troops invaded Yugoslavia along with other Axis forces. In addition to the parts of western Slovenia they already held, they occupied southern Slovenia as well.

A bitter war against local resistance fighters followed. Then in 1943, after the Italian armistice with the Allies, the Germans invaded Italian-held areas. Some Italians fought in local partisan units.

Slovenia joined NATO in 2004. Italy has provided Air Policing services over Slovenia.

SOLOMON ISLANDS

WHILE NEITHER THE ROMANS NOR THE ITALIAN GOVERNMENT may have ever invaded or fought in the jungles of the Solomon Islands, many Italian Americans did. An astonishing one in twelve US servicemen in World War II was of Italian ancestry.

The most famous Italian American soldier of World War II was surely Marine Gunnery Sergeant John Basilone, who grew up in Raritan, New Jersey. He had enlisted in the US Army in the 1930s but subsequently joined the US Marine Corps. Basilone won a Medal of Honor on Guadalcanal for manning a machine gun nest that helped to defend Henderson Field in 1942. He returned to the United States after the campaign on Guadalcanal to support war bond drives. He met and married Lena Mae Riggi, who was a sergeant in the Women's Marine Corps Reserve. Basilone insisted on rejoining his unit to participate in the invasion of Iwo Jima, where he won a Navy Cross and was killed in action. His story was featured in Stephen Spielberg's 2010 TV miniseries, *The Pacific*. Every year residents of Raritan, New Jersey, celebrate John Basilone Day with a parade to commemorate his life.

Frank Petrarca, who was killed on the island of New Georgia, also won a Medal of Honor for his service in the Solomons.

SOMALIA

T HE ROMANS KNEW THE COASTLINE OF SOMALIA, as far as the Horn of Africa, well.

It was an area of sea familiar to Roman merchants making the voyage through the Red Sea either to trade at local ports or to pass into the Indian Ocean. The port of Opone was located on the coast of what is now Somalia, and among other things, slaves and tortoiseshell were for sale there.

However, it was in the late nineteenth century that Italy started taking a serious military interest in Somalia. As in Eritrea, commercial settlements in the area were the first stage of Italian involvement. In the late 1880s, two local rulers signed deals making their territories Italian protectorates. Gradually, further deals were done to expand Italian control in the region, with territory being added from British East Africa even after World War I. And in the 1920s, the Italians fought a tough war to impose direct Italian rule over some areas rather than protectorate rule.

Italian Somalia constituted the part of Somalia lying along the Indian Ocean's coast south of the Horn of Africa. The part lying along the coast north of the Horn constituted, at that stage, British Somaliland. In June 1940, Italy declared war on Britain, and in August 1940, troops from Italian-controlled Ethiopia invaded British Somaliland.

After bitter fighting at the Battle of Tug Argan, British forces withdrew to Berbera on the coast. From there, they were evacuated by sea.

However, Italian control of British Somaliland did not last long. British forces invaded Italian Somalia from Kenya in January 1941. With little realistic hope of resisting the powerful British advance through Somali territory, Italian forces mainly withdrew into the better defensive territory of Ethiopia. In March 1941, a British seaborne invasion launched from Aden retook British Somaliland and linked up with the British forces advancing through Italian Somalia.

This was not entirely the end of Italian military operations in Somalia during World War II, as a small guerrilla campaign of resistance was maintained until 1943.

However, after the war, Italy was once again given control of Italian Somaliland, on the condition that the territory would achieve independence within ten years. Over 5,000 Italian troops were sent to the territory to help prepare Somali troops. In 1960, both British-controlled and Italian-controlled Somalia became independent and united as the Somali Republic.

Somalia has had difficult times in recent decades, and Italian troops have returned there as part of international efforts. In particular, in March 1993, an Italian peacekeeping force was sent to Mogadishu. Italian forces withdrew after March 1994; but then in early 1995, the 26th Italian Naval Group headed to Mogadishu to work with the US and Pakistan navies on Operation United Shield, to ensure the safe withdrawal of the last international forces.

In recent years, Italian personnel have taken part in the European Training Mission in Somalia.

Pasta, known in Somalia as *baasto*, was brought to this nation by Italians in 1889 and is now the national dish.

SOUTH AFRICA

HARD TO BELIEVE, WITH THIS COUNTRY being so distant, but armed Italians have had a bit of involvement with Africa's southernmost nation.

For a start, the Romans may well have been aware of the Cape of Good Hope, whether or not any of them ever made it that far.

In the very early days of Rome, that great seafaring people, the Phoenicians, may already have rounded the Cape. The Greek historian Herodotus tells of an Egyptian pharaoh, Necho, who sent a Phoenician fleet south along the African coast from the Red Sea to see if it was possible to circumnavigate Africa and return to Egypt via the Mediterranean. The fleet accordingly set out and, according to Herodotus, returned to Egypt via the Pillars of Hercules in the third year of their voyage. Herodotus is not always the most reliable of historians, and it is hard to know how much trust to put in this story. However, one detail included by Herodotus does lend the story some support. He says that when the Phoenicians were rounding the southern tip of Africa and heading west, they said that the sun was on their right, to the north. At the time, with limited knowledge of the world and the movement of the sun, it's not necessarily the sort of detail that people would make up, and Herodotus himself writes that he did not believe their claim.

An amazing document from the Roman period, the *Periplus of the Erythraean Sea*, shows remarkable knowledge of the Indian Ocean. In part, the text lists details of the coast south of Somalia up to the southernmost location it describes, a port called Rhapta, where ivory was available in great quantities, far south along the African coast. Then it refers to an area even farther south, where the unexplored ocean bends toward the west and mixes with the western sea. This again seems to suggest the Romans had at least a secondhand knowledge of the Cape of Good Hope.

However, it was, of course, in the late fifteenth century that Europeans were really going to come face to face with the Cape of Good Hope and what is now South Africa. OK, it was the Portuguese who have claimed the most credit for developing the route through the Atlantic to the Cape and around it to India, but Italians were heavily involved in early Portuguese explorations in the area as well. As with Brazil, the Florentine banker Bartolomeo Marchionni helped make some of Portugal's early ventures in the area possible. For instance, he helped finance the *Anunciada*, one of the ships in the second armada to head for India, an armada that Bartolomeu Dias, the man who had first rounded the Cape, also chose to join. Not a great decision as it turns out, since he and his ship didn't make it around the Cape this time and were lost. And on the fourth armada to India, two Italians, Thomaz de Carmona, or Cremona, and Giovanni Buonagrazia, both commanded ships.

But South Africa was never to become Portuguese (or Italian). In 1510, Francisco de Almeida, first viceroy of the Portuguese Indies, managed to get him and a large percentage of the contingent with him killed in an attempt to raid cattle from a Khoikhoi village in the vicinity of Table Bay. It was to be the Dutch and then, of course, the British who took control in South Africa, setting the scene for the Boer Wars of the late nineteenth century. And that's when more armed Italians commenced operations in South Africa.

Italians fought on both sides in the war. For instance, a grandson of Giuseppe Garibaldi, also called Giuseppe Garibaldi, served bravely with the British forces.

An Italian volunteer unit served with and fought alongside the Boer forces, as well. At the heart of this unit was the extraordinary Camillo Ricchiardi. Ricchiardi had already had a career in the Italian military— he'd been a war reporter and fought in the Philippines—when he turned up to fight alongside the Boers in South Africa. Significant numbers of Italians had traveled to South Africa already by the time of the wars. Some, like the Anglo-Italian Sir John Molteno, occupied high positions. Molteno fought as a Boer commando in the Amatola War of 1846, before becoming the first prime minister of the Cape Colony and leading it in the Ninth Frontier War in 1877. He is now noted for his liberal approach to the development of South Africa. Many of the Italians who moved to South Africa came to work in the mines after diamonds and gold were found there in the nineteenth century, and a proportion became sympathetic to the Boer cause. During the Boer Wars, the Italians developed a particular skill in scouting and blowing up bridges and rail tracks.

In 1941, the collapse of Italian East Africa led to an influx of Italian prisoners of war into South Africa, and after the war, many of them stayed on to settle there.

During the Second World War, Italian submarines did at times operate in the waters off South Africa. In particular, the Italian submarine *Leonardo da Vinci* (named, of course, after the man who, among his many other inventions, thought about the concept of submarine warfare) launched a number of attacks in the area in April 1943. In command of the *Leonardo da Vinci* was the well-known submarine commander Gianfranco Gazzana-Priaroggia; in just over a week, he sank four ships off the coast of South Africa. On April 17, he torpedoed and sank the Dutch freighter *Sembilan*. Then on the 18th, with torpedo and gunfire he sank the British freighter *Manaar*. And on April 21,with torpedo and gunfire he sank the American Liberty Ship *John Drayton* and the British tanker *Doryssa*. Of the British tanker's crew of sixty-four, only eleven managed to survive the experience.

The crew of the *Leonardo da Vinci* and Gazzana-Priaroggia, however, were never to return to their base at Bordeaux, as their submarine was sunk during the return journey in May. Gazzana-Priaroggia was posthumously awarded the Italian Gold Medal of Valor and the German Knight's Cross of the Iron Cross. A modern Italian submarine is named after him.

And the Italian submarine *Bagnolini* will always rest in African waters. Having already been damaged by air attack, the *Bagnolini* was due to rendezvous with German U-178 for an emergency refueling. But when U-178 reached the rendezvous spot about five hundred miles off Cape Town, all it could find of the *Bagnolini* was an oil slick after it had been sunk by British Catalina aircraft.

After the Italian armistice with the Allies in September 1943, the Italian submarine *Ammiraglio Cagni,* which was headed for Singapore to collect a consignment of rubber and tin for the Axis war effort, turned around and managed to escape Axis capture, reaching an Allied port at Durban in South Africa. It was received with full military honors and returned to Italy in 1944 to support the Allied war effort.

In 2014, the Italian aircraft carrier *Cavour* and her escorts also visited South Africa.

SOUTH KOREA

MARCO POLO DISCUSSES KUBLAI KHAN'S INVASION of Korea in the thirteenth century. Polo informs us that, after a twenty-day march, the Khan's army found the Korean leader, Najan, "lying in bed with his wife, and disporting with her, for he loved her dearly." Najan of "Choreha," presumably a better lover than a fighter, was defeated and captured. He was put to death by being rolled in a carpet and beaten to death so that his imperial blood would not be shed on the earth or in the air.

Italian missionaries were early visitors to Korea in the late sixteenth century. And the Italian Navy was active at times in Korean waters in the late nineteenth and early twentieth centuries. For instance, during the Russo-Japanese War, after a Japanese attack on Russian warships at Inchon in 1904, the Italian Navy's ship *Elba* helped rescue Russian sailors from the sea. And in 1905, as the Japanese advanced, an Italian naval detachment was rushed to Seoul to protect Italian diplomats.

During the Korean War, Italy deployed a Red Cross Field Hospital unit in support of UN forces. Could the Italian docs have swapped martini recipes with the nonfictional Hawkeye Pierces and Trapper Johns of the US Army?

Italian Americans also fought during the war with great bravery, including Joseph Vittori, who, after participating in the South and Central Korean campaigns, was posthumously awarded the Medal of Honor for his heroism in fighting an enemy counterattack on September 16, 1951, at hill 749 near the DMZ.

SOUTH SUDAN

IT IS, AT THE TIME OF WRITING, the world's newest country, and it has faced some difficult times.

Generally speaking, unlike the countries to its north and east, South Sudan has been a little too far south and a little too far west to be on the receiving end of much Italian military involvement, but it has seen some.

In the Roman period, what is now South Sudan was mainly south of any of the Nubian kingdoms that had much contact with the Roman and Byzantine worlds. Even Alodia, the southernmost of the Christian Nubian kingdoms, seems to have been somewhat to the north. However, it is likely that trade routes from Roman Egypt did extend south into this area along the White Nile. Roman coins have been found as far south as El Obeid, just over a couple hundred miles from the South Sudan border. And in AD 61, it's even possible Roman soldiers reached this far south. In that year, a small number of Praetorian Guard soldiers, two of them centurions, were sent south, possibly on a scouting mission to prepare for a Roman invasion of the area. They reached the city of Meroë and then pressed on to an area of extensive marshes, which it has been suggested may have been in the area of Malakal. The planned invasion, if indeed it was planned, never happened, though.

In the nineteenth century, one Italian with experience in the Italian Army did take an intense interest in the area. Gaetano Casati was born in 1838 and joined the Italian Army in 1859. By 1866, after taking part in a campaign against brigands, he had reached the rank of captain. Then he set off for Africa. He served in the Egyptian Army in Sudan, following in the footsteps of other Italian explorers, particularly Orazio Antinori, Carlo Piaggia, and Giovanni Miani (Miani had acquired guns and ammunition from Napoleon III for his venture). Casati spent time exploring the Bahr-el-Ghazal basin, and then he managed to get caught up in a major war in the area. He finally escaped to the coast with German doctor, naturalist, and local governor Emin Pasha and Henry Morton Stanley. Another Italian officer who served in the Egyptian Army with some success in what is now South Sudan and explored the area was Romolo Gessi.

At the beginning of World War II, though, it was British forces that were based in what are now the countries of Sudan and South Sudan. That meant that in June 1940, the border between those countries and Italian-occupied Ethiopia was a war zone. Italian troops rapidly moved across the border to take areas along it; for instance, the villages of Qaysān and Kurmuk, just north of the current border between Sudan and South Sudan. And Italian bombers reached deep inside South Sudan. On July 6, for example, two Italian aircraft bombed Malakal; and on July 23· Italian aircraft attacked Doro, now in South Sudan. However, in October 1940, British and Allied forces in the area went on the offensive. In January 1941, the advancing forces occupied Pochala and Italian troops were forced to pull out of Kurmuk.

The territory that is now South Sudan has faced hugely difficult times in recent history. Civil war in Sudan led to the eventual independence of South Sudan, and then civil war within South Sudan ensued. Italian military personnel have taken part in UNMIS, the United Nations Mission in Sudan; and as civil war exploded in independent South Sudan, Italian Air Force personnel helped evacuate civilians from Juba, the capital of the country.

SPAIN

THE ROMAN INVASION OF WHAT IS NOW SPAIN took place over a long time and involved a number of campaigns and numerous clashes. The emperors that ruled Rome at the apex of its power, Trajan and Hadrian, both grew up in what is now Spain.

The Romans first arrived in Spain during the Second Punic War. With Hannibal off to invade Italy, the Romans took the opportunity to attack the Carthaginian Empire that Hannibal's family had built up on the Iberian Peninsula.

After a long series of campaigns involving multiple armies and commanders, the Romans eventually defeated the Carthaginian forces in Spain and took control of areas previously controlled by Carthage, mainly along the southern and eastern coasts of Spain.

And Rome's campaigns in Spain had only just begun. The first decades of the second century BC saw assorted rebellions and clashes; and then in 181 BC, the First Celtiberian War broke out after more tribes rebelled. The result was a Roman victory, and the war ground to a halt in 179 BC.

Then in 155 BC, the Lusitanian War broke out, involving much action on what is now Spanish soil. A massacre by Roman troops ended that war in 150 BC; but war erupted again in 146 BC as a man who would become legendary, Viriathus, led the Lusitanians against the Romans. This bitter war, fought both on territory that is now Portuguese and on territory that is now Spanish, dragged on until 139 BC, when Viriathus was assassinated by three of his own men.

Meanwhile, to the north, the Romans had become engaged in a titanic struggle against the city of Numantia. The war finally ended in 134 BC when Numantia fell to besieging Roman forces.

In 132 BC, the Romans took the Balearic Islands.

War broke out in Spain in 80 BC, in which Roman commander Sertorius allied with local rebels to take on pro-Sulla Roman forces. Sertorius was eventually assassinated by his own side.

Plenty more fighting linked to Rome's civil wars followed in Spain. Then in 29 BC, Augustus launched the Cantabrian Wars to take control of an area in northern Spain that remained outside Roman control. Within ten years, the war was mainly finished. More minor clashes would ensue, but after a process of conquest taking about two hundred years, the Roman occupation of Spain was finally finished.

In the early fifth century, invaders who had crossed the Rhine and then crossed Gaul arrived in Spain, producing yet more fighting.

And Italians were fighting again in Spain during the Middle Ages. For instance, Benedetto Zaccaria commanded Castilian forces in the late thirteenth century; and Spain became deeply involved in wars in Italy in the fifteenth and sixteenth centuries.

During the Renaissance, the Spanish Borgia family would rise to the height of the papacy with the ascension of Pope Alexander VI. His bastard son, Cesare Borgia, would launch many an invasion in Romagna before his ultimate exile and imprisonment in Spain.

And more Italians fought in Spain after the Renaissance too. (More Spanish troops fought in Italy as well.) For example, during the Napoleonic Wars, Italians could be found fighting on both sides. Significant numbers of Italians troops were in Napoleon's forces in Spain, but the British commanders also had Italians on their side. For example, at the Battle of Castalla in Spain in 1813, two Anglo-Italian divisions were among the forces that repelled desperate French assaults on their defensive position near Alicante. And about 115 Italians were among those serving on Admiral Nelson's ships at the Battle of Trafalgar in 1805.

Italians again fought in the Carlist Wars in Spain in the nineteenth century; and in 1870, an Italian, Amadeo of Savoy, a son of King Victor Emmanuel II, was selected to be King of Spain. He found the job impossible, and in 1873, he had had enough and gave it up.

In the twentieth century, Italian troops played a central role in ensuring victory for Franco's Nationalists in the Spanish Civil War. This Italian-assisted victory had long-term consequences on the development of Spain that were felt into the Cold War.

The Italian effort during the Spanish Civil War started with air power, as Italian aircraft attacked the Republican fleet in the Straits of Gibraltar. They then airlifted Nationalist troops from Africa to Spain, a crucial step in giving Franco the ability to challenge the Republican government on the Spanish mainland.

Soon Italy was also sending tanks and trainers to help the Nationalist side; and then it was sending troops to fight the CTV, Corpo Truppe Volontarie (Corps of Voluntary Troops), supported by heavy artillery and aircraft.

An Italian offensive in March 1937 against Madrid—the Battle of Guadalajara—achieved only limited gains against determined Republican opposition, and Mussolini gave orders to increase Italian efforts. In October of that year, the Italian presence was openly and officially admitted.

Italian troops fought on all fronts in the war and in a large number of clashes. Italian aircraft also saw extensive action, and 175 pilots died in action. Three Italian planes participated in the bombing of Guernica. At sea, Italian Navy surface ships and submarines also sank Republican vessels and merchant ships.

Italian troops played a decisive role in some of the key actions of the war. In the north in August 1937, they were heavily involved in the capture of Santander. In the spring of 1938, they took part in the Aragon Offensive, which struck a decisive blow against the Republican forces in that part of northeastern Spain. And in early 1939, they played a leading role in an offensive in Catalonia that eventually reached the sea and cut the Republic in half. In April 1939, the Nationalist victory was complete.

Over three thousand Italians, however, fought on the Republican side in Spain, joining units such as the Garibaldi Battalion of the International Brigade.

During World War II, Spain remained neutral, though it was friendly to the Axis cause. The Italian Navy took advantage of a derelict tanker, the 4,900 ton *Olterra* moored in the waters near Algericas, by installing members of the X Flottiglia MAS inside its hull. From this base in Spanish waters, they launched a series of attacks against shipping in the Bay of Gibraltar with two-man minisubmarines called *Maiale* (pig).

Spain joined NATO in 1982.

SRI LANKA

THE ROMANS WERE WELL AWARE OF SRI LANKA, and details of two specific visits there are known. In the first century AD, a freedman of tax collector Annius Plocamus ended up on the island, resulting in a delegation being sent from Sri Lanka to Rome. And a later visit by a certain Sopatros, probably in the fifth century, is also recorded. But finds of late Roman coins and their local imitations suggest rather more extensive direct, or possibly indirect, contacts.

Marco Polo visited Sri Lanka in the twelfth century, and other Italian explorers followed. Italians probably took part in the Portuguese exploration and colonial occupation of parts of the island in the sixteenth and seventeenth centuries, before the Dutch and then the British became the dominant colonial powers on the island.

In 1943, the Italian ship *Eritrea* had been ordered to support the Italian submarine *Cappellini* in the east. After hearing of the Italian armistice with the Allies, it escaped Japanese attempts to capture it and instead headed for the Allied port at Colombo in Sri Lanka.

ST. KITTS AND NEVIS

CHRISTOPHER COLUMBUS WAS THE FIRST EUROPEAN to encounter the islands, coming upon them in 1493 during his second voyage.

Britain and France (and then eventually just Britain) were to become the colonial powers in the islands. However, this did not stop another Italian from invading them.

In October 1629, a Spanish fleet appeared off Nevis and attacked a number of British ships. It then continued to St. Kitts, where it anchored in sight of a French fortification. The French fired at it, and the fleet sent in an invasion force led by an Italian engineer. The invasion force succeeded in scaring the French off the island, but it was not to be a great day for the Italian officer who led the invasion. He was shot and killed.

Piedmontese troops were sent to the nearby French Caribbean island of Martinique in 1805, shortly after a French attack on St. Kitts and Nevis. It is unclear whether they were involved in subsequent operations.

ST. LUCIA

SOME HAVE SUGGESTED THAT COLUMBUS WAS the first European to visit this island as well. Others doubt that the route he took would have brought him to St. Lucia.

St. Lucia is named after a martyred saint. The island's national day is celebrated on December 13, also the saint's feast day, the day on which she was martyred in Syracuse on the island of Sicily sometime early in the fourth century AD.

Napoleon ran St. Lucia for a time. A small time, in fact, from 1802–1803. The British had it before him, and they had it again after him.

An 1844 history of the island records the European population as being mainly of either British or French origin, but it does mention Italians and Savoyards as a significant group.

The Italian warship *Flavio Gioia* called in on St. Lucia in the late 1880s.

Italian submarines were active not far from St. Lucia during World War II.

ST. VINCENT AND THE GRENADINES

ON JANUARY 22, 1498, Genoese Christopher Columbus caught sight of the main island of the group and named it St. Vincent. It was Saint Vincent's feast day.

And that's pretty much it from the point of view of Italians invading.

SUDAN

THE ROMAN PERIOD SAW A NUMBER OF CONFLICTS between the forces of Roman Egypt and the powers to the south.

One of the most notable was the invasion of areas in what is now Sudan in 22 BC by Publius Petronius, in an attempt to end raids north into Egypt. He attacked and defeated a Meroitic army at Pselchis; and then, despite the pleas of Queen Candace, captured and sacked the city of Napata before withdrawing.

And in AD 61, during the reign of Nero, a small group of Praetorian Guard soldiers was sent south to Meroë and beyond, possibly as a scouting party for an invasion that never happened. Meroë also shows plenty of evidence of trade with the Roman Empire. The third century saw extensive fighting between the forces of Roman Egypt and a people called the Blemmyes. Roman ships also knew the Red Sea coast of what is now Sudan very well, and the Roman military had a base on Farasan Island in the Red Sea, to the south of Sudan.

Italian soldiers would invade Sudan from Egypt in the nineteenth century. This time, though, they were serving as mercenary officers in the Egyptian Army. Gaetamo Casati, Romolo Gessi, and Giacomo Messedaglia had fought in the Risorgimento and with the Egyptian Army, and they all spent considerable time in the Sudan. Gessi and Casati and Messedaglia also became well known as explorers of the region, and Messedaglia was even made governor of Darfur.

And as Italy took control of Eritrea at the end of the nineteenth century, it invaded part of Sudan. After defeating raiders from Sudan at a battle at Agordat in Eritrea in 1890, Giuseppe Arimondi advanced into Sudan in 1894 and seized the town of Kassala.

At the end of the nineteenth century, Italy even had a chance to take shared control of Sudan. British General Kitchener was looking for military support for his campaign in Sudan, and in return for that, Britain offered the Italian government shared control of the region. Rome rejected the offer.

Italian troops, though, were in action in Sudan again during World War II, when Sudan, under British control, was hostile territory. After Italy declared war on Britain, Italian troops rapidly crossed the border to take targets along it; for instance, Qaysān, Kurmuk, Gallabat, and, once again, Kassala, which they fortified.

A British counterattack in November 1940 retook Kassala in heavy fighting. After losing a high proportion of their tanks, however, the British forces were unable to press on into Eritrea, and a heavy Italian attack followed. But in January 1941, the advancing British forces occupied Pochala, and Italian troops were forced to pull out of Kurmuk.

The fighting also saw the Italian Air Force in action over Sudan. Italian fighters attacked a Rhodesian air base near Kassala, destroying a number of planes, and Italian aircraft also bombed Port Sudan. The Italian Navy was in action off the coast of Sudan.

Italy has supported UN operations in Sudan; for instance, sending Task Force Leone to Khartoum in 2005.

SURINAME

S URINAME'S COLONIAL HISTORY WAS most closely tied with the Netherlands and Britain, so this really isn't going to be a big chapter.

Christopher Columbus, however, did sail along what is now the coast of Suriname in 1498, and he was followed shortly after by Florentine Amerigo Vespucci.

In the seventeenth century, the region was almost the site of a Tuscan colony. English captain Robert Thornton was sent by Fernando I of Tuscany to explore the possibilities of setting up an Italian colony on the north coast of South America. Thornton did make it to the area and explored the territory, mainly in what is now French Guiana, Suriname's eastern neighbor, but the plans for the colony never came to anything.

Italian submarines were operational in the waters off Suriname during World War II, at a time when Suriname was hostile territory.

SWAZILAND

W ELL, ITALIANS DIDN'T HAVE A LOT OF INVOLVEMENT with Swaziland in military terms, but we have come up with a few stories.

A number of Italians fought alongside the Boer during the Boer Wars, and it's possible some of the Italians operated inside Swazi territory during this period. Certainly, Camillo Ricchiardi (see South Africa) was at Komatipoort, only about thirty-three miles north of the Swazi border, during the final Boer retreat to the border of what was then Portuguese South-West Africa and is now Mozambique.

And during World War II, it was in Lourenço Marques (now Maputo), then the capital of South-West Africa, that Italian intelligence agent Alfredo Manna was kidnapped by British agents. He was taken across the border into Swaziland so that he could be officially arrested there.

Ultimately, the biggest military connection between Italy and Swaziland is not Italians invading Swaziland, but Swazis invading Italy, even though Swaziland is one of the smallest countries in Africa.

During World War II, the King of Swaziland, Sobhuza, agreed to send volunteers to fight for the Allied cause in return for promises of greater autonomy from the British colonial authorities. A few thousand Swazis volunteered and served in a variety of locations, including Italy.

SWEDEN

OBVIOUSLY, FOR A LONG TIME SWEDEN has been known for being passionate about neutrality. Having said that, it is a country with a long military history as well. And having said that, Italy hasn't played a huge part in it.

Numbers of Roman coins have been found in Sweden, but these seem to be either the result of trade or plunder. In a recent archaeological excavation on the island of Öland, a late-Roman gold coin was found at the site of what seems to have been a massacre in a fort. But whoever was doing the massacring, it's unlikely it was the Romans. Assorted classical authors refer to a great island in the north called Scandza or similar names. The Romans had some sense of what was up in the Scandinavian and Baltic areas, but maybe not in much detail.

However, on a number of occasions, Italians have fought for Sweden.

For instance, when the Swedish Army under the French general Pontus de la Gardie took Narva in Estonia in 1581, an assault by Italian mercenaries proved decisive.

And again, during the Thirty Years War, the Swedish Army of Gustavus Adolphus faced Italian commanders and Italian soldiers, but also seems to have made use of them on occasion—although not always with the most successful (from the Swedish point of view) results. One Quinti del Ponte is supposed to have infiltrated the Swedish ranks and organized an ambush of Gustavus by Neapolitan cavalry. Another Italian serving with the Swedes, John Baptista, is also alleged to have plotted against Gustavus.

After the collapse of Napoleon's cause in central Europe, French and Italian deserters and prisoners of war were recruited into the Swedish Army, and they fought in Norway. They were in good company, though, because the man in control of Swedish foreign policy at the time, Jean-Baptiste Bernadotte, had been born in France and had been one of Napoleon's marshals before becoming crown prince of Sweden and turning Sweden against Napoleon. Quite a career. His wife, née Désirée Clary, who had been one of Napoleon's old girlfriends, became Queen of Sweden.

After the start of World War II and after Operation *Barbarossa*, Sweden, desperate to be adequately armed in a world suddenly at war, bought from Italy sixty Reggiane Re.2000 fighter planes. These, somewhat ironically, were then used to intercept German as well as Allied aircraft that entered Swedish airspace.

Modern Italy and Sweden have assorted military links.

SWITZERLAND

THE ROMANS TOOK CONTROL OF THE TERRITORY of what is now Switzerland in a number of different stages.

For instance, in 121 BC, Quintus Fabius Maximus defeated the Allobroges, who were a tribe that occupied parts of what is now eastern France and a little bit of Switzerland. And in 58 BC, Caesar decisively defeated the Helvetii at the Battle of Bibracte, a victory that set the scene for the establishment of Roman sites like Noviodunum/Nyon and Colonia Raurica in western Switzerland. In 15 BC, Tiberius and Drusus seized Raetia, a territory that included much of what is now Switzerland. And in 6 BC, Augustus celebrated his triumph over the tribes of the Alps with a massive trophy constructed at what is now La Turbie in France, where much of it is still visible.

These were not the last Italians to fight over what is now Swiss territory. For instance, the Ticino area of southern Switzerland saw extensive fighting by Italians in the late Middle Ages. After the city of Como decided in 1239 to side with Italian-born Emperor Frederick II, at that time ruler of Switzerland, he took control of Bellinzona, the capital of the region. This area was regularly disputed between the Italian powers of Como and Milan. Milan took the city in 1242, but then Como took it back in 1249. Finally, in 1340, the Viscontis took Bellinzona, and Milan would hold it long term. In 1403, Milan temporarily lost control to Alberto di Sacco, who then sold it to the Swiss. Milan sent troops into the area; and after a decisive victory at the Battle of Arbedo in 1422, retook Bellinzona. Swiss forces attacked in 1441 but failed to take Bellinzona. Another attack in 1478 led to the Milanese suffering a defeat at the Battle of Giornico, but Milan hung onto Bellinzona. In 1499, though, when Louis XII of France attacked Milan, it lost control of Bellinzona, which shortly afterward became Swiss.

During the Thirty Years War, the so-called Spanish Road, which linked Hapsburg-held territory in Italy with Hapsburg-held territory in Germany via Switzerland, became a key strategic target for French forces, resulting in extensive fighting.

And the Napoleonic Wars would see more Italians fighting in Switzerland. In 1798, French forces invaded Switzerland and occupied it. Shortly afterward, Andrea Massena, born in Nice (when Nice was Sardinian), was given a major French command in Switzerland and told to resist advancing Austrian and Russian forces. Massena not only managed to resist an Austrian advance on Zurich, but at the Second Battle of Zurich in September 1799, he also achieved a major and strategically important victory over a combined Russian and Austrian force.

In the spring of 1800, Napoleon, whose family was from San Miniato, famously crossed the Alps through the St. Bernard Pass in what is now Switzerland. He soon led the French to victory over the Austrians in the Italian town of Marengo.

In the closing days of World War II, Mussolini considered but rejected the notion of a retreat into neutral Switzerland.

While Switzerland may be known for its bankers, it was the Italians who invented double-entry bookkeeping and the Medicis who pioneered merchant banking. And without Columbus's discovery of the New World, the Swiss would not even have chocolate!

Today in Switzerland, just under 7 percent of Swiss citizens are Italian speaking. The pope continues to be protected by guards who must all be Swiss, Catholic bachelors between the ages of nineteen and thirty. There were 112 Swiss guards protecting the pope as of 2010.

SYRIA

T HE INITIAL ROMAN INVASION OF SYRIA isn't a hugely dramatic story. In
the aftermath of the war against Mithridates and Tigranes, Pompey
decided to wrap up the Seleucid Empire. He had Antiochus XIII killed in
64 BC, but apart from that, his acquisition of what was left of the empire,
including much of what is now Syria, was mainly peaceful.

However, although the beginning of the Roman occupation of Syria
wasn't that dramatic, the northeast of the country soon became part of the
battleground between Rome and, first, the Parthian Empire, and then the
Sassanid Empire.

The Parthians invaded parts of eastern Syria after their crushing defeat
of Crassus at the Battle of Carrhae in 53 BC. And during the civil war
between Pompey and Caesar, and then in the wars after Caesar's death,
the Parthians took the opportunity to invade much of Roman-controlled
territory in the area before finally being forced out again.

Trajan advanced eastward in the area in 114 at the start of his great
push, which took him as far as what is now Iran and the Persian Gulf.

In 165, Avidius Cassius again drove eastward, taking the key
Syrian site of Dura-Europos before advancing into what is now Iraq and
taking Ctesiphon.

More imperial incursions to the east followed, including that by
Emperor Septimius Severus.

But the Romans weren't the only ones campaigning. In the third
century, the Sassanid king Shapur I pushed into Syria before being defeated
at the Battle of Resaena in Syria in 243. In 253, though, at the Battle of
Barbalissos, also in Syria, Shapur would have his revenge.

Eventually, it was a Roman ally, Odaenathus of Palmyra—at that
time, Palmyra was a powerful city-state—who stopped the Sassanid
attacks and forced Shapur to retreat. This, though, would be the start of
a different problem for the Romans in Syria. In 270, Queen Zenobia of
Palmyra (contested by ISIS and Syrian forces at this writing), seeing a
Roman Empire torn apart by infighting, took her chance and created the
Palmyrene Empire, seizing large parts of Rome's empire in the east.

Her empire did not last long. The emperor Aurelian marched through
what is now Turkey and defeated her forces at the Battle of Emesa (modern-
day Homs) in Syria, before marching to Palmyra itself and capturing both
the city and Zenobia.

More border changes in the region would follow, including a big Sassanid leap westward after Julian's disastrous attack on Ctesiphon in 366.

And Italian warriors would return to the area in the Middle Ages with the Crusades. Assorted actions inside what is now Syria involved Italian crusaders, but it's worth mentioning Bohemond of Taranto in particular, one of the leaders of the First Crusade who became Bohemond, Prince of Antioch, ruler of the Principality of Antioch, a state that was created by the crusaders. The Principality included parts of what is now Turkey as well as a large section of what is now Syria. Bohemond had much military success in his career, but he suffered a major defeat at the hands of the Seljuk Turks in the Battle of Harran, fought somewhere near the eastern Syrian city of ar-Raqqah.

During World War II, Italian aircraft headed for Iraq made use of French Vichy bases in Syria on their journey to Iraq.

TAJIKISTAN

EARLY ITALIAN EXPLORERS WERE certainly in the vicinity of Tajikistan at times. Marco Polo, for instance, describes the Pamirs; and it is possible, though by no means certain, that he passed through what is now southeastern Tajikistan on his route toward Kashgar in China.

And Italian military forces were in the region during the Afghan War. For example, Italian aircraft were based at Manas, Kyrgyzstan, to the north of Tajikistan and operated on routes to Afghanistan to the south of Tajikistan. Early in the war, the United States and its allies were allowed to use an air corridor in Tajikistan.

TANZANIA

DID THE ROMANS EVER COME CLOSE to controlling Tanzania?

It's not as an odd question as it at first seems, because although nobody is suggesting that Roman legions ever marched through the streets of Zanzibar, it does seem that part of Tanzania was at one time controlled by a foreign kingdom that itself almost came under Roman control.

According to the *Periplus of the Erythraean Sea*, written probably early in the time of the Roman Empire, a coastal area of east Africa, possibly located in the region of modern Tanzania, was called Azania, with a major port at Rhapta and where ivory was in plentiful supply. Ships from the Roman Empire did reach there. Ptolemy, writing probably some time after the *Periplus*, describes a ship captain called Diogenes who was blown off course while returning from India, and who decided to head south along the coast toward Rhapta to explore. Another Roman captain called Theophilos took twenty days to sail south from the Horn of Africa to Rhapta, thousands of miles from the empire.

What's more, according to the text of the *Periplus*, this territory was controlled by the ruler of a region of the Arabian Peninsula called Mapharitis, with a major port called Muza. These seem to have been located in the western part of what is now Yemen. It might seem unlikely that the people of Muza could exert control over a part of Tanzania, as the *Periplus* claims, but in a time when travel by sea was often far easier and safer than travel by land, it's not implausible. In more modern times, for instance, the Sultan of Oman also controlled Zanzibar.

Rome never did fully control the part of Yemen that ruled Azania, but it came close. In about 25 BC, Aelius Gallus, Prefect of Egypt, set out on a major expedition with the intention of conquering a large chunk of the Arabian Peninsula, including this area. Basically, though, the expedition was a bit of a disaster; and after roaming around large parts of the Arabian Peninsula for six months and taking assorted towns and villages, he had to relinquish it all and head home empty-handed (see Yemen).

In 1502, Italian captain Thomaz de Carmona, or Cremona, part of Vasco da Gama's India Armada, managed to catch up with the rest of the fleet at Kilwe in what is now Tanzania, where da Gama managed to extort tribute from the local ruler.

The royal Italian warship *Staffetta* called in on its long cruise around Africa in 1887–1888. And a military man from an old Italian family, Georg Leo Graf von Caprivi de Caprera de Montecuccoli, was head of the German Navy from 1884 to 1888 and then German chancellor from 1890 to 1894, at the time when Germany was imposing colonial rule on the majority of the area that would become today's Tanzania.

Italian prisoners of war were held in what is now Tanzania during World War II, and significant numbers of Italians settled there after the war.

The Italian Navy has recently trained with the Tanzanian Navy and seeks to cooperate on matters such as fighting maritime crime.

THAILAND

THAILAND IS ONE OF THOSE COUNTRIES that was near the end of trade routes from the Roman Empire, but it seems clear that some links did exist. Roman coins have been found in Thailand. For instance, a third-century bronze coin of Victorinus, minted in Cologne, was found at U Thong in central Thailand and another was found at Wat Khlong Thom. By the mid-second century AD, Roman ships themselves may well have reached this far.

Contact between Italians and Thailand was less during the Middle Ages, but may have occurred. Italian travelers like Niccolò de' Conti (see Malaysia) certainly traveled in the region. And when the Portuguese opened up the sea route to India via the Cape of Good Hope in the late fifteenth century, Italians played a major role in exploring the seas and lands farther east.

As early as 1510, for instance, Florentine merchant Girolamo Sernigi sent a fleet of four to Malacca in what is now Malaysia. The ships got dragged by the local Portuguese commander into an attack on Goa and then on Malacca itself. The Portuguese took Malacca in 1511 and, shortly afterward, sent an envoy to the King of Siam at Ayutthaya. The result of this early Portuguese contact was permission for the Portuguese to send people to live in Ayutthaya and to send Portuguese military aid to the king, including guns and sometimes even mercenary soldiers. It is likely at least some Italians were involved in these links with Thailand.

In the mid-nineteenth century, the Italian warship *Principessa Clotilde* called in, in order to establish links between the governments of Italy and Siam.

And in the late nineteenth century, Italian architects and engineers played a significant role in developing modern infrastructure in Thailand. Also, Thailand's links to Italy at the time were seen in some sense as countering pressure on Thailand from the British colonial presence in Burma and Malaya, and the French colonial presence in Laos, Cambodia, and Vietnam.

When fighting from World War II reached the region in December 1941, two Italian ships, the *Volpi* and the *Sumatra*—these ships were intended to be used as auxiliary cruisers in the event of war—were caught in Phuket Harbor in Thailand. Their crews scuttled them on December 8, rather than allowing them to be captured. But by October 1944, the

Japanese, then in control of the harbor, had already raised the *Sumatra*. They intended to repair it fully, and work was in progress on raising the *Volpi*. In response, the British attacked them with chariot submarines *Tiny* and *Slasher* and sank the *Sumatra* once more and did further damage to the *Volpi*.

Italian submarines operated in the waters off Thailand, heading to the Japanese and German submarine base at Penang, Malaysia, just to the south of Thailand's border.

In 2013, Italy and Thailand signed a defense cooperation agreement.

TOGO

A SMALL COUNTRY THAT HAS SEEN very little in the way of Italian military involvement.

However, a military man from an old Italian family, Georg Leo Graf von Caprivi de Caprera de Montecuccoli, was head of the German Navy from 1884 to 1888 and German chancellor from 1890 to 1894, at the time when Germany was imposing colonial rule on the area that would become today's state of Togo.

Italian military aircraft have flown Italian Air Force and charity medics into Togo in an operation to restore sight to patients.

TONGA

R IGHT OUT IN THE PACIFIC, this collection of islands is not exactly a place most people would associate with Italy. Yet Italians did play a vital role in bringing European influence to the area and did, sort of, invade it.

Alessandro Malaspina was born in Tuscany and ended up a senior naval officer in the Spanish Navy. In 1793, he turned up with two ships on the Vava'u group of islands in the north of Tonga. He came to explore the islands, but he also came to claim then in the name of Spain; and in May 1793, after his crew spent some time enjoying the company of the local women and with a crowd of locals looking on, Malaspina, the boy from Tuscany, took control of Tonga. Well, sort of. It seems fairly clear that the local ruler and the locals themselves had no real idea of the significance of what Malaspina was up to; and shortly afterward, he and his crews sailed off over the seas, headed home.

In the end, Tonga became a British protectorate, not a Spanish or Italian one.

An Italian submarine named *Alessandro Malaspina* was operational during World War II. On June 14, 1941, it sank the Greek freighter *Nikiklis* southwest of the Azores. Seventeen of the freighter's twenty-eight crew members were rescued, but the rest died. The *Malaspina* was lost at sea in September 1941.

TRINIDAD AND TOBAGO

Y EP, COLUMBUS MADE IT HERE TOO.
Christopher Columbus, on his third voyage of exploration, came across Trinidad on July 31, 1498, the first European to do so, and took on water there. He named the island Trinidad, after the Holy Trinity and three hills. Later in his voyage, he also encountered Tobago. He called that Bellaforma, but unlike Trinidad, it's not a name that's lasted.

As elsewhere, Columbus's arrival meant trouble for the locals. Many inhabitants were seized as slaves, and eventually the islands were colonized. And some of those colonists were Italian.

In 1783, the Spanish decision that Trinidad was too thinly populated resulted in the Cedula of Population. Spain offered free land to anybody who was Catholic and who would swear allegiance to the Spanish crown. Among those who responded to the offer were Italians.

Among the Italians who came to Trinidad in the next few decades was Count Giuseppe Caracciolo, who had served in the Russian Army before immigrating to Trinidad in 1801.

The Italian warship *Flavio Gioia* called in at the Port of Spain in the late 1880s.

And Italians were once again headed for the waters off Trinidad and Tobago during the Second World War, when Trinidad and Tobago (as part of the British Empire) were enemy territory.

On August 1 or 2, 1942, the Italian submarine *Enrico Tazzoli*, under the command of submarine ace Feccia di Cossato, sank the Greek freighter *Kastor* with a torpedo one hundred miles east of Trinidad. Four crew members died, but thirty-one were rescued.

In May 1943, the *Tazzoli*, now converted to a transport role, left Bordeaux on a blockade-running mission, headed for Japan. It was never seen again.

TUNISIA

TUNISIA IS, OF COURSE, THE SITE OF Rome's great enemy, Carthage. Cato the Elder used to end all of his speeches in the senate with the words, *"Carthago delenda est"*—"Carthage must be destroyed."

During the First Punic War, the main Roman action on African soil was an invasion by Marcus Atilius Regulus in what is now Tunisia, with a Roman army. He won a couple of victories, but was then decisively defeated in a battle near Tunis in 255 BC.

Toward the end of the century, the Romans were invading again. After Hannibal had taken the war to Italy, Scipio took the war to Africa. After landing near Utica, he defeated a Carthaginian force at the Battle of the Great Plains in 203 BC, and then went on to defeat Hannibal himself at the Battle of Zama the next year. But it was not the end for an independent Carthage just yet.

In 149 BC, the Romans forced the Carthaginians into the Third Punic War; and in 146 BC, Scipio Aemilianus captured Carthage and destroyed it. Rome had its first African colonial territory in what is now Tunisia.

This territory saw assorted fighting during the Roman period; for instance, the defeat of the forces of the emperors Gordian I and Gordian II by forces loyal to the emperor Maximinus Thrax at the Battle of Carthage in 238.

In AD 439, Carthage was captured by the Germanic Vandals who had crossed from Spain and advanced along the North African coast.

And Italian soldiers invaded Tunisia again in the Middle Ages on a number of occasions. For example, in 1087, Pisa and Genoa launched a campaign against parts of Tunisia. Or again, starting in 1135, Tunisia became the center of the Kingdom of Africa for Roger II of Sicily. And then, in 1284, Roger de Lauria seized the island of Jerba. Charles I of Naples was instrumental in getting his brother, King Louis IX of France, to launch a disastrous crusade against Tunis.

More Italian fighters would end up invading the area in the period after the Middle Ages. For instance, Gabrio Serbelloni, born in Milan, led imperial troops in the capture of Tunis in 1573; and then endured a siege by Ottoman forces before the city fell. He was taken as prisoner to Istanbul, from where he was ransomed by the Venetian ambassador in 1575.

And during the period of the Barbary Pirate threat, Italians would once again attack Tunisia. In 1784, 1785, and 1786, Angelo Emo, last Grand Admiral of the Republic of Venice, led successive attacks on Tunis.

During the nineteenth century, France became the European colonial power in Tunisia. In 1940, in an attempt to keep Italy out of the Second World War, France offered Mussolini control of Tunisia, but he rejected the offer, opting instead for war.

In the autumn of 1942, after Allied landings in Algeria and Morocco, Italian and German forces raced into French-held Tunisia to prevent the Allies from occupying it. The Allies had hoped for a quick liberation of Tunisia, but the rapid Italian and German reaction prevented this.

Italian troops played a part in the Axis victory at the Battle of Kasserine Pass in February 1943. General Giovanni Messe, commanding German and Italian troops in the 1st Italian Army, mounted a dogged, determined, and courageous defense against Allied troops advancing from the east. The 7th Bersaglieri, in particular, distinguished themselves at the Axis victory at Kasserine. Rommel commented, "The German soldier has impressed the world, however the Italian Bersagliere soldier has impressed the German soldier."

Angelo Spinelli was an Italian American who grew up in the Bronx and became a US Army photographer who served in the 1942 invasion of North Africa—Operation Torch. On Valentine's Day in 1943, he was captured near Kasserine Pass in Tunisia. Spinelli would spend over two years in multiple German POW camps. A nonsmoker, he bartered his cigarette ration with German guards in exchange for a camera and film. He documented life behind the lines in POW camps with photographs published in his remarkable book *Behind the Wire*.

After bitter fighting, the last Italian and German troops in Tunisia surrendered in May 1943.

TURKEY

I TALY HAS A LONG AND DEEP HISTORY of military involvement with Turkey. Virgil poetically traced the founding of Rome back to the escape of Aeneas from Troy, whose precise location was later revealed by Heinrich Schliemann to be on the west coast of Turkey.

In the early second century BC, Rome expanded eastward and clashed with the Seleucid Empire, which at that point controlled large parts of what is now Turkey, as well as extensive other territories in the Middle East. Despite having the assistance of Rome's great enemy Hannibal, the forces of Antiochus III were decisively defeated by the Romans and their ally, Eumenes III of Pergamum, at the Battle of Magnesia in 190 BC. As a result of this defeat and the peace deal that followed, Eumenes picked up a big chunk of Turkey. When he died in 133 BC, he left the territory in his will to Rome, and the Romans turned part of it into a province.

However, before they took most of the rest of what is now Turkey, Rome had one major problem to deal with: a king known as Mithridates the Great. He was King of Pontus, located in the north of what is now Turkey, and while Rome was expanding its power base from the west, Mithridates had other plans. First, he invaded kingdoms to the west of the Black Sea and to the north, and then he looked south and east. He clashed with Roman ally Nicomedes IV of Bithynia. As a result, Nicomedes, with Roman forces in support, invaded Pontus.

It wasn't a great decision—Mithridates smashed the Bithynian army. He then advanced to take the whole of Asia Minor before arranging for Romans and Italians to be slaughtered in cities across the area. Nicomedes fled to Rome. Mithridates subsequently advanced into Greece and was welcomed as a liberator.

Rome amassed forces to retaliate. While Sulla dealt with matters in Greece, another Roman commander, Fimbria, landed in Asia Minor and attacked Pergamum. Sulla, however, gave Mithridates an apparently lenient peace deal that allowed him to retain much of his power and territory.

In the Second Mithridatic War in 83–81 BC, Lucius Licinius Murena invaded the Kingdom of Pontus but was defeated.

And then in 74 BC, Nicomedes IV of Bithynia died and left his kingdom to Rome. Mithridates didn't like the idea of Rome having Bithynia, and he attacked. After Mithridates's initial successes, Pompey managed to destroy his army in a night battle. Mithridates fled to the north coast of the Black Sea before committing suicide, and Rome ended up controlling the vast majority of what is now Turkey, either directly or as protectorates. Those client kingdoms gradually came under full Roman control. For instance, the Kingdom of Cappadocia ceased to exist in AD 17, and the remnants of the Kingdom of Pontus ceased to exist in AD 62.

However, the east of what is now Turkey would become part of the battleground between Rome and its eastern neighbors, first the Parthian Empire and then the Sassanid Empire.

Lucullus and Pompey both pushed into this zone during their wars against Mithridates and his ally, Tigranes of Armenia. However, in 53 BC, the Roman general Crassus suffered a crushing defeat by the Parthians at the Battle of Carrhae. A period of instability in the region, accompanied by Parthian intrusion, followed during the civil war between Pompey and Caesar and after Caesar's death. And Mark Antony's expedition east in 33 BC was a disaster.

The Roman-Parthian War of AD 58–63 over the succession to the throne of Armenia, which at that time included much territory in what is now eastern Turkey, ended in a sort of draw.

In AD 114, the emperor Trajan began his big push to the east. Annexed territories included Nisibis, a key city in the region (now Nusaybin in eastern Turkey); but then he died in 117, and his successor Hadrian abandoned many of Trajan's plans. Another Roman-Parthian war over Armenia in 161–166 ended in a Roman victory. Nisibis was lost again in 194, but then in 195, Septimius launched his great drive to the east. He retook the city before pushing into what is now Iraq. But then in 217, the emperor Macrinus was defeated in battle by the Parthians near Nisibis. Soon the Parthian threat was replaced by a Sassanid threat, and in the 230s, Severus Alexander campaigned against Sassanid king Ardashir. But after some Roman success, Ardashir advanced again and took both Nisibis and Carrhae, and then advanced even farther and sacked Antioch.

Just when some Romans probably thought it couldn't get worse, it did. At the Battle of Edessa in southern Turkey, Shapur captured most of a Roman army and Emperor Valerian himself. Roman ally Odaenathus of Palmyra had to step in to stop the Sassanid onslaught, but this in itself was a sign of trouble to come. Shortly after, Zenobia of Palmyra exploited the chaos in the Roman Empire to establish her own short-lived Palmyrene Empire, necessitating a campaign by the Emperor Aurelian to end it. More fighting followed under Emperor Carus; and then Emperor Galerius smashed the Persian army at a battle in 298, thereby securing the eastern frontier, including Nisibis, for decades.

Constantine established Constantinople as a major eastern Roman power base and was headed for a campaign against Persia when he died. However, Julian's disastrous expedition to Ctesiphon in 363 lost Rome a huge portion of territory again, including Nisibis. Eventually, the situation settled down when both empires had to deal with other threats from the north.

And Italian soldiers returned to the area during the Middle Ages.

The Crusades had a focus on the Holy Land but also saw extensive action in Turkey, much of it involving Italians. For example, Bohemond, Prince of Taranto, was one of the leaders of the First Crusade, and he led it across Asia Minor. He captured Antioch with the help of, among others, Genoese reinforcements who had arrived by sea. After the First Crusade had achieved its goal in the Holy Land, Bohemond established himself as Prince of Antioch. And, of course, the Fourth Crusade, with heavy Venetian involvement, attacked and sacked Constantinople in 1204.

But Italians didn't just fight against the Byzantines; some of them fought for the Byzantines. For instance, Italian mercenary commander Roger de Flor led a mercenary band to Constantinople in 1303 and achieved a victory over the Turks, before being killed by rival mercenaries. And Venetian and Genoese ships and soldiers formed a major part of the force that tried desperately to prevent Constantinople from falling to the ultimately successful Ottoman assault in 1453.

Genoa helped support the Empire of Trebizond in the north, which lasted a few years longer than Byzantine Constantinople; while in the south, Venice was involved with the the rulers of Karaman until they were crushed by the Ottomans in 1474.

Italian fighting men would return in the period after the Middle Ages. For instance, during the War for Candia (1645–1669), the Venetian fleet made repeated attempts to close the Dardanelles. In 1649, in the Battle of Focchies fought off the Turkish coast near Smyrna/Izmir, a Venetian fleet attacked an Ottoman fleet that had managed to slip through the Dardanelles, and destroyed it. And in 1656, Venetian naval commander Lorenzo Marcello clashed with a larger Ottoman fleet and decimated it, leaving only a fraction of the Ottoman ships to escape.

In 1911, the Italian-Turkish wars broke out and Italian warships returned to Turkish waters. For instance, five torpedo boats under Captain Millo entered the Dardanelles on a reconnaissance mission.

At the end of the First World War, with Turkey defeated, Italian warships were part of the Allied armada that entered the Dardanelles; and Italian troops were part of the Allied force that eventually occupied Istanbul.

However, it was in the south of Turkey where an Italian invasion would cause rather more international controversy. Italy wanted control of territory in defeated Turkey, and so did Greece. Italy landed troops in Antalya and then, expanding their area of control, occupied places like Konya and areas of the coast in the direction of Smyrna/Izmir, including Bodrum. The Greeks landed at Smyrna/Izmir as well. In the end, as Mustafa Kemal began to establish Turkish central authority again, Italy gave up on its dreams of a new Turkish empire and withdrew its forces from southern Turkey in 1921.

Turkey remained neutral during World War II. However, Italian military personnel did conduct at least one operation in Turkish waters during the war. Italian naval frogmen attached mines to ships in the Turkish ports of Alexandretta/Iskenderun and Mersin in an attempt to prevent the transport of vital chromium to Britain.

Turkey has long been a fellow member of NATO with Italy.

TURKMENISTAN

I TALIANS HAVEN'T HAD A LOT OF military involvement in Turkmenistan, but they have had some.

The most intriguing story is from the Roman writer Pliny, who refers to 10,000 Roman prisoners captured by the Parthians at the Battle of Carrhae in 53 BC. They were shipped east to serve the Parthians by protecting the Parthian Empire's borders in Margiana, most of which is in current Turkmenistan. It has been suggested that Parthian documents found south of Ashkhabad, the capital of Turkmenistan, refer to the commander of a legion now involved in agricultural work.

The Caspian has also seen assorted military activity by Italians. In the fourteenth century Luchino Tarigo sailed up the Don from the Black Sea, transported his boat across land, and then sailed down the Volga into the Caspian. However, it's unclear whether he ever entered the waters of what is now Turkmenistan. In 1428, another Italian, Giovanni de Valle from Venice, operating on the Caspian under the orders of the Khan of Darband, did attack ships sailing from Astarabad. Astarabad is now in Iran, only about forty miles south of its current border with Turkmenistan.

And Italian troops have been in action again on Turkmenistan's border recently. An Italian contingent was based at Bala Murghab in Afghanistan, very close to the border and controlling the road connecting that region with Turkmenistan.

TUVALU

A SPANISH EXPLORER, ALVARO DE MENDAÑA Y NEYRA, first encountered the islands of Tuvalu on a Pacific voyage of exploration in 1568, and Italians may have been part of his expedition.

However, it was really only in the nineteenth century that Europeans began to take a close interest in the islands. The island of Niulakita has at times been known as Sophia Island because in 1853, Italian Captain Agostino Tortello, in a yacht called, yes, *Sophia*, arrived there and called it that. The islands would later come under British control.

UGANDA

NOT A COUNTRY ITALIANS HAVE had a huge amount of military involvement with.

Italians did play a significant role in opening up various parts of Uganda to Europeans.

For instance, Romolo Gessi had fought alongside British troops in the Crimean War. He ended up serving under British General Gordon in the Sudan, where he explored and mapped Lake Albert Nyanza in Uganda.

Major Gaetano Casati from Lesmo in Italy spent time in the 1880s exploring the western Ugandan kingdom of Bunyoro. And in 1906, Prince Luigi Amedeo, Duke of the Abruzzi, who would go on to command the Italian Adriatic fleet in World War I, commanded an expedition exploring the Ruwenzori Range. The prince himself reached many summits, and one of the peaks in the range, Mount Luigi di Savoia in Uganda, is still named after him.

Italian prisoners of war in Uganda during World War II worked on assorted projects, including in 1944 building a flax factory at Kisiizi, which became a hospital in 1958. Some Italian-speaking Maltese were also imprisoned in Uganda during World War II.

In recent years, trainers from the Italian armed forces have been active in Uganda at Bihanga, about 150 miles west of Kampala, training troops from the Somali security forces as part of the European Union Training Mission to contribute to the training of Somali security forces (EUTM).

UKRAINE

Y ES, THE ROMANS MADE IT TO UKRAINE.
To be fair, a quite extensive Greek presence had long existed on the Black Sea coast of what is now Ukraine, particularly in Crimea (currently under Russian control), long before the Roman period, so it was perhaps inevitable that the Romans would turn up eventually.

Crimea became a major focus for Rome in the first century BC when it was fighting one of its most determined enemies, Mithridates VI, aka Mithridates the Great. The heartland of his kingdom was Pontus, in the northeast of what is now Turkey. Mithridates, though, who came to the throne in about 120 BC, expanded his power across Asia Minor and around parts of the Black Sea, including Crimea. After many battles and three wars, Mithridates was defeated by Pompey in 63 BC and fled to Crimea, determined to raise another army and fight on. Instead, faced by rebellion from his own men, he committed suicide. And with the death of Mithridates, Roman influence began to spread in the region.

However, it was not until the first century AD that a solid Roman military presence was established there. In the middle of the century, Sarmatians threatened the region and besieged Chersonesus. An expeditionary force was sent under Plautius Silvanus Aelianus in order to save the city, and a passage in a manuscript by Romano-Jewish historian Josephus suggests the presence of three thousand Roman troops in the Bosporus region in AD 66. More evidence suggests a Roman presence in the area under Trajan; and archaeological sites give firm proof of significant Roman military presence, particularly around Chersonesus from the second century on. The Roman military did not, however, just appear in Crimea. They also had a presence at Olbia and Tyras, both now in what is Ukrainian territory.

The Roman military presence in Crimea seems to have been at its height in the second and early third centuries AD, but Rome faced increasing conflict with peoples moving in from the north in the late third and fourth centuries.

The Byzantines subsequently had a presence in the area, and so— too soon again—did the Italians. In the thirteenth century, Venetians and Genoese struggled for power and influence on the coast of Crimea and other parts of the Black Sea coast, with the Genoese becoming the dominant power. They had a string of colonies and some impressive fortifications, including the castle at Sudak. But the most significant of their colonies were at Feodosia, then called Caffa. It grew rich on trade with the east. By 1311, it had a Catholic bishop, and by the second half of the fifteenth century, a population of over 70,000. But it would not last. The expansion of Ottoman Turkish power in the region would mean the end of Genoese dominance, though an Italian community in the area would live on.

That was not the end of Italian military personnel in the region.

For instance, in 1794, Catherine the Great sent her Neapolitan-born admiral Guiseppe de Ribas to set up the major Russian naval base at Odessa. For a long time the city itself would have a very Italian feel to it, due to the presence of Italians, including many merchants, there.

During the Crimean War, the Kingdom of Piedmont-Sardinia allied itself with Britain and France and sent a force of over 15,000 troops to invade Crimea. They fought well and distinguished themselves at the Battle of Tchernaya on August 16, 1855. The Russians attacked in an attempt to end the siege of Sevastopol, but after heavy fighting, the attack was contained and the attackers forced to retreat. The deployment of Piedmontese troops to the Crimean War would later help win French support for a war against Austria, which would lead to Italian unification.

Italians serving in the Austro-Hungarian Army in the First World War fought in Ukraine.

And in another example, World War II would also see an extensive Italian military invasion of the area. Italian forces achieved success in the first stages of the invasion of Russia in 1941. The CSIR, the Italian Expeditionary Corps to Russia under General Givoanni Messe, took part in the battles at Dnepropetrovsk and Kiev and the capture of Stalino as it moved through Ukraine, and it sent troops to occupy Odessa after its capture.

Another feature of the war was the return of Italian forces to Crimea. The Italian Navy operated MAS motor torpedo boats and small submarines in the Crimea during 1942 and 1943, using bases that included the once Genoese port of Feodosia. They conducted a bitter struggle against well-equipped Soviet naval units in the area. Both sides suffered significant casualties before the Italian Navy was forced to suspend operations in 1943 due to the Soviet advance.

UNITED ARAB EMIRATES

THE ROMAN MILITARY NEVER REACHED the part of the Arabian Peninsula that is now the United Arab Emirates.

However, the Romans were aware of the Persian Gulf and the trade routes that it contained. And Roman glass has been found at Mleiha in the United Arab Emirates.

The Venetians were well aware of the Persian Gulf and its trade routes during the Middle Ages. And then the Portuguese turned up, after opening the sea route to the east around the Cape of Good Hope.

During the Gulf War in 1990, the Italian armed forces operated out of facilities in the United Arab Emirates. For instance, a detachment of ten Italian Tornado aircraft was based at Al Dhafra, flying 226 raids during the war and losing one aircraft. The crew was captured and shown on Iraqi television.

In recent years, the Italian armed forces have again used facilities in the United Arab Emirates. For instance, Italian air force personnel of the Task Force Air of Al Bateen have operated in support of operations in Afghanistan; and recently, the flagship of the EU Naval Force, the Italian destroyer ITS *Andrea Doria*, called in on Dubai. Italy has also supplied military equipment and training to the United Arab Emirates.

UNITED KINGDOM

THE ROMANS HAD LONG BEEN AWARE of the presence of Britain, but they finally arrived in force in 55 BC. According to Suetonius, they came in search of pearls that were much prized by the women of Rome. Colchester became a significant town in Roman Britain, and remains a center of oyster production to this day. Julius Caesar, on the lookout for new victories after rampaging across Gaul, took Roman troops onto British soil for the first time. It wasn't a great success for Caesar, as storms in the English Channel threw his plans into disarray. He withdrew to Gaul fairly rapidly.

He returned in 54 BC and made a rather more determined invasion of the island. This time, he managed to penetrate some distance inland and achieve a kind of victory over local British leader Cassivellaunus. However, in the end, once again, the Romans withdrew.

It was not until almost a century later, in AD 43, that the Romans, during the reign of Emperor Claudius, invaded Britain and managed to impose long-term occupation on most of what is now the United Kingdom.

The British tribes were not united in opposition to Rome. Roman forces advanced in the east and fairly soon took Colchester, and then expanded control across other parts of Britain. The future emperor Vespasian campaigned in the southwest; and soon Roman forces entered what is now Wales, where they encountered fierce fighting.

And all was not well for Rome in the east of the island. In AD 60 or 61, the mighty Iceni tribe under their queen Boudicca rose in revolt. The rebels enjoyed some success against Roman forces before eventually being crushed, with much attendant slaughter.

Eventually, the Roman invaders focused on the drive north, which would take them into what is now Scotland. However, despite repeated pushes into the area, Rome would never firmly control much of what that territory. Agricola, for instance, thrust north before Hadrian built his seventy-three-mile wall to establish the long-term frontier. Hadrian's Wall, now a UNESCO World Heritage Site, was mainly constructed by three Roman legions (about 15,000 men) with around two million tons of stone over at least six years. Hadrian's Wall is a tangible reminder of the impact of Italian invasions on Britain; it may also have provided inspiration for George R. R. Martin's dividing wall in *A Game of Thrones*.

Under Antoninus Pius, the Antonine Wall was built farther north, temporarily sealing a large chunk of what is now Scotland within the empire, but then that was abandoned. In another example, Septimius Severus campaigned in the north, but again, his temporary conquests achieved little. Constantius and his son Constantine both campaigned in the north.

Christianity became widespread in Roman Britain especially after the conversion of Constantine, who was acclaimed emperor in York in 306. The Romans also introduced rabbits to Britain. No Roman invasion, therefore, would have meant no *Watership Down*.

However, as Roman power in Britain weakened in the late fourth and early fifth centuries AD, peoples from north of Hadrian's Wall and peoples from across the North Sea began raiding inside Roman-controlled Britain. Eventually, Roman power in Britain ended entirely as much of the army left for Gaul to pursue Constantine III's ambitions there. Britons probably started fighting other Britons then, as Britain fragmented.

In 1154, an Englishman made his way to Rome and became Adrian IV, the first and only English pope thus far.

Italian bankers, with their double-entry bookkeeping, made it to Britain in the Middle Ages, long before the Medici. In the thirteenth century, for example, the Ricciardi of Lucca would lend Edward I about £400,000 to finance his wars.

Italians would return to Britain not only to collect debts but also to attack. For instance, in 1338, Italians were a major component in the fleet that sacked Southampton. And in 1588, the Spanish Armada actually included a lot of Italians. It wasn't simply Italians attacking Britain either. Italians were employed to fight on British soil as well. For instance, in 1547, Italian mercenaries were part of a force sent to fight Kett's Rebellion in Norfolk. Two years later, Italian mercenaries were in the force that crushed the Prayer Book Rebellion in Devon and Cornwall. And at much the same time, one Italian mercenary called Petruccio Ubaldini was fighting with English forces against the Scots while another Italian, Migliorino Ubaldini, was a military engineer helping the Scots defend their cities against the English.

Charles Edward Stuart, Bonnie Prince Charlie, grew up at the Jacobite court in Italy before landing in Scotland to lead the Forty-Five Rebellion. After his defeat at Culloden, he returned to exile in Rome, where he lies buried at St. Peter's Basilica.

Giuseppe Garibaldi first visited the United Kingdom in 1854, landing at Newcastle, where he was presented with a sword and telescope by a group of English miners. He declared that, "Should England at any time in a just cause need my arm, I am ready to unsheathe in her defence this noble and splendid sword received at your hands."

During the Crimean War, the "thin red line" of British infantry fought alongside Piedmontese troops.

In 1864, following his conquest of Sicily, Garibaldi made a triumphal return to Great Britain. He met with luminaries such as Lord Tennyson; "Bertie," the Prince of Wales; and Florence Nightingale. Thousands of Englishmen thronged the streets of London and many Garibaldi biscuits were consumed. Only Queen Victoria, scenting the odor of revolution about Garibaldi, was not amused by the Italian patriot, sniffing, "The Queen much regrets the extravagant excitement respecting Garibaldi, which shows little dignity and discrimination in the nation ..."

Britain and Italy fought World War I together as allies, but not the Second World War.

Perhaps not a fan of Garibaldi biscuits, Mussolini declared war on Britain on June 10, 1940. Italian military personnel would soon see action on British soil — or actually, over British soil and in the waters off British soil.

In September 1940, the Italian Air Corps was sent to Belgium to take part in the Luftwaffe's Battle of Britain, which was Hitler's attempt to make an invasion of Britain possible. During October and November of that year, bombers and fighters of the CAI (Corpo Aero Italiano) carried out a number of raids on ports in southeast England, including Harwich, Felixstowe, and Ramsgate. The slow-flying CR.42 biplanes of the Italian Air Force were no match for the RAF's Hurricanes and Spitfires. A Beaufighter pilot later reported that CR.42s "just disintegrated" when hit. The Macchi fighters that were deployed after the Battle of Britain were a distinct improvement, though underarmed compared to the German Messerschmitt, the Me 109.

In 1982, Italian Argentine general and president Leopoldo Galtieri invaded the Falklands/Malvinas, triggering a war with the United Kingdom.

Italy and the United Kingdom have been allies in NATO and have fought alongside each other recently in Afghanistan and Iraq.

UNITED STATES OF AMERICA

IN 1492 CHRISTOPHER COLUMBUS sailed west from Europe to the New World and changed the world forever. The intrepid navigator was not the first European to reach what would become known as the Americas, but the impact of this "Italian Invasion" was profound, and its effects are being felt to this day.

Columbus would later be mythologized as the man who dared sail off the edge of the world. Ditties would instruct schoolchildren that "in fourteen hundred ninety-two, Columbus sailed the ocean blue." More recently, Columbus has come under fire by those who point to his lust for gold, his tolerance for slavery, and the sufferings of Native Americans.

Columbus cannot, however, be blamed for all the sins of European colonialism. Slavery was widespread throughout the world in the fifteenth century, and he needed to deliver a return on Ferdinand and Isabella's investment in his venture. At the end of the day, Columbus was an unbelievably brave visionary who transformed our world.

The Italian connection to Columbus's voyage of discovery went deeper than his origins in Genoa. It was Italian merchant bankers based in Seville who financed Columbus's journeys, not the apocryphal sale of Queen Isabella's jewelry.

Amerigo Vespucci, a Florentine explorer, led at least three voyages to South America shortly after Columbus. His cartographical skills probably ensured that his own name would be used to label the New World.

And in 1524, Florentine Giovanni da Verrazano explored what is now New York Bay, inspiring the bridge that was later built in his honor.

Soon Italians would be settling in the land. For instance, in 1657, three hundred Italians emigrated and settled in New York.

And we should mention here the Italian de Tonti brothers. Henri de Tonti explored the Mississippi with La Salle in 1682. He subsequently fought in wars against British and Iroquois forces. His younger brother, Alphonse de Tonti, was also an officer in the French Army and helped found the French base at Detroit.

William Paca, who was later elected governor of Maryland, was an Italian American signatory of the Declaration of Independence. Philip Mazzei (1730–1816) was a Tuscan aristocrat who immigrated to Virginia and acted as an agent for the colony, purchasing arms for the Patriot cause. He was a great friend of Thomas Jefferson and wrote that "All men are created equal" even before Jefferson penned it in the Declaration of Independence in 1776. The two men shared a love for both liberty and wine; Mazzei helped Jefferson to plant grapes at Monticello. The Mazzei family has been making wines in Chianti since the fifteenth century and continue to do so to this day.

Italian naval commander Alessandro Malaspina led a Spanish naval expedition up the west coast of North America in the late eighteenth century.

Vincenzo Gambi was an Italian pirate who fought under Jean Lafitte at the Battle of New Orleans in 1815. After the American victory, Gambi was pardoned and rewarded with American citizenship by President Madison. He was, nevertheless, decapitated with an ax by one of his own crew in 1819.

An English packet ship named *Waterloo* brought the Italian patriot Garibaldi to New York on July 29, 1850. He declined most of the honors that were offered him and instead took up with other members of the nineteenth-century Italian diaspora. The general worked humbly as a laborer in sausage and candle factories on Staten Island.

In 1860, Garibaldi would lead his "Thousand" on a legendary conquest of Sicily against a Bourbon army of over 40,000. That would ultimately unite the two halves of Italy under the crown of Savoy. At a critical point in the campaign, Captain Palmer of the US Navy would provide much needed gunpowder from the hold of his ship, the steam frigate *Iroquois*, to the Garibaldini when a ceasefire was arranged in Palermo between the combatants.

Garibaldi's masterful handling of his outnumbered and ill-equipped irregular forces in 1860 caught the attention of the world, and also the admiration of Abraham Lincoln. Even as Italy was on the path to unification, the United States was splitting apart with the dawn of its Civil War. After the April 1861 attack on Fort Sumter by Confederate forces, President Lincoln gave serious consideration to recruiting Garibaldi to lead Union forces against the Confederacy. The American minister to Belgium, Henry Shelton Sanford, was directed to negotiate for the services of General Garibaldi. These negotiations broke down over Garibaldi's insistence that he have supreme command of all Union forces and that all African American slaves be emancipated immediately. Lincoln did not issue his Emancipation Proclamation until 1863.

Although Garibaldi did not accept a commission in the Union Army, thousands of Italians and Italian Americans did fight in the US Civil War. In the spring of 1861, the 39th New York infantry regiment was formed and became known as the Garibaldi Guard. These soldiers were issued red woolen shirts. It must be noted that the Guard was not exclusively Italian, but rather contained many Hungarians, Germans, Irish, etc. This unit would fight in many battles of the Civil War, including First Battle of Bull Run and the Battle of Cross Keys. The Guard's finest hour was surely in July 1863 at Gettysburg, where it defended the heights of Cemetery Ridge. Its monument can be found there today.

Italians, with their proud sea-faring tradition, served in the Union Navy as well. Bancroft Gherardi, whose family was Tuscan, graduated from the US Naval Academy in Annapolis, served during the Mexican-American and the US Civil Wars, and rose to become a rear admiral in the US Navy.

Perhaps the most prominent Italian to fight in the Civil War was Colonel Luigi Palma di Cesnola. He was born in Rivarola, Piedmont, in 1832. His military career began at the age of fifteen, and he served with Piedmontese forces during the Crimean War before moving to New York City. In 1862, he became an officer in the 11th New York Cavalry, and he later served in the 4th New York Cavalry. Di Cesnola's distinguished service in multiple engagements, including the Battle of Brandy Station, one of the largest cavalry actions of the war, brought him to the attention of Lincoln. Shortly before his assassination, Lincoln rewarded di Cesnola with an appointment as American consul in Cyprus. While serving as consul, the soldier turned diplomat became an archaeological enthusiast, accumulating a vast collection of Cypriote antiquities. In 1876, he returned to New York City and founded the Metropolitan Museum of Art with his personal collection. He served for twenty-five years as the first professional director of the famous museum.

Many Italians also served in the Confederate forces during the Civil War. The large Italian community in Louisiana, for example, was recruited to serve in the Garibaldi Legion of New Orleans. Union and Confederate soldiers wore feathered headgear in imitation of the elite Italian Bersaglieri that had first been created by the Kingdom of Piedmont in 1836.

After the Civil War, Italians and Italian Americans would fight in the Indian wars on the western frontier. No less than six Italians were members of Custer's 7th Cavalry at the time of the Battle of Little Bighorn. They were First Lieutenant Charles DeRudio (b. Belluno), Private Augustus DeVoto (b. Genoa), Private James John (b. Rome), Private Frank Lombard (b. Naples), and Trumpeter John Martin (b. Sola Consalino). Somewhat surprisingly, none of these men were killed with Custer at the Little Bighorn on June 25, 1876.

The trumpeter, John Martin—or Giovanni Martini—played a vital role in the dramatic events of that fateful day as he carried Custer's final message to Captain Benteen. The famous message, found in the West Point Museum today (and reproduced in our photo section), reads: "Benteen, Come on. Big Village, Be quick. Bring packs. W.W. Cooke. P.S. Bring packs." Some historians have interpreted this as a call for ammunition, while others see it as a last desperate plea for immediate reinforcement. Martin, a fortunate musician who had served as a drummer boy in the Italian Army, died in 1922 in Brooklyn.

In 1892, President Benjamin Harrison issued a proclamation to celebrate the four-hundredth anniversary of Columbus's discovery of the New World. That same year, Ellis Island opened its doors, marking the acceleration of a huge wave of Italian emigration that would flow to American shores over the next sixty years or so.

After the shattering Italian defeat at Adwa in 1896 (see Ethiopia), Italian American organizations raised money for the soldiers and their families. The *Progresso Italo-Americano* of New York, for example, raised 55,000 lire.

Italy joined the Allied powers in World War I in 1915, while the United States entered the war in 1917.

In 1918, Ernest Hemingway volunteered to serve as an ambulance driver on the Italian front. He was wounded by shrapnel and received the Italian Silver Medal of Valor.

The Italians sustained a major defeat at the Battle of Caporetto in the fall of 1917. Italy would lose over 600,000 men fighting in the Great War and would make only modest territorial gains at the Treaty of Versailles.

Discontent over the war and its aftermath helped pave the way for the ascension of Mussolini, a wounded World War I veteran, to power in 1922. In 1933, Commander Italo Balbo of the Italian Air Force led a squadron of Savoia-Marchetti S.55 X seaplanes from Rome, across Europe, and to the United States in a display of fascist might.

On July 28, 1941, the US Congress authorized the construction of the Pentagon. The design for the Pentagon was based on the fifteenth-century Italian Star Fortifications. Michelangelo had used a similar pattern to build defensive earthworks for Florence. After December 7, 1941, construction of the Pentagon accelerated rapidly, with 13,000 laborers working night and day to open the building in 1942.

On December 11, 1941, only four days after the Japanese attack on Pearl Harbor, Mussolini made a speech to a subdued crowd at the Piazza Venezia, declaring war on the United States of America. Many Italians were troubled by the notion of going to war against a nation that had never threatened Italy and where so many of their cousins and blood relatives lived.

As we noted in our earlier work, *America Invades*, on July 10, 1943, American and other Allied forces began the invasion of Sicily. On June 4, 1944, Rome was liberated by the Allies, and American jeeps drove into St. Peter's Square, accidentally violating the neutrality of the Vatican state. The Swiss guards, immensely relieved by the lifting of the Nazi siege of the Vatican (some Nazis had even advocated kidnapping the pope), politely requested that the Americans move their vehicles.

A submarine attack on New York planned by the Italian Navy for December 1943 never occurred due to the Italian surrender, which followed the fall of Sicily. The plan had been for midget submarines to sneak up the Hudson and bring the war home to America.

After the armistice in 1943, many Italians fought alongside American forces in the Co-Belligerent forces until 1945. By March 1944 there were, for example, over four hundred planes operating in the Co-Belligerent Air Force. Many Italians also joined the Partisan movement that supported Allied war aims as well.

As we have mentioned in several other chapters, many Italian Americans served their adopted country with great pride in World War II. About one in twelve Americans in the armed forces was of Italian descent.

Joe DiMaggio, the famous Yankee Clipper, joined the United States Army Air Force in 1943 but did not see combat. His parents had been classified as enemy aliens during the war. Joe's younger brother, Dom DiMaggio, was classified as 4F but managed to enlist in the US Navy, where he played baseball for the Norfolk Naval Training Station Nine.

Since World War II, Italy and the United States have enjoyed peaceful friendship, with all mutual invasions being cultural or touristic. Italy and the United States were founding members of the NATO alliance in 1949.

On November 22, 1963, President Kennedy was assassinated in Dallas, Texas. Eight months earlier, Lee Harvey Oswald had purchased via mail order a bolt-action rifle, a Mannlicher Carcano Model 91/38. This gun was an Italian infantry rifle that had been manufactured by the Royal Arms Factory in Terni in 1940.

Recently, Italian forces have served alongside American troops in the former Yugoslavia, Afghanistan, and Iraq.

URUGUAY

I TALIANS HAVE HAD MAJOR INVOLVEMENT with what is now the country of Uruguay right from the start of European contact with the area. In fact, something like 40 percent of Uruguayans have Italian ancestry.

In the 1520s, Anglo-Italian explorer Sebastian Cabot, working at the time for the Spanish crown, headed for the region. In February 1527, he took his squadron into the Río de la Plata estuary and spent months exploring it. And in August, he set up the first Spanish settlement in Uruguay, building a fort there called San Salvador.

Italians continued to play a role in the region as Spain extended its control across the region and developed its colonial rule.

In 1724, one Italian was to play a particularly significant role in the development of the nation's capital, Montevideo. In that year, the Spanish took the area from the Portuguese and started sending in their own settlers to establish control, including a certain Giorgio Borghese—or Jorge Burgues, as he was known in Spanish—who was born in Genoese territory. Due to the pioneering role Giorgio played in establishing the new regime, he eventually became governor of Montevideo.

In 1841, a particularly famous Italian immigrant moved to Montevideo, one Guiseppe Garibaldi. Initially, he didn't come to fight, but when the Uruguayan Civil War began in April 1843, he took command of an Italian legion that was fighting alongside the Colorados, against President Oribe's Blancos. Garibaldi rapidly proved himself a talented military commander, and he wore the South American poncho and sombrero that would later become famous in Italy. Over the course of five years, the legion led by Garibaldi fought a series of skirmishes to defend the Uruguayan capital, Montevideo. They fought under a black flag with a volcano at its center that symbolized mourning for Italy and the hidden fires that smoldered beneath the surface. The famous Redshirts (*camicie rosse*) of his troops were supposedly shirts made in Montevideo and originally destined for local butchers, dyed red to hide blood. His campaigns included the capture of Colonia del Sacramento, and victories at Cerro and the Battle of San Antonio del Salto in 1846. In 1848, he departed from South America, heeding the call of revolution that was sweeping Europe that fateful year.

Italian warships, like the *Eurydice,* had on occasion already been sent to South American waters to protect Italian interests; and in 1865, the Italian Navy established a base at Montevideo for its South American naval division. Among numerous other operations, the division in 1868 worked with other European naval ships to protect their civilians during a conflict in Uruguay.

Italian immigration increased as the nineteenth century advanced, and it continued on a large scale in the twentieth century. Many Italian Uruguayans came to play major roles in the life of Uruguay, including in the military and political spheres. A number of Uruguayan presidents were of Italian origin, including Demicheli, Sanguinetti, and Baldomir Ferrari. And from 1931 to 1938, Italian Uruguayan Gabriel Terra was president. Terra saw Mussolini's Italy as an important friend, and Mussolini in turn saw Uruguay as the most Italian country in North and South America. Italian funding provided for a massive dam on the Río Negro. Italian fascist summer camps for Italian Uruguayan children were established in the country.

Nonetheless, when World War II broke out, Uruguay remained neutral. And an event in 1942 did little to encourage pro-Axis feeling in Uruguay.

The *Montevideo* was originally a British-built Italian steamer called the *Adamello.* It had been interned at the beginning of the war, and then it was seized, renamed, and given a Uruguayan crew under a Uruguayan naval officer. In February 1942, the *Montevideo* set off for New York. It didn't make it. Off Puerto Rico, in early March 1942, the Italian submarine *Tazzoli,* under the command of Fecia di Cossato, torpedoed and sank the

Montevideo, killing fourteen of the crew in the attack. In 1945, Uruguay declared war on Germany.

In 2011, an agreement on cooperation in the field of acquisition of security and defense systems was signed between the Italian and Uruguayan governments.

UZBEKISTAN

ALEXANDER THE GREAT'S INVADING FORCES did make it into Uzbekistan. So, too, would any Italians who were accompanying them. With such a diverse army as he had, it's certainly not impossible that Italians were amongst either the actual fighting troops or with Alexander on a noncombat basis.

Alexander's family had connections with Italy. His uncle, Alexander I of Epirus had led a military expedition to Italy to aid the city of Tarentum, and, coincidentally or not, there is some evidence of Tarentines with Alexander in the east. The writer Athenaeus does refer to Italian entertainers with Alexander at Susa, in what is now Iran: Philistides from Syracuse, a juggler; Alexis from Tarentum, who sang Homer's poetry; and Heracleitus from Tarentum, a singer and lyre player.

A Greek inscription and two Latin inscriptions have been found in southern Uzbekistan on the Surkhan River. It has been suggested that one refers to the Fifteenth Pannonian Legion and may be connected with Roman prisoners captured by the Parthians.

Italian explorers did spend some time in what is now Uzbekistan. For instance, the Polo brothers spent three years in Bukhara.

In recent years, military personnel from Uzbekistan have attended the Italian Military Academy.

VANUATU

ITALY IS NOT THE EUROPEAN NATION that has had most connections with the Pacific island nation of Vanuatu. It has, however, had some.

For instance, Italian Admiral Alessandro Malaspina commanded a Spanish naval expedition that landed on Espiritu Santo in the late eighteenth century.

And the United States did construct air and naval bases on Espiritu Santo during World War II, so some Italian Americans must have served here.

But one fascinating Italian link to Vanuatu is musical. Ezio Pinza, an opera singer born in Rome, was in the original Broadway production of *South Pacific*, (a musical linked to the American experience on Espiritu Santo during World War II). My own mother (CRK) heard him sing "Some Enchanted Evening" on Broadway.

VATICAN CITY

THE HISTORY OF THE VATICAN IS, of course, closely linked to the history of Italy in numerous senses, so this can be only a summary of a few of the key points.

All roads lead to Rome. The Eternal City is home to the Roman Catholic Church, which leads the largest Christian church in the world with over a billion followers. In AD 64, St. Peter was martyred (crucified upside down) in Rome during the reign of Emperor Nero. The Old St. Peter's Basilica, completed in about 360, was built on his gravesite. Today millions of tourists and religious pilgrims flock each year to St. Peter's Basilica, which lies at the heart of the Vatican, and crane their necks at the Sistine Chapel. Today Vatican City is a 110-acre walled enclave within Rome, with a population of less than one thousand. Yet this tiny part of our world has a violent, blood-soaked history, having been invaded by Italians and others many, many times.

It's hard to be certain about the course of early Roman history, but certainly during the Roman period, Rome itself—including the territory that later became the Vatican—was repeatedly seized in civil wars by those aspiring to grab power.

During the medieval period, an almost bewildering variety of forces competed for control of Rome at different times, including Germanic peoples, Byzantines, Normans, the Papacy, Italian factions, and the Holy Roman Empire. Many of these armies contained Italians. A period of conflict in the fourteenth century also saw Cola di Rienzo take power in Rome, declare himself Tribune of the Roman People, and announce the (rather theoretical at that stage) unification of Italy. He would later become a source of inspiration for the Risorgimento movement of the nineteenth century.

In the same period, Cardinal Egidio Albornoz controlled a mercenary army fighting on behalf of the papal cause in central Italy. Albornoz assisted Rienzo's return to Rome in 1354.

During the Renaissance, Alexander VI, a Borgia pope, would lead the church for a time. He made his illegitimate son, Cesare Borgia, Bishop of Pamplona at the age of fifteen. With the help of Machiavelli and Leonardo da Vinci, the pope's son campaigned with papal troops in Romagna, capturing towns such as Piombino and Urbino. After his father's death, Cesare was arrested by Pope Julius II and held in the Vatican until his permanent exile to Spain. Julius II himself became known as the Warrior Pope because of his military campaigning.

One of the most infamous invasions of the Vatican took place in 1527. A renegade imperial army, including Italian troops (for instance, the mercenary Fabrizio Maramaldo), went on the rampage when it didn't get paid. What followed was the Sack of Rome as the attacking troops stormed into the city. Widespread looting followed. The Swiss Guard were largely massacred on the steps of St. Peter's, but their sacrifice helped Pope Clement VII to escape.

Napoleon proudly proclaimed his Italian heritage, declaring, "I am of the race that founds empires." Napoleon began his military career serving in the armies of revolutionary France. When his troops arrived in the Papal States in June of 1796, they were said to have "lit their pipes with altar candles." In 1798, the French occupied the Papal States and proclaimed a Roman Republic. An invasion by Neapolitan forces restored the Papal States shortly afterward, although Napoleon's forces would invade again in 1808.

For most of the nineteenth century, France would be a guardian of papal power in Italy.

This would put French forces in conflict with Giuseppe Garibaldi. Garibaldi, the great Italian patriot, was violently anticlerical, denouncing the priesthood as an "emanation from hell" and the "very scourge of God." Garibaldi would fight many battles around the Vatican with the hope of annexing Rome to Italy. In 1849, he marched his Legionaries into Rome and proclaimed the Roman Republic. They were besieged and driven out by a French army led by Marshal Oudinot.

In 1867, Garibaldi led the irregular Garibaldini or Redshirts in his final invasion of Lazio against the Papal and French forces. The battle cry of the Garibaldini was *Roma o Morte* (Rome or death). The general was defeated at the Battle of Mentana, after which he was arrested and sent back to exile on the Isle of Caprera.

During the Franco-Prussian War in 1870, Napoleon III, desperate to defend France, was compelled to withdraw the French garrison from Rome. King Victor Emmanuel II saw his chance to fulfill his long-cherished dream of capturing Rome.

When Pope Pius IX, whom a conclave had declared infallible the same year, was presented with a demand that he submit to the protection of the Kingdom of Italy, he exploded, "Fine loyalty! You are all a set of vipers, of whited sepulchres, and wanting in faith." The Pope's Army was outnumbered six to one by the Italian forces, who also threatened to bombard Rome with a navy. The pope knew that all was lost but refused to submit without "a bit of resistance" to show the world that he acted under duress.

On September 11, 1870, the Italian Army, not just irregulars of the Garibaldini, finally began an invasion of the Papal States. The defending papal forces were, in some sense, surprisingly well equipped with the latest weaponry. Their infantry were armed with the breech-loading Remington model 1868. Their leader, General Kanzler, was competent and had been the victor of the Battle of Mentana just three years before.

The papal forces were one of only three armies in the world at the time (along with England and France) that were equipped with a Claxton gun, a forerunner of the machine gun. This type of gun had been invented by an American—F. S. Claxton—and featured six horizontally mounted 25mm canons. A Claxton gun, likely of Belgian manufacture, was concealed in one of the towers of the San Giovanni gate. But even the pope's machine gun could not save Rome.

By September 18, the Eternal City was surrounded. Italian forces, led by General Cadorna, had orders to attack anywhere in Rome except for the Leonine City, which included the Vatican and the Castel Sant'Angelo. No one wished to see an artillery shell land on St. Peter's Basilica or wound the Holy Father.

The battle for Rome was fought on September 20. Thirty-two Italian soldiers were killed, along with twelve in the papal army. At last, Rome was Italian.

Finally, in 1929, the Lateran Pact would establish the present-day state of the Vatican City.

The Swiss Guards protect the Pope in the Vatican today.

VENEZUELA

ITALIANS HAVE PLAYED A MAJOR ROLE in the history of Venezuela, including in its military history.

For instance, Christopher Columbus explored the coast of Venezuela in 1498; and the very name of the country, Venezuela, is derived from the name of Venice. The following year, Alonso de Ojeda turned up with Italian explorer Amerigo Vespucci. The gulf they explored was named Venezuela—little Venice.

In the nineteenth century, a number of Italians became prominent in the military forces of Simon Bolivar, operating in the area. Agostino Codazzi from Lugo, for instance, after fighting for Napoleon, moved to Venezuela and he joined Bolivar's forces. He became, eventually, a leading cartographer and governor of Barinas. Carlo Castelli from near Turin was another Italian who had fought for Napoleon and ended up joining Bolivar's forces and becoming a powerful figure in Venezuela.

Later, Guiseppe Garibaldi II would find himself in Venezuela fighting against Cipriano Castro, and he wasn't the only Italian fighting Castro.

In the Venezuela Crisis of 1902–1903, Italy was one of the European nations demanding Castro pay foreign debts and reimburse foreigners who had suffered damage in the conflict inside Venezuela. Consequently, the Italian Navy joined a naval blockade of Venezuela until a deal was reached under pressure from President Theodore Roosevelt.

VIETNAM

HAS ITALY EVER INVADED VIETNAM? Well, not exactly, but she has had some surprising military involvement over the course of Vietnam's history.

Romans do seem to have reached Vietnam in small numbers in the second century AD. At Oc Eo in southern Vietnam, gold coins of the emperors Antoninus Pius and Marcus Aurelius have been found; and in 166, Romans claiming to be delegates from Marcus Aurelius seem to have arrived at Rinan in Vietnam before traveling to the Chinese court.

In the Middle Ages, Italian explorers, including fifteenth-century Italian explorer Niccolò de' Conti, also made it as far as Vietnam.

Trade is not, of course, the same as war. Some Italians did manage to fight in Vietnam, though.

It was the French who colonized Southeast Asia in the era of European imperialism.

The son of an Italian soldier, Joseph-Simon Gallieni, played a key role in crushing resistance to French rule and establishing French colonial administration in Tonkin in the 1890s.

Lieutenant Colonel Rossi commanded the 13th Demi-Brigade of the French Foreign Legion from 1954 to 1956 during the first Indochina War. Many other Italians served with the French Foreign Legion in the area at the time, including some who fought at the disastrous (for the French) Battle of Dien Bien Phu in 1954.

Italy, along with other NATO allies, managed to stay out of the American portion of the Vietnam War. Many Italian Americans, however, fought with US forces during that war. No fewer than seven Italian Americans won the Medal of Honor for their service during the Vietnam conflict.

In 1979, Italy did participate directly in Vietnam by dispatching a small squadron of two cruisers and a support ship to aid the rescue of the Vietnamese boat people in the South China Sea.

YEMEN

Yes, THE ROMANS DID INVADE YEMEN.
It was an area they knew extremely well, due to the busy trade routes between the Red Sea and India that passed along the coast of Yemen; and due to their trade with the area in, among other items, frankincense. But the Roman military were also well aware of the area.

Emperor Augustus decided it would make sense to conquer the Sabaean Kingdom in the region of what is now Yemen, and he sent Aelius Gallus to do it. They captured assorted towns along the route, finally making it as far as the Sabaean capital at Ma'rib before being forced to retreat due to sickness among the troops. As part of the operation, though, Roman ships did attack and destroy the port of Aden, then called Eudaimon.

In the early years of the twentieth century, the Italian Navy attacked Yemen again. During the Italo-Turkish War of 1911-1912, the Italian Navy attacked a number of targets in Yemen, particularly shelling the port of Al Hudaydah.

In the 1920s, the idea emerged in Italy of an Italian protectorate over Yemen, and Mussolini sent weapons and spies into Yemen to try to prompt an attack on British-controlled Aden. When conflict later flared between Yemen and Saudi Arabia, in 1933, Mussolini made some effort to get Italy involved by sending warships into Yemeni waters. Britain, however, successfully maintained its position as the prime colonial power in the area, and Mussolini turned his attention to the other side of the Red Sea.

Prior to World War II, the Italian Navy did consider plans to capture Aden in the event of war with Britain. So when the Italian Navy in East Africa responded to Mussolini's declaration of war on Britain in June 1940, the Italian submarine *Galileo Galilei* was sent to patrol off Aden. On June 16, the submarine sank a Norwegian tanker a few miles south of Aden. A couple days later, the *Galilei* engaged in a gun fight with HMS *Moonstone*. When HMS *Kandahar* turned up as well, the submarine crew was forced to surrender and the captured *Galilei* was towed into Aden.

But it wasn't just the Italian Navy that had plans for Aden. The Italian Air Force also launched a number of air raids against Aden, doing a certain amount of damage.

Italian military personnel took part in the 1963–4 United Nations Yemen Observation Mission (UNYOM). And in recent years, Italian naval vessels have taken part in international antipiracy operations in the Gulf of Aden.

ZAMBIA

ONLY TWO COUNTRIES HAVE NAMES that in English start with a Z. The two countries, Zambia and Zimbabwe, are next door to each other; and from the point of Italian involvement, they have one or two similarities as well.

Zambia used to be run by the British and used to be called Northern Rhodesia (whereas Southern Rhodesia became Zimbabwe). In 1905, Victor Emmanuel III was asked to adjudicate the border between British and Portuguese control, and in the end he created a line that still separates Angola from Zambia.

However, Italy did have a bit of later involvement with the area.

In World War II, troops from Northern Rhodesia ended up in East Africa in territory previously controlled by Italy, and the country received a number of Italian prisoners, including 1,500 from the Middle East.

After Northern Rhodesia became independent Zambia in 1964, Italian Air Force trainers helped train pilots for the Zambian Air Force at Livingstone, Zambia.

ZIMBABWE

A ROMAN COIN OF ANTONINUS PIUS was allegedly found in Zimbabwe. A Roman coin could conceivably have traveled inland from the Indian Ocean, where Roman ships did sail, but even if it did genuinely travel there during the Roman period, it doesn't necessarily prove that any Roman ever set foot in what is now Zimbabwe.

During the fighting in East Africa in World War II, Italian troops did come up against Rhodesian units. But the fighting all took place a long distance from what was then Southern Rhodesia and is now Zimbabwe.

However, the war years did see the arrival of many Italians in Southern Rhodesia. Internment camps were constructed there, and Italians, including some from Ethiopia and Somalia, were imprisoned there. East of Masvingo, the beautiful Chapel of St. Francis, also known as the Italian Chapel, was built during the war by Italian prisoners. Seventy-one Italian prisoners who died during their captivity are now buried in wings of the chapel that were attached after the war.

During the struggle for majority rule in Southern Rhodesia that led to the eventual creation of Zimbabwe, Italians in the country supported both sides. Giovanni Arrighi, for instance, was an Italian academic working in the country in the 1960s. He was arrested and briefly imprisoned on charges of supporting the movement for majority rule. But Italians also fought in the Rhodesian Army against the guerrillas that were fighting for majority rule.

After majority rule finally came to Zimbabwe, Italian troops played a small, brief, but still significant role in the country in the 1990s. In 1993, Italian troops were sent to neighboring Mozambique as part of the United Nations Operations in Mozambique (ONUMOZ) mission. An important role played by the Italian contingent was protecting the vital Beira Corridor, which links Zimbabwe, through Mozambique, to the sea.

CONCLUSION

A SUMMERTIME VISITOR TO THE PIAZZA SANTA CROCE in Florence will find the picturesque square transformed into an arena. The Florentines are about to start playing *Calcio Storico*, or ancient football (soccer). This bruising game is based on a tradition dating back at least to the sixteenth century. Each team has twenty-seven men, and the rules are "Anything goes." Punches are thrown. Wrestling matches break out for the full fifty minutes of the match. Some players are carried off in stretchers and no substitutions are allowed. The fighting spirit of Italians is commemorated in this event that is half-sport/half-Renaissance spectacle. Petrarch would be pleased to see that ancient valor is not dead in Italian hearts. It even draws a crowd!

The Roman Empire was, at its height, a formidable institution. The philosopher Friedrich Nietzsche called "the Imperium Romanum, the most grandiose form of organization under difficult conditions which has hitherto been achieved, in comparison with which everything before and everything since is patchwork, bungling, dilettantism."* Nietzsche may have held an idealized view of what was often a chaotic Roman Empire, but he did have a point. Roman legions, lacking aviation and modern technology, still managed to invade or fight in at least 26 percent of all the world's countries, based on modern geography.

After the fall of Rome, Italy languished for many centuries. The Christian Church in the West made Rome its home base and spread its spiritual power and influence throughout the world. The Renaissance revived the notion of Italy with Machiavelli and others, but in political terms it still remained a "geographical expression," due to the division among competing Italian states.

Napoleon, who had deep Italian roots, had himself crowned King of Italy. His empire stirred nationalist longings in many Italian hearts, reviving the dream of a united Italy. With help from his nephew, Napoleon III, Italy would unite into one nation around the middle of the nineteenth century. Italy fought and bled in the First World War. As we have seen, Mussolini sought ineptly to revive the imperial glories of ancient Rome with invasions of Ethiopia, Albania, Greece, and others.

After the devastation of World War II, Italy has rebuilt herself and taken an honorable position among nations. Her armed forces have served in many lands around the world, including participating in many UN peacekeeping missions. Her proud naval tradition continues, as two Italian aircraft carriers are available to patrol the Mare Nostrum and call at ports around the globe.

The aggressive instincts of her people have been largely rechanneled into commercial endeavors and sports, where she has excelled. Italy has won four soccer World Cups at time of writing, most recently in 2006. *Forza Azzurri!* The Romans used their arms to conquer. Modern Italians must now rely on their charms to market their products in the global marketplace. Where once Roman and Italian warriors strode, Italians, in fields such as fashion, gastronomy, soccer, and sports cars, have indeed conquered our world again.

* Friedrich Nietzsche, *The Anti-Christ*, trans. R. J. Hollingdale, (New York: Penguin, 1968), Section 58.

THE ROMAN EMPIRE

in 117 AD, at its greatest extent

Mare Germanicum

Oceanus Atlanticus

Britannia

Belgica

Lugdunensis

Aquitania

Narbonensis

Germania Superior

Noricum

Raetia

Pannonia

Tarraconensis

Lusitania

Baetica

Corsica

Italia

Sardinia

• Roma

Dalmatia

Dacia

Moesia

Thracia

Macedonia

Epirus

Achaia

Sicilia

Mauretania

Africa

Mare Internum

Pontus Euxinus

Bithynia et Pontus

Asia

Galatia

Lycia

Cappadocia

Cilicia

Syria

Cyprus

Iudaea

Armenia

Assyria

Mesopotamia

Arabia Petraea

Aegyptus

Cyrenaica

AFRICA

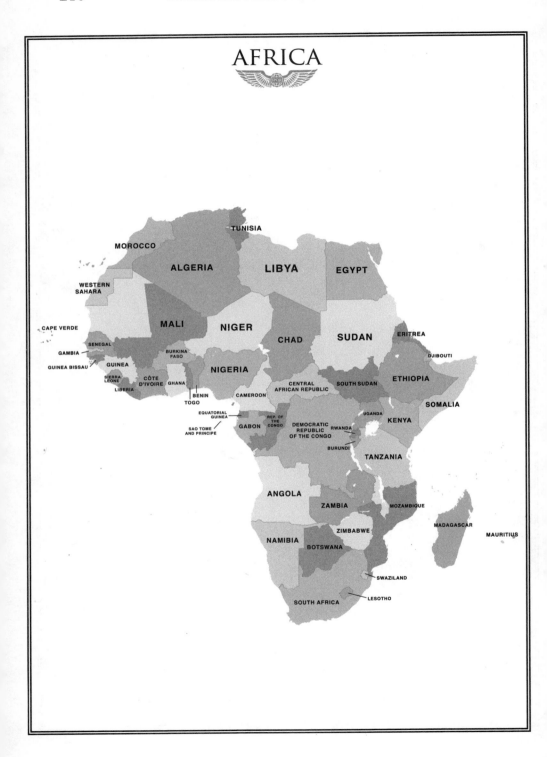

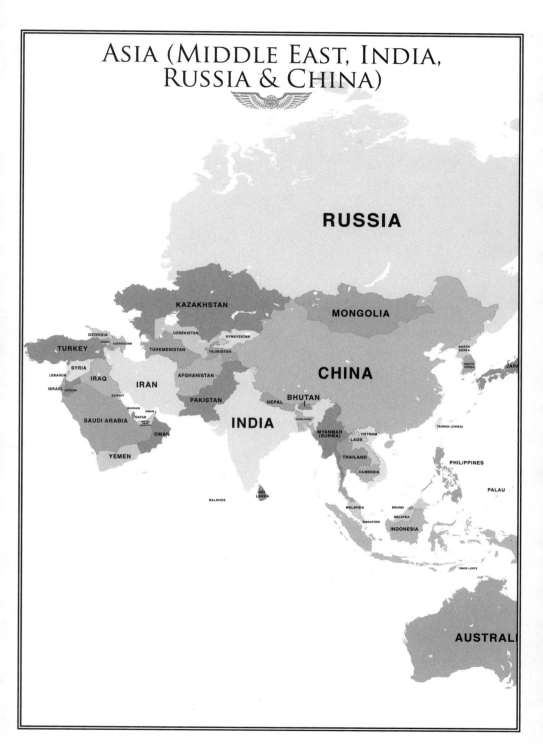

ASIA (MIDDLE EAST, INDIA,
RUSSIA & CHINA)

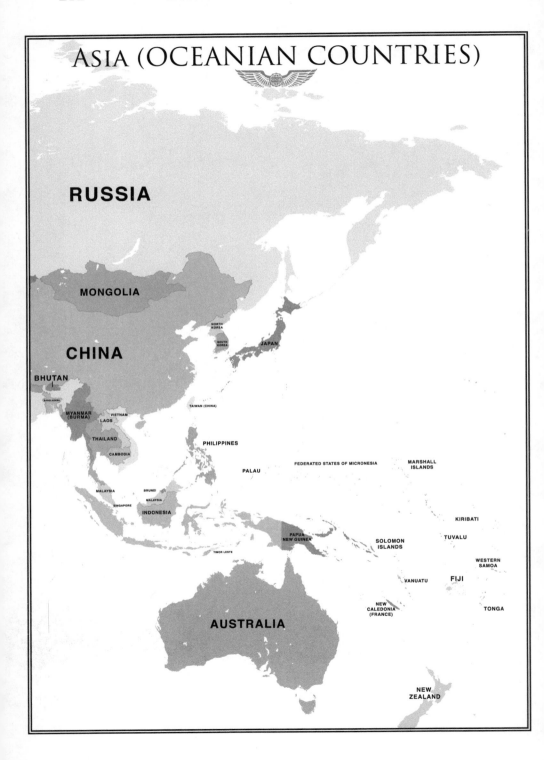

ASIA (OCEANIAN COUNTRIES)

RUSSIA

MONGOLIA

NORTH KOREA

SOUTH KOREA

JAPAN

CHINA

BHUTAN

BANGLADESH

MYANMAR (BURMA)

VIETNAM

LAOS

TAIWAN (CHINA)

THAILAND

CAMBODIA

PHILIPPINES

FEDERATED STATES OF MICRONESIA

MARSHALL ISLANDS

PALAU

MALAYSIA

BRUNEI

MALAYSIA

SINGAPORE

INDONESIA

KIRIBATI

TUVALU

PAPUA NEW GUINEA

SOLOMON ISLANDS

WESTERN SAMOA

TIMOR LESTE

VANUATU

FIJI

NEW CALEDONIA (FRANCE)

TONGA

AUSTRALIA

NEW ZEALAND

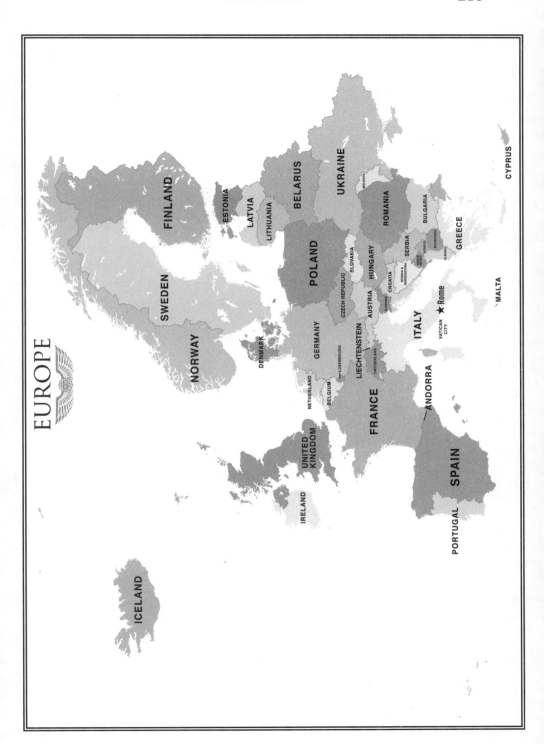

EUROPE

ICELAND

NORWAY

SWEDEN

FINLAND

ESTONIA

LATVIA

LITHUANIA

BELARUS

UKRAINE

DENMARK

UNITED KINGDOM

IRELAND

NETHERLAND

BELGIUM

LUXEMBOURG

GERMANY

POLAND

CZECH REPUBLIC

SLOVAKIA

HUNGARY

MOLDOVA

ROMANIA

BULGARIA

SERBIA

LIECHTENSTEIN

SWITZERLAND

AUSTRIA

SLOVENIA

CROATIA

BOSNIA &
HERZEGOVINA

MONTE
NEGRO

KOSOVO

MACEDONIA

ALBANIA

GREECE

FRANCE

ANDORRA

ITALY

VATICAN
CITY

★ Rome

MALTA

CYPRUS

SPAIN

PORTUGAL

NORTH AMERICA

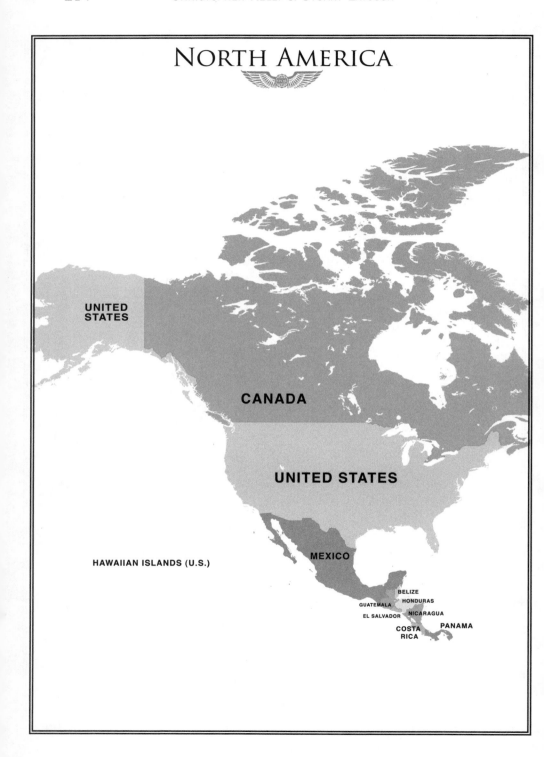

UNITED
STATES

CANADA

UNITED STATES

HAWAIIAN ISLANDS (U.S.)

MEXICO

BELIZE
GUATEMALA   HONDURAS
EL SALVADOR   NICARAGUA
COSTA   PANAMA
RICA

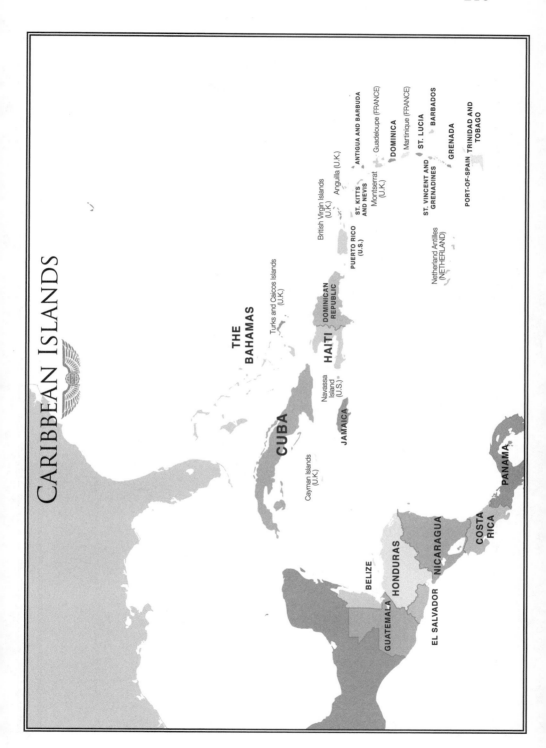

CARIBBEAN ISLANDS

THE BAHAMAS

Turks and Caicos Islands (U.K.)

Cayman Islands (U.K.)

CUBA

Navassa Island (U.S.)

JAMAICA

HAITI

DOMINICAN REPUBLIC

British Virgin Islands (U.K.)

Anguilla (U.K.)

PUERTO RICO (U.S.)

ANTIGUA AND BARBUDA

ST. KITTS AND NEVIS

Montserrat (U.K.)

Guadeloupe (FRANCE)

DOMINICA

Martinique (FRANCE)

ST. LUCIA

ST. VINCENT AND GRENADINES

BARBADOS

GRENADA

Netherland Antilles (NETHERLAND)

PORT-OF-SPAIN TRINIDAD AND TOBAGO

BELIZE

GUATEMALA

HONDURAS

EL SALVADOR

NICARAGUA

COSTA RICA

PANAMA

SOUTH AMERICA

VENEZUELA

COLOMBIA

GUYANA

SURINAME

FRENCH GUIANA
(FRANCE)

ECUADOR

PERU

BRAZIL

BOLIVIA

PARAGUAY

URUGUAY

ARGENTINA

CHILE

APPENDIX

Note by Christopher Kelly: The author of An Adventure in 1914 *was Thomas Tileston Wells (1865–1946), my maternal great-grandfather. The text was written in late 1914 or early 1915. At the time of his adventure, Wells was a forty-eight-year-old lawyer from New York who served each summer as the American consul general to Romania. He was married to Georgina Betts Wells (1868–1956) and had two children, John Wells (1895–1951) and my grandmother, Georgina Lawrence Wells Van Rensselaer (1902–1997), who was an eleven-year-old girl in 1914. (CRK)*

—AN ADVENTURE IN 1914—

WITH MY WIFE, SON, AND DAUGHTER, I LEFT PARIS early in the morning of July 13th for a little trip through the Austrian Tyrol and the region of the Dolomites. That afternoon we arrived at Belfort near the frontier between French and German Alsace; saw the lion carved in the rock which commemorates the heroic defense of the town in 1870 against the Germans, the heavy forts and many soldiers, but we did not then think that these soldiers and forts would be so soon engaged in deadly contest. We then went on in the train and stopped a few minutes on the French frontier town of Petit Croix. We went from Petit Croix to Altkirch and Milhause, or Mulhausen as it is called in Germany, where the terrible battles were fought in the early part of this war, these cities being repeatedly taken and lost by both sides. All these names have since become familiar to us owing to the war.

We spent a couple of days at Zurich. One day we went up the lake in a steamer and took tea at the other end. The country about this lake is not very high, but the lake is very picturesque; and when it is clear you can get glimpses of the distant snow-covered mountains beyond the hills which immediately border the lake.

When we left Zurich, we went right through in the train to Innsbruck in the Tyrol. On our way we passed the picturesque lake of Walensee, surrounded by high mountains, and then crossed the Rhine into the little principality of Liechtenstein; and as the train stopped for a few minutes near the capital, Schaan-Vaduz, we got out to be able to say that we had been in that country. This little state has no taxes as its prince personally pays all the expenses. He has vast estates and generally lives in Vienna.

Then the train went on into the Austrian territory. We went up the valley of the Ill River with towering snow-covered mountains on either side, and finally reached the Arlberg tunnel, which brought us into the upper Inn valley. We went on down that valley until we came to the beautiful old city of Innsbruck. In the dining car on that train, my son and I happened to sit opposite the great M. Pachitch,[1] the Prime Minister of Serbia, and we had a nice chat with him, but did not mention politics. He was dissatisfied with the service and the lunch and wrote out a complaint, but he gave the waiter a tip of 5 kronen[2]—an unusually large sum....

We then went back to Innsbruck and arrived there on Thursday, July 23rd, and as we were walking about the streets in the rain, we saw a great crowd looking into the newspaper offices and reading the notice of the Austrian ultimatum to Serbia that required an answer within forty-eight hours, the acceptance of which would have meant that Serbia had abandoned its independence. I immediately thought that there would be a European war as I did not believe that Russia would permit the crushing of Serbia. Serbia could not accept the Austrian demands, which seemed to be entirely unjustified, especially as the archduke and his wife were murdered by an Austrian subject, in Austrian territory. Moreover, the Serbian government had warned the Austrian government that there was a plot to kill the archduke and advised him not to go to Sarajevo where, as you may remember, he and his wife, the Duchess of Hohenberg, were murdered on the 28th of June.[3] Therefore, I thought the ultimatum was a mere excuse for starting a great European war, and events have proved that I was right.

I wished to go right back to Paris where our heavy luggage was, but my family could not believe that war was coming and wanted to keep on the journey as planned. I gave in....

After leaving the large town of Bruneck, you have some beautiful views of the snow-white mountains; and presently, as the train turns and twists up

---

1   Nikola Pašić (1845–1926) later became the President of Yugoslavia. The Austrians accused the Serbian government of complicity in the assassination of Archduke Ferdinand. It is unclear to this day whether Pašić had any foreknowledge of the conspiracy to kill the archduke and his wife.

2   About one US dollar in 1914.

3   Gavrilo Princip was a Bosnian Serb who participated in the assassination of the Archduke Ferdinand on June 28, 1914. He was a citizen of Austria-Hungary; Sarajevo was in Bosnia, which had been annexed to Austria in 1908. Too young to be executed according to Hapsburg law (age nineteen at the time of the assassination), Princip was imprisoned, where he died of tuberculosis in April 1918.

the valley, you have your first sight of the Dolomites. These mountains are different from the other mountains of the Alps, and the name comes from a geologist of the name of Dolomieu who first examined the magnesian limestone formation of which they are made....

While we were in Cortina, rumors of the coming war became more and more frequent, and I kept getting more and more alarmed; and finally I persuaded my family to leave, which we did on Thursday, the 30th of July. Already soldiers were being mobilized; and even in the little village of Cortina, we constantly heard military bands and bugles, and saw soldiers marching away to Toblach to take the train for centers of concentration. We also heard a great deal of rifle practice going on....

I might say that in Cortina they speak Italian, although the country belongs to Austria, and in some of the neighboring villages they speak German....The country generally is Italian in sentiment, and the people nearly all wish that their country belonged to Italy rather than to Austria....

When we got to Botzen late in the afternoon of July 31st, we saw that the people were very much excited about the war. Cannons, camp ovens, and other military supplies filled the approaches to the railway; and as we arrived at the hotel, a police official notified our driver that he must leave that night for his regiment and that his horses were required immediately to drag cannon. That night at dinner, we heard military bands marching about the town, followed by soldiers, who in turn were followed by all the reservists, who were not yet in uniform, and they in turn by all the young women. All kept marching about the town with halts occasionally to listen to speeches, singing and shouting until four o'clock in the morning.

We got off the train at Trent, which is the town where the Great Council of the Church, called the Council of Trent, was opened in 1545.... It has a beautiful cathedral and other interesting churches; and as we went into the cathedral and the churches, we found them all full of women kneeling, praying, and crying because their husbands, sons, or sweethearts were leaving for the war. It was a very sad sight and one never to be forgotten.

We then went on by train to a little place called Mori and then changed to a narrow-gauge railway that was to take us to Riva[4] at the northern and Austrian end of Lake Garda, where we arrived in the early afternoon. On the way, we constantly passed trains full of soldiers and trains with cannon and other military supplies. In the villages, we saw trainloads of soldiers leaving and kissing good-bye to their wives and children; and very sad they looked, although they tried to keep up their courage by singing patriotic songs. These people were very much to be pitied because they are really

---

4   Riva del Garda has been a part of Italy since 1918.

Italian and their country should belong to Italy, as I hope it soon will, for they have been oppressed by the Austrians since the country was given to Austria in 1814. None of these people care anything about the war, or for the matter of that, anything about Austria, except that they mostly hate it.

Riva is one of the most beautiful places in the world.... We went to the great hotel called the Lido Palace Hotel,[5] which is on the lake and has a beautiful garden running out to a little promontory on the lake, but the hotel had a strange look. For although there must have been a hundred, or perhaps two hundred waiters and servants, there was no one in the hotel except an American couple and ourselves; and it gave you a creepy feeling to see such a big and beautiful place, meant for so many people, so deserted. My wife wanted to spend several days at Riva, but that was made impossible by the manager telling us that the hotel would close the next day. So we had a swim in the lake and a row on it, and took tea on the terrace of the hotel gardens and arranged to leave the next morning by the early boat. Frequently in the night, we heard bugle calls and other sounds of military activity, and there were two searchlights on the lake, which were constantly being turned in all directions, and occasionally a flash of light would come through the windows into our rooms. All of this gave us a very unpleasant feeling and made us appreciate that we were in a country that was already at war, and that martial law was in force.

The next morning, Sunday August 2nd, we made an early start to the morning boat that takes you to the Italian end of the lake.... When we got to the quay from which the boat sailed, we stopped, and my family got out of the 'bus and went on board the boat. I stayed behind to see the trunks taken down and put safely on the boat. When the trunks were on the boat, I prepared to follow, but was stopped by a man in a brown and rather dirty civilian suit, with a beard that had not been shaved for several days, who told me that the two other Russian spies had been caught, and that now that he had me, all three of us would be shot that afternoon. I protested that not only was I not a Russian spy, but that I was an American. The police official, for such I suppose he was, called up some soldiers with rifles and fixed bayonets, and two of them grabbed me, each holding one of my arms, and they made me go to a room nearby which apparently is used for the customs house. There I again protested that I was an American, and they asked for my passport. I had no passport and told them so, but showed my letters, my visiting cards, and finally my Letter of Credit to prove that I was an American, none of which, however, convinced the police spy. My son then came back from the boat, he having observed there was some trouble, and I asked him to get me my bag but told him to say nothing to anyone, but simply to fetch the bag. This he did, and I got out of the bag a letter that I had obtained before leaving America from Secretary of State Bryan[6] "directed to the Diplomatic and Consular officers of the United States of America, introducing Mr. T. Tileston Wells." The letter is as follows:

Department of State,
Washington
June 20, 1914

To the
Diplomatic and Consular Officers
Of the United States of America.

Gentlemen:
At the insistence of the Honorable William F. McCombs, Chairman of the Democratic National Committee, I take pleasure in introducing to you Mr. T. Tileston Wells of New York City, who is about to proceed abroad.

I cordially bespeak for Mr. Wells such courtesies and assistance as you may be able to render, consistently with your official duties.

I am, Gentlemen,
Your obedient servant,
W. J. Bryan

After the police spy had read this letter, he took it to some officers in uniform who were standing a little way off. They read the letter, and as they did so, I could see them looking around at me from time to time. After a very short time, the police spy came back, handed me back my letter, and told me that I could go. He made no excuse or apology, but I was very pleased to go and did so readily. I went on the boat where my wife and daughter were seated, and sat down opposite to them but saying nothing at the time, fearing that if I showed any excitement that the police official might change his mind and come back. I can assure you that I counted the seconds until the time to go came, and was greatly relieved to see the ropes cast off and the boat start.

---

6   William Jennings Bryan (1860–1925) ran twice for President of the United States and famously delivered the Cross of Gold speech in 1896.

A few minutes after leaving, we made another landing at Tarbole, also in Austrian territory; but after leaving there we soon got into Italian waters, and as the boat was Italian, I felt that I was thoroughly out of Austria and was very glad of it.

When we left Riva, as we had tickets all the way to Paris and through Milan, we decided that after landing at the south end of the lake at Desenzano, we would go by train to Milan; but as we came down the lake, we stopped at the little Italian town of Limone. There we got that morning's local Italian papers which said that the French army was mobilizing and that Italy had decided to remain neutral in the great war. Therefore, knowing that the French army would require all the French railways for some days, we felt that it would be impossible to go right through to Paris and, therefore, we decided to go to Venice instead to stay until the time was more favorable for going on to Paris....

There were about seven hundred Americans at Venice at this time, many of them in great distress as they had planned their trips and got their tickets on lines that the war made impossible. A great many had paid for passages home on the German lines which were not running, or had paid for passages from the north and could not get there, either through Germany or France. Getting back to America from Italy was difficult because in the first place, all Americans wanted to get home at once; and in the second place, the German steamers were not running at all, and few of the English and French were. Moreover, it was feared that Italy might join in the war, which would interfere with her ships sailing. Then again, there was a great shortage of coal in Italy which made sailing from her ports difficult....

Very soon after the war broke out, the English government chartered a special train to take all the English people in Venice to Genoa, and there provided the White Star SS *Cretic*[7] to take them to England. Nothing of the kind was done for Americans in Italy so far as I have been able to learn, and the appropriation that Congress generously made to help Americans abroad was largely squandered in a great junketing party for the benefit of the agents who were sent out to relieve the distress, and who traveled hither and thither at Uncle Sam's expense.

The hotelkeepers at Venice were very good and told us we need not pay our bill to them until we got back to America. This in spite of the fact that many of them were embarrassed by the effects of the royal decree,

---

7   SS *Cretic* sailed from 1902 until 1928, and was used as a troopship to bring American soldiers of the American Expeditionary Forces to Europe in 1918. She was part of the White Star Line from 1903 to 1923.

which exempted banks from paying depositors more than 5 percent of their deposits per month. I suppose that measure was necessary, but it worked a good deal of hardship, as you can well imagine.

Food supplies at this time in Venice were, however, abundant and cheap, because a royal decree forbade their export, cutting off the market, and the supply was much greater than the demand. You could get eggs in Venice for less than a cent apiece, and milk and butter and meat, including fowls and chickens, as well as vegetables and fruits.

However, there was great suffering in Italy caused by this war. Quantities of Italian laborers have sought work for many years past outside of their own country, not only in America, but in South America, Austria, France, and Switzerland. Almost all work stopped in the countries that were at war; and the times have been very bad lately in South America, so that thousands of poor Italians had to return to Italy. We saw many of these refugees with their children and babies and bundles.

They aroused pity, I can assure you. How Italy is going to take care of all these industrious but unfortunate people, who unwillingly had to come back at this time, I do not know; but perhaps their situation has been improved to a certain extent by taking the places of some of those who were mobilized by the Italian army or navy. When the war started between the great countries who are now fighting, Italy slowly began to mobilize her army and navy, getting them ready for war, and has been slowly but steadily at it ever since.

This brings up the question as to whether Italy is likely to join in the war. It seems to me that she is, because the sentiment in favor of the war and against Austria is growing all the time; and moreover, it appears to be for the interest of the country to do so. Austria is the hereditary enemy of Italy; and the people of the north of Italy especially remember too well the persecutions they suffered during Austrian occupation not to hate that country—which they do to a man cordially—so that it never would have been possible for the Italian government to have gone to war with Austria and Germany against France and England, because the people would not have stood it and there would have been a revolution immediately. However, Italy had no need under the terms of the Triple Alliance of joining in the war. Her reasons are more than an excuse, as the crushing of Serbia by Austria was contrary to the interests of Italy; and as Italy was not consulted in advance about the note that produced the war,[8] she was not

---

8   On July 23, 1914, Austria delivered an ultimatum to Serbia demanding a response within 48 hours; when a positive response was not received the path to war was set in motion.

obliged to join in it. If she had been consulted about the note, she would have objected to it and then it would not have been sent. It was because the Austrians and Germans knew that Italy would not permit the note to be sent, if she were consulted, that they did not consult her.

However, there is every reason to believe that both Germany and Austria brought every possible pressure to bear, both by threats and offers of reward, such as giving Italy the Trentino,[9] which is the country about Trent and Riva of which I have already told you. However, nothing availed, and Italy has up to the present time remained neutral. But the feeling is growing in favor of a war against Austria, and I have no doubt that a pretext for the war will soon be found, especially now that the Marquis of San Giuliano, so long the Minister of Foreign Affairs and rather well disposed to Austria, has resigned from the Cabinet.

At Venice, we spent a great deal of time reading the extras of the papers with the so-called latest news of the war, and in the evening we would go to the Piazza of San Marco and sit down at a table in front of Florian's,[10] order some black coffee which we would slowly sip, and discuss the war news, and listen to the splendid band.

> **Note by CRK.** *Wells proceeded from Venice to Rome. On September 3, 1914, they observed the fumata rise above St. Peter's indicating the selection of a new Pope—Benedetto Diecimo Quinto, or Benedict XV. Wells and his family then went to Naples, where they managed to board a British steamer that departed on September 10. The ship stopped briefly at Almeria in Spain, in Gibraltar, and at the Azores. Wells expressed anxiety about the possible presence of German cruisers that could be hunting for merchant and passenger ships, though none were encountered. They arrived safely in Boston about two weeks after their departure from Naples.*
>
> *On May 23, 1915, Italy, as predicted by Wells, declared war on Austria-Hungary.*

---

9   Germany and Austria-Hungary did offer the possibility of some of Trentino (as well as French Tunisia) to Italy. The Allies, however, were prepared to offer all of Trentino, along with Gorizia and Trieste in order to convince Italy to join the Triple Entente.

10   Caffe Florian remains a popular tourist destination in Venice. (See www. caffeflorian.com)

GLOSSARY

Aeronautica Militare: Italian Air Force, from 1946 to present

Alexander VI (1431–1503): Borgia pope born in Valencia, served as pope from 1492 to 1503

Augustus (63 BC–14 AD): Caesar Augustus (Octavian), founder of the Roman Empire

Aurelius, Marcus (121–180 AD): Emperor-philosopher, author of the *Meditations*

Barbarossa (Operation): Hitler's invasion of the Soviet Union which commenced on June 22, 1941; the largest invasion in history

Basilone, John (1916–1945): US Marine who won the Medal of Honor and Navy Cross, killed on Iwo Jima

Bersaglieri: An elite corps of the Italian Army founded by the Kingdom of Sardinia in 1836; noted for their distinctive feather headdress

Bonaparte, Napoleon (1769–1821): Born Napoleone Buonaparte in Corsica, Emperor of the French 1804–1815, King of Italy 1805–1814

Borgia, Cesare (1475–1507): The illegitimate son of Pope Alexander VI who inspired Machiavelli

Caesar, Julius (100–44 BC): Roman general who ended the Republic and became a dictator; author of *Commentaries*

Caproni (1908–1950): Italian aircraft manufacturer, built the first Italian aircraft in 1911

Cavour (1810–1861): Camillo Benso, Count of Cavour, Italian statesman who guided Piedmontese foreign policy during the Risorgimento

Claxton gun: Invented by American F. S. Claxton, this was a horizontally mounted weapon that had six 25mm cannons; a machine gun prototype from around 1868

Co-Belligerent Forces: Italian army, naval, and air forces that fought on the Allied side in World War II following the arrest of Mussolini in 1943

Columbus, Christopher (circa 1450–1506): Genoese explorer and navigator who "discovered" the New World on behalf of the Spanish monarchy

Condottieri (*singular* condottiero): Italian commanders, often mercenaries, who fought on behalf of Italian city states and the pope during the late Middle Ages through the Renaissance

Constantine the Great (272–337 AD): Roman emperor who converted to Christianity and shifted the empire toward Byzantium and the east

Corpo Truppe Volontarie (CTV): Italian Corps of Voluntary Troops that fought on the Nationalist side in the Spanish Civil War, 1936–1939

CR.42: Fiat Cr.42 Falco, single-seat biplane flown by the Regia Aeronautica before and during WWII

de' Conti, Niccolò: (1395–1469): Venetian merchant and explorer who journeyed to Asia

Di Cesnola, Luigi Palma (1832–1904): Colonel in the Union Army in the US Civil War, US consul to Cyprus, first director of the Metropolitan Museum of Art

Douhet, Giulio (1869–1930): Theoretician of aerial warfare, author of *The Command of the Air*

Esercito Italiano (1861–Present): Italian Army

Eurofighter Typhoon: Twin engine fighter jet developed by a European consortium that includes the Italian government, now in service with the Aeronautica Militare

Garibaldi, Giuseppe (1807–1882): Born in Nice, became an Italian general during the Risorgimento, captured Sicily from the Bourbons on behalf of the Kingdom of Italy

Hadrian, Publius Aelius Hadrianus Augustus (76–138 AD): Emperor of Rome, ordered the construction of a seventy-three mile wall in Northern Britain

Hannibal (242–circa 182 BC): Carthaginian general and enemy of Rome

IFOR: Implementation Force; NATO-led peacekeeping force in Bosnia Herzegovina

ITS: Italian Ship (NATO designation)

Leonardo da Vinci (1452–1519): Italian scientist, inventor, and artist of the Renaissance; painted the *Mona Lisa* and conceived the tank, submarine, and parachute

Macchi Aeronautica: An Italian company that built the 200 and 202 fighters that served the Regia Aeronautica in WWII

Machiavelli, Niccolò (1469–1527): Florentine historian and philosopher, author of *The Prince*

Marina Militare: Italian Navy from 1946 to present

Martini, Giovanni (1852–1922): Also known as John Martin, served as trumpeter for General George Armstrong Custer at Little Big Horn; carried Custer's last message

MAS: *Motoscafo armato silurante* or torpedo-armed motorboat used by the Regia Marina in WWI and WWII

Mazzei, Philip (1730–1816): friend of Thomas Jefferson, winemaker

Mazzini, Giuseppe (1805–1872): Journalist and chief ideologue for the unification of Italy

Mithridates the Great (134–63 BC): Also known as Mithridates VI and Mithridates of Pontus; from Asia minor, an enemy of the Roman Republic

Montecuccioli, Raimondo (1609-1680): A Modena-born general of various mercenary forces; he famously said, "For war you need three things: Money, Money, and Money."

Mussolini, Benito (1883–1945): Known as Il Duce; led the Kingdom of Italy from the 1922 March on Rome until his deposition in 1943; led the Italian Social Republic from 1943 until his execution in 1945

NATO: North Atlantic Treaty Organization. Italy was a founding member in 1949. Its official motto is in Latin—*Animus in consulendo liber*—which means "a mind unfettered in deliberation." The motto is derived from a speech by Cato the Younger to the Roman Senate.

Nero, Claudius Caesar Augustus Germanicus (37–68 AD): Emperor of Rome during the Great Fire; philhellene

Pastene, Giovanni Battista (1507–1580): Genoese explorer who traveled to South and Central America

Petrarch, Francesco (1304–1374): Italian humanist and poet of the Renaissance

Philhellene: Lover of Greek culture

Pigafetta, Antonio (1491–1531): Venetian explorer who accompanied Ferdinand Magellan

Polo, Marco (1254–1324): Venetian merchant and traveler, author of *The Travels of Marco Polo*

Pompey the Great (106–48 BC): Roman general who shared the First Triumvirate with Caesar and Crassus; defeated by Julius Caesar in civil war at the Battle of Pharsalus

Redshirts: Followers of General Giuseppe Garibaldi, also known as Garibaldini (see Thousand)

Regia Aeronautica: Royal Italian Air Force (1923–1946)

Regia Marina: Royal Italian Navy (1861–1946)

Risorgimento: Historic period in which Italy was unified, roughly from 1815 to 1871

Saint Patrick's Battalion: Irish volunteers that served in the papal military forces

San Marco Regiment: Italian Marine unit that traces its origin back to La Marina Regiment, which was first formed in 1713

SM.82: Savoia-Marchetti SM.82, tri-motor bomber used by the Regia Aeronautica in WWII

Thousand: The Thousand followers of Garibaldi (see Redshirts) that liberated Sicily from Bourbon rule in 1860

Titus, Flavius Caesar Vespasianus Augustus (39–81 AD): Flavian emperor of Rome who besieged Jerusalem

Trajan, Caesar Nerva Traianus (53–117 AD): Emperor of Rome at its height

Vespasian, Titus Flavius Caesar Vespasianus Augustus (9–79 AD): Roman general who became emperor in 69 (the year of the four emperors) and ruled until his death in 79

Vespucci, Amerigo (1454–1512): Italian explorer and navigator after whom North and South America are named

INDEX